Celtic History and Mythology

An Enthralling Guide to the Celts and their Myths, Gods, and Goddesses

Free limited time bonus

Stop for a moment. We have a free bonus set up for you. The problem is this: we forget 90% of everything that we read after 7 days. Crazy fact, right? Here's the solution: we've created a printable, 1-page pdf summary for this book that you're reading now. All you have to do to get your free pdf summary is to go to the following website:

https://livetolearn.lpages.co/enthrallinghistory/

Once you do, it will be intuitive. Enjoy, and thank you!

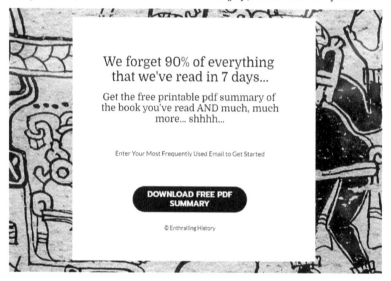

We forget 90% of everything
that we've read in 7 days...

Get the free printable pdf summary of
the book you've read AND much, much
more... shhhh...

Enter Your Most Frequently Used Email to Get Started

**DOWNLOAD FREE PDF
SUMMARY**

© Enthralling History

Table of Contents

Part 1: Celtic History

An Enthralling Overview of the Celts

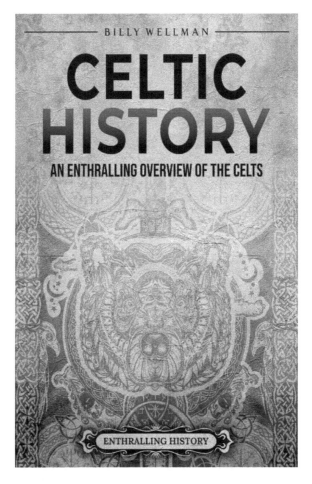

Introduction

You would be hard-pressed to find anyone in the English-speaking world who hasn't been enchanted by or at least interested in Irish history at one point or another. Ireland is a land of magic, mystery, and ancient customs that reach back millennia.

What makes the Emerald Isle so fascinating can be largely attributed to the Celts, the ancient people who inhabited what is now known as Ireland all the way back in 500 BCE; they even began trickling onto the island as early as five hundred years prior to that.

In the following chapters, we will break down what made the Celts so quintessential to Ireland's history: their daily lives, folklore and Celtic legends, the Celtic language, holidays, and rituals, and what Celtic culture looked like once Christianity arrived on the scene. Fortunately, many remnants of Celtic culture and beliefs remain today, which we will also discuss.

The purpose of this book is to provide an accessible and interesting overview of the Celts, their culture, society, and the effects of their presence, which are still felt today. It is meant to be a historical overview of who the Celts were, how and why they found themselves in Ireland (or Hibernia, as the Romans dubbed it), and what that meant for the people who were already living on the Emerald Isle.

Through this book, you will learn about the Celts in a way that uses easy-to-understand language; you can enjoy this book whether you're a history buff, just getting into learning about your Irish roots, or a beginner at reading about history.

But why should we want to know about the Celts? Any resource about history, especially about a people so influential and pivotal to the course of regional and world events, is essential to understand events that happen around us today. We can only understand the present by first looking into the past. The Celts are the reason we celebrate Halloween each year. They are also the reason Irish Gaelic persists as a language. The Celts left behind intricate metalworking and carving designs, and they may even be the reason Europeans began wearing pants!

This book, *Celtic History: An Enthralling Overview of the Celts*, is the essential resource you need to help you dive into your study of this intriguing and influential culture. Enjoy!

SECTION ONE:
Celtic Ireland — The Basics
(500 BCE–400 CE)

Chapter 1: Who Were the Celts? An Overview

The Celts were really a conglomeration of several ethnic groups and tribes that are now identified as a group of people who shared a common language and linguistic roots. For example, the Gauls, an ethnic group that eventually melded into the Germanic tribes, was a Celtic group conquered by the Romans. Germanic, Roman, and Gallic influences eventually evolved into the French people.

It is now widely accepted that the Celts, although still diverse and widespread in Britain, Ireland, and western Europe during their heyday, were bound together by their beliefs and linguistic similarities.

Who is a "Celt?"

The first time the word we can identify as "Celt" was used to identify a group of people was by the Greek geographer and historian Hecataeus. He used the term *Keltoi* to refer to a group of people who were living in what is now southern France. Herodotus, the famed historian, also wrote about the *Keltoi* in the 5th century BCE.

These people, the *Keltoi*, called themselves Celts. There are several theories on where the name came from, but scholars generally agree that "Celt" is from the Celtic language, not anything that outside people named them. For example, the Apache in the United States refer to themselves as "Diné," which means "the people." The term Apache was assigned to them by their enemies, and fittingly, that is what "Apache" means.

The Celts may or may not have come up with this demonym (a name for a people), but it is certain they used the name to refer to themselves even if they did not originally come up with the name. It is true that the Gauls and Celts were interchangeable in terms of tribal customs, language, cultural similarities, fighting styles, and areas they inhabited. Those very closely related societies only split off after the Roman occupation of Britain and western Europe.

From Where Did the Term "Celt" Originate?

There are several theories as to how the Celts could have adapted the Greek *Keltoi*. One theory is that the name "Celt" could have come from "the offspring of the hidden one" because the Gauls (interchangeable with the Celts when the Greeks wrote in 500 BCE) professed to be descendants of the ruler of the underworld. After all, *Hel* is Germanic in origin and is used to describe the place of the underworld and to refer to the goddess Hela.

Another theory for the name Celt is that it comes from a root word in the Celtic language meaning "to hide" or "to heat." We may never truly know the exact origin of the name, but we can assume that besides it being the Greek term for these western Europeans, the Greek *Keltoi* means "the tall ones."

Whether they came up with their demonym or not, the Celts definitely used that name to refer to themselves. In fact, in what is now Spain and Portugal, the Roman naturalist Pliny the Elder noticed that families used *Celtici* as a surname. This would offer the conclusion that these people identified as Celts culturally and ethnically even earlier than the 1ˢᵗ century BCE when Julius Caesar and Pliny the Elder recorded these findings.

"Celt" and "Celtic" Today

Today, the term Celt refers to the ancient tribes we've been discussing above. The adjective Celtic typically refers to their cultural similarities and art styles, but it more often means a shared language that linked these disparate and far-flung tribes together.

In today's modern world, Celtic simply refers to the languages, cultures, ancient pagan beliefs, inscriptions, and especially the art styles of Ireland, Wales, Scotland, Cornwall, Brittany, and the Isle of Man. These different locations reflect the far-reaching dominance of Celtic culture for what has now been millennia.

Celts and Their Origins

The people eventually consisting of the many tribes and groups eventually known as Celts originated in central Europe in the 13th century BCE, long before they came across the waters to Ireland. The archaeological evidence is scarce and does not start to appear until about the 8th century BCE near Salzburg, Austria.

Hallstatt culture.

However, prior to that very well-preserved evidence, we know the Celts migrated from central Europe because we see evidence of their settlements as far as what is now known as Czechia (the Czech Republic). They made their way into western France, and over time, the massive range of Celtic tribes spread all across western Europe. They covered what is now known as France, Germany, Spain, and Portugal.

The Celts made their home in the Upper Danube region. Water is essential to life, and these people found they could trade and travel using the Danube River. They could also use it to irrigate their crops. The early success of the Celts and their subsequent explosion across the European continent can be attributed in large part to the security and prosperity they received from the Danube River.

It is in this Danube cradle that historians and archaeologists refer to the early Celts as the Late Bronze Age Urnfield culture. The Urnfield name comes from their unique but unified burial practice of burying urns containing the cremated remains of their dead. This way of interring the deceased is pretty much the only extant archaeological evidence of these early Celtic tribes (and remember, the name "Celt" was not used by those people or anyone else for another eight hundred years).

From the Urnfield culture, these people migrated and changed and were then known as the next Celtic bead in the string of Celtic cultures, the Hallstatt culture. This culture was named for the amazing site found near Salzburg, Austria, that we mentioned earlier. This other precursor to the Celts was successful and powerful around what is now western Austria, some parts of Czechia and eastern Austria, Switzerland, southern Germany, and eastern France, which is quite the territory. Those living on the western side of this extensive area were the people who would eventually spread farther west all the way to Britain and Ireland—the official Celts.

The Hallstatt proto-Celts did not prosper from conquest or violence. They did have brave warriors and did not shy away from fights when the situation called for violence, but these people became prosperous because of the incredible mineral ore deposits in the areas they inhabited. These deposits included copper, iron, and salt, which have always been valuable and attractive commodities. The Hallstatts traded with the neighboring tribes and, in turn, received things like gold and amber. In fact, the interspersal of all these goods throughout Europe and even as far south as the Mediterranean (where cultures like the Etruscans lived) helped the Hallstatts have a stable and prosperous existence for close to eight hundred years.

Hallstatt amber necklace found in a woman's grave.
Wolfgang Sauber, CC BY-SA 4.0 <https://creativecommons.org/licenses/by-sa/4.0>, via Wikimedia Commons; https://commons.wikimedia.org/wiki/File:NBAM_Hallstattzeit_-_Bernsteinkollier_2.jpg

This trading is evident in gold and amber found in Hallstatt burial sites, as well as Danube iron and copper found dispersed south and east of the Hallstatt territories. The Hallstatts did not die out. As people groups do, they simply evolved and adapted to the times. The Hallstatt culture declined around 400 BCE simply because natural resources started drying up. It was time for a child of the Hallstatts and a grandchild of the Urnfield culture to emerge: the Celts.

Celtic Society

Celtic society operated much like the cultures before it. This was a time before monarchies, dynasties, and feudalism pervaded Europe. This was a time of tribal alliances, relative ease of migration, and flexibility of borders, a time before the Romans became obsessed with conquest and control.

Tribes made alliances through marriages between important members (chieftains' children and the offspring of advisors, the equivalents of nobles and royalty), and these often led to building up trade between tribes. It also meant that if there were intertribal rivalries that needed to be settled through battle, those allied tribes could fight together against a common enemy.

The Celts were many various tribes that spread across Britain and Ireland and western Europe for about eight hundred to nine hundred years, from 500 BCE until the arrival of Christianity in Ireland (but even then, this only shifted their cultural dominance, not the existence of the Celts themselves).

These tribes were never centralized with an overarching ruler or oligarchy, but they were tied together by similar tribal codes, a colorful mythology and belief system, close ties to seasonal changes and the harvest, and, most of all, a common language.

The Celts were organized within each tribe by a hierarchy based on the chieftain's ability to protect the tribe and make wise decisions based on property disputes, harvest activities, and even criminal offenses when necessary. Later on, once the Celts had more interactions (usually in the form of wars or conquests) with the Romans, oligarchical governmental structures began to take shape, although these always retained a uniquely Celtic flavor. The bravest and strongest warriors became advisors to the chieftain, along with the mysterious Druids who led the Celtic religion.

Fascinatingly, the Celts (unlike many of their synchronous counterparts) did not define much of their lives by gender roles. Women and men could inherit property equally, and marriage was seen as a partnership rather than a business or political contract. Women could not be married against their will; a prospective husband needed to have his prospective wife's abject approval before any marriage agreement could take place.

Other than the contrast of women having more rights than their counterparts in other societies, we know little else about how the Celts conducted their affairs as men and women before their arrival on the Emerald Isle. The records are scant, and what does exist discusses a matriarchal society, but these are not from reliable sources, as they come from Romantic authors and early feminists in the last three hundred years.

However, what is mentioned by contemporaneous sources about the Celts is interesting. Strabo, a Greek geographer born in 64 BCE, wrote, "Men and women dance together, holding each other's hands," which was completely unlike the Greeks and Romans. In those cultures, genders were strongly separated by legal and cultural measures. Roman and Greek writers also write of Celtic women being as fierce, tall, and strong as the men, and this can be attested to by the story of Celtic Queen Boudicca, who famously led a rebellion against the Romans in 60 CE.

Although the pagan goddesses the Celts worshiped, as well as the women in their day-to-day lives, had it better than their female counterparts in other societies, this was still a far cry from modern-day women's rights. Whatever was "egalitarian" or "matriarchal" to the extremely patriarchal Greeks and Romans, the Celts' number one enemies, could have been something as simple as a woman not having an arranged marriage. We cannot take these outsider sources at face value—they must always be examined using the lenses through which they were originally observed.

Ancient Celtic Women: Still Largely a Mystery

Because most of what we know about the early Celtic cultures (and we know next to nothing about the Urnfield culture or the Hallstatts) was written by outsiders, we have to take that into consideration when discussing the roles of men and women in society.

The ideal Celtic goddess was powerful, both in war and by her ability to bring forth life—we cannot say for certain that ordinary Celtic women were revered in the same way. However, as we discussed above, Celtic women enjoyed an extraordinary amount of freedom compared to Roman women and especially the Briton women who came after them. "Extraordinary" is a term we can apply liberally. Celtic society was not strictly separated between the sexes like other cultures of the same time, as well as ancient societies that came before and after.

Whatever sources we have that were written about Celtic women were written with the undeniable bias that the Celts, Gauls, and Germanic people were barbarians, and the writers' viewpoints cannot help but be flavored by their own opinions.

For example, Celtic women's ferocity to defend their families and property most likely arose from myths that were extremely popular about the Celts during the medieval period, which came much later than these first writings. The best sources we have to indicate the position of women in Celtic society prior to their arrival on Irish soil are the artifacts that have been found in their gravesites.

As often happened in the past (think the 18th, 19th, and even 20th centuries), archaeologists, all male, assumed that if a grave was decked out with items of precious value, such as weapons, jewelry, and fragments of expensive fabrics, and if the grave was grand and/or intricately decorated, that grave belonged to a man. It is only within the past century or so that anthropologists and archaeologists have bothered to examine whether human remains were men or women.

Since the traditional gender of these buried people has been uncovered, it has been extremely enlightening to discover that Celtic women, especially in the prosperous Hallstatt culture, were buried with full honors and goods for use in the afterlife, such as the enormous bronze mixing krater (a bowl with a handle on either side imported from Greece) that was found in the grave of a Hallstatt woman in France. Along with this ridiculously expensive and valuable item, she was buried with what was typical for women: tweezers, ear picks, combs, and jewelry. However, this particular woman, dubbed the Lady of Vix since Vix is the name of the site, also had numerous figures of dogs and young girls buried with her. These were molded and carved from expensive materials like glass and bronze and more ordinary materials like clay and jet. We do not know their purpose.

Gorgon head decorates a krater (huge urn) found at the Vix Grave.
*WikiRigaou, CC BY-SA 4.0 <https://creativecommons.org/licenses/by-sa/4.0>, via Wikimedia
Commons; https://commons.wikimedia.org/wiki/File:Vix_krater.jpg*

The Lady of Vix is not the only example of an ancient Celtic woman receiving a lavish burial; it is simply the most famous. Without the misogynistic and imperial lens of the past and by donning more objective glasses and using the modern instruments they have on hand, archaeologists can say with confidence that Celtic women were largely honored upon their deaths, which leads us to believe they did enjoy a higher status than their contemporaries.

Basic Celtic Beliefs

The Celts were first bound together over vast territories and history through their language, but the next binding factor was their religious beliefs. It is difficult to describe a centralized Celtic belief system; rather, Celtic peoples throughout the ages, including today, have similar beliefs that bind them together.

One of the most central beliefs of the Celts was the sanctity of places in nature like holy groves and clear, fresh springs. Certain groves of trees were considered sacred because they were thought to be the dwelling places of the gods, often the goddess Nemetona. Once these sacred groves were found and ceremonially cleansed, they were blocked off on four sides to mark them as sacred places.

One religious belief that those of us reading this today might find intense is the importance the Celts placed on the human head, which was said to be the seat of the soul. That idea on its own may not be so astonishing, but from it sprung practices that may seem questionable through our modern eyes. Roman writers say the Celts worshiped the skulls of their ancestors, but a more likely practice was the embalming and preserving of enemies' heads after victory in battle. Preserving the heads and skulls of conquered foes is much more likely than cutting off the heads of beloved ancestors.

The Druids: An Introduction

Some people today claim to practice the Druidic religion, but it is simply a modern interpretation of what the ancient Celtic Druids did during the height of their religious power and prominence. The bottom line is we do not know much for sure about the ancient Celtic religious system, especially before the Celts moved westward and settled in Britain and Ireland. There is no centralized piece of Celtic writing that survives. In fact, the Druids, the leaders of society as chieftains, were so secretive that their body of beliefs, rituals, practices, and herbal knowledge was passed onto their acolytes orally.

The word "Druid" is shrouded in mystery. Even today, we are not sure why the Celtic judges, chieftains, medicine men and women, priests, teachers, and any other position of learning are referred to as "Druids." The name is attributed to the Celtic root meaning "to know" since the Druids were the most learned level of Celtic society.

However, unlike many of the people groups we refer to today, the Druids likely did call themselves something that sounded like that name. There is a Welsh term that refers to prophets as *dryw*, which has a similar pronunciation. Female Druids in Irish mythology were known as *ban-druí*.

The main idea behind introducing the Druids here is that as the Celts (whom the Romans referred to as Gauls) made their way west over the centuries (at the end of the Iron Age and into what we call the Classical Era), the Druids were the knowledge holders, the secret keepers, and the storytellers. Even today, we have a certain idea of mystical rituals in the forest conducted underneath the full moon, nature worship, and even human sacrifice. The Druids were part of the highest layer of Celtic society, along with the Celtic nobles, but they made sure to keep most of their knowledge secret. What we think we know comes from Irish mythology (in every myth, after all, is some grain of truth), which was promulgated through the Emerald Isle and the medieval world well after the Celts were part of the Irish narrative.

A nineteenth-century depiction of a Druid.
https://commons.wikimedia.org/wiki/File:An_Arch_Druid_in_His_Judicial_Habit.jpg

Chapter 2: Celtic Arrival in Ireland

The people we are getting to know, the Celts, began arriving in Ireland around 500 BCE. It was not a sudden migration, nor was it marked by the mass exodus of people to one location. The Celtic migration to Ireland can be likened to a small trickle of people who sailed through a period of several hundred years. Some historians think that some Celts began coming to Ireland prior to 500 BCE—the common window is between 800 and 400 BCE, but this is a rather unestablished idea. The year 500 BCE is what is generally accepted as the approximate time Celtic people began to call Ireland their home.

It may seem strange that a people so far-reaching and spread out so as to cover areas of what is now France, Germany, Switzerland, Austria, Spain, Portugal, and even as far south as Turkey would simply stop at some islands they landed on. Why did the Celts not continue their westward expansion past Britain and Ireland? There are several factors that contributed to the Celts' expansion into Britain and Ireland and their settlement there, especially in Ireland.

One reason they could not continue westward was that seafaring technology did not yet exist in Europe to make such strenuous ocean voyages as would be required of sailors from Ireland to the Americas. Another reason is that about a millennium after the Celts arrived and settled in Ireland, the Romans put an end to any possibility of the Celtic culture expanding anywhere else.

Did the Celts Invade Ireland?

From our present-day perspective, at first glance, the Celtic expansion from western and central Europe may remind us of a conquest-hungry people like the Norsemen or the Normans, but the Celtic expansion of and settlement in Ireland was slow, gradual, and, on the whole, peaceful.

The Norsemen, or the Vikings as we commonly call them, invaded England violently in the late 8th century CE, which was long after the arrival of the Celts in Ireland. There are marked differences between these two people groups arriving on the soil of Britain and Ireland (the Norsemen also conquered Ireland, famously naming Dublin from the words of their own language, meaning "black pool"). "Viking" is actually a profession, which is why the invaders are known as Vikings. The Scandinavians who rapidly and violently made it to Britain and other parts of Europe are actually called Norsemen (a distortion of "Northmen"). Viking is a title like sailor, farmer, or soothsayer.

Contrary to the bombastic and bloody Norse invasion of lands in Europe, the Celts more or less slowly settled in Ireland and made it their primary home base. After all, it's easier to feel at home in a land where you can build a culture, a society, a life, and shared history without being threatened on all sides by hungry empires (like the Greeks, the Romans, and even the Scythians at times).

The Normans would also come to call Britain their home, but that happened over two hundred years after the Norsemen invaded England at the hands of William the Conqueror, which happened in 1066. Both the Norsemen and the Normans came to forcefully take land, turn the locals into slaves and subjects, and rule the land on their terms. Sometimes, there were negotiations, but on the whole, the arrival of these two bloodthirsty groups centuries after the Celts' arrival on Irish soil spelled death and destruction for those inhabiting the islands, including the Celtic peoples themselves.

However, the Celts who settled in Ireland and Britain did so unassumingly, integrating themselves into the system that was already in place or finding land that was uninhabited to make their own. These Irish Celts are the ones we think about today when we discuss the ancient Celtic people and culture.

The Celts' arrival in Ireland allowed them to build a stronger cultural connection between tribes and chiefdoms. They never fully centralized but realized that allies were better than enemies, especially with the ever-looming Romans across a short stretch of water.

Travel and Trade

Just like the proto-Celtic cultures before them, the Irish Celts essentially insinuated themselves into existing Irish society, eventually becoming the dominant culture from about two hundred years after their initial arrival all the way to about 400 CE. The Gauls and Celts (the overlap on the European continent was such that there were almost no distinguishing features of the two peoples until the Celts left for Ireland, with the Gauls living in modern-day France under Roman occupation) always prospered because of alliances and trade. This was no different once the Celts reached Ireland.

The Celts brought iron tools to Ireland and the knowledge of how to forge and use them. Although most of the tools were farming and cooking implements, there were definitely weapons among those items the Celts introduced to the people already living in Ireland.

When the Celts arrived in Ireland, they were likely seeking new trading posts at first, but they eventually began to settle. One can go to Ireland today and see why the Celts were enchanted with the verdant green, lush landscape. They themselves contributed heavily to the Irish language and culture that we know and love today.

What probably began as reconnaissance for a trade mission allowed the migrating Celts to forge more alliances westward, ending up as a sort of homecoming for the ancient Celts.

Who were the people already inhabiting Ireland when the Celts arrived? We don't actually know a whole lot about them. We do know that the Celts did encounter Irish inhabitants because of gravesites and remnants of ancient villages. We do not know much else because although the Celts did develop a writing system, *ogham*, there are no surviving written records about with whom the Celts traded.

Written Language System

Although it is likely that the *ogham* language was inscribed upon perishable items like cloth and wood, the surviving examples of *ogham* are carved into stone monuments. The majority of these surviving examples represent personal names. The reason for this assumption is that several sounds of the language are missing from the stone monuments, although they were obviously used and survived. Therefore, there were likely plentiful Celtic writings in *ogham* that were too fragile to have survived throughout such a long time.

However, there are other theories about how *ogham* writing came to be used by the Celts in Ireland. Because *ogham* more than slightly resembles what we refer to as the Germanic runic alphabet (in popular culture, these are the "Viking runes," like in Tolkien's maps and metalheads' tattoos), anthropologists, linguists, and historians have suggested that perhaps *ogham* is simply a copy of Germanic runes. Because the Germanic runic alphabet does have those sounds missing from the surviving written examples of *ogham*, this theory explains that the sounds never disappeared at all.

Another theory is that *ogham* is simply a transliteration of the Latin alphabet, although Celtic consonants like /z/ and /w/ do not exist in the Latin alphabet. The reason this theory has any traction at all is that we know there was heavy contact between the Romans and the people of Britain, especially when these *ogham* monuments would have been inscribed.

Ogham monuments in Dunloe, Ireland.
Berthold Strucken, CC BY-SA 4.0 <https://creativecommons.org/licenses/by-sa/4.0>, via
Wikimedia Commons; https://commons.wikimedia.org/wiki/File:Dunloe_(Ogham_Stones).jpg

Since the discovery (or perhaps recovery) of this system, there have been countless theories put forward about its origins, including the two mentioned above. It is important to note that the word *ogham* only refers to the writing method—the act of using a blade to carve into a hard surface. The group of letters themselves is known as the *Beith-luis-nin*, which is like saying "alphabet" (alpha and beta being the first letters of the Greek alphabet). *Beith-luis-nin* gets its name after the first three letters in the writing system.

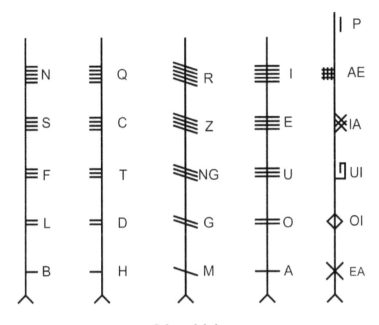

Ogham alphabet.
Runologe, CC BY-SA 4.0 <https://creativecommons.org/licenses/by-sa/4.0>, via Wikimedia Commons; https://commons.wikimedia.org/wiki/File:All_Ogham_letters_including_Forfeda_-_%C3%9Cbersicht_aller_Ogham-Zeichen_einschlie%C3%9Flich_Forfeda.jpg

Unfortunately, there is so much more that we don't know about Celtic writing and *ogham* than what we do know. Much like the disappearance of the English colonists at Roanoke, Virginia, and the location of the Ark of the Covenant, the Celts still hold many secrets, even after all these centuries.

Life after Arriving in Ireland

Despite what was to come, the Celts were relatively unmolested by the encroaching Romans, and for the most part, they did get along with other tribal peoples of Europe, such as the vast Germanic tribes and the Gallic peoples (who were a Celtic group but developed a more separate identity than the Irish Celts). However, this does not mean the Celts did not know how to fight. They were fierce warriors who put their metalworking skills to the test by creating helmets, greaves, gauntlets, spears, and swords for battle. They saw the wisdom in nonviolence, but they could defend their families, farms, homes, and villages if necessary.

Most Celts were farmers, and they supplemented their crops by hunting wild game in Ireland's lush forests. They grew corn, barley, and rye, but eventually, wheat overtook all of these in prominence. When it came to hunting, wild boar was a staple, but venison was also hugely popular. The Celts also hunted foxes, beavers, and even bears. A bear provided fat for helping wounds heal, fur for clothing and bedding, and meat for an entire village.

To cook these morsels, the Celts used a cooking method in which they dropped heated stones into a large pot to make water boil. They added meat, vegetables, and herbs to this mixture, which was all cooked with stones. They kept the fire for the stones extremely hot so that they would always have a way to keep the water boiling.

Celtic Influence on Irish Culture

As we've mentioned above, very little is known about the inhabitants of Ireland before the Celtics came to have a major presence on the island. However, we do know the language that eventually developed into Irish Gaelic (still taught in Ireland today) came from a mixture of several Celtic languages and indigenous Irish tongues. As the Celts developed into a more Irish and less nomadic people, they adopted Irish Gaelic as their uniting tongue.

Although very little is known about the indigenous inhabitants of Ireland before the Celts, it is said that they had been there about seven or eight thousand years before the Celts first arrived. Ireland's topography is not the best for preserving organic materials (except in peat bogs), so not much is understood about the culture that reigned in Ireland before the Celts. There was a Bronze Age people called the Beakers, so-called for their style of beaker-shaped pottery, which does survive today. They may have shown the early Irish how to work with bronze, and they perhaps taught the Celts the same.

However, because the Celts were a major Iron Age culture in their own right, many artifacts and archaeological sites remain from their civilization. Besides the language evolution, which can still be seen and studied today, the Celts brought a unique sense of artwork, craftmanship, mythology, and even fighting methods, all of which are renowned today. The Celtic peoples who settled in Ireland more than 2,500 years ago are the ancestors of most of the Irish population, and so whatever indigenous groups preceded them have faded into history. In fact, the DNA of modern Irish people is mostly Celtic/Gaelic; this also includes the population of Northern Ireland. Irish Travellers (Romani) are the exception, but they were genetically similar until around the 1600s.

Essentially what we know is that early Irish culture influenced the Celts by providing linguistic characteristics that became Irish Gaelic, but all in all, the Celts *did* become an Irish culture a few hundred years after their arrival on Irish soil.

Chapter 3: Daily Life in Celtic Ireland

Farming

Most inhabitants of Ireland during the Bronze Age were farmers. The Iron Age, which followed, was really no different. These metal alloys could be used to create farming implements, which made it easier to complete more work in less time. Farmers could not only feed just their families but also trade surplus crops to purchase more farm implements or livestock or add on to their houses. Sometimes, crop surpluses were even used to purchase slaves.

Farming in Celtic Ireland during this time was virtually the same as it was in Britain. These methods remained the same for centuries. The Celts began to organize plots of farmland into regular rectangular shapes, and they would grow different crops on these plots and use some for animal grazing and some for cultivating hay. The animals the Celts raised normally slept indoors at night, either in a precursor to a small barn or under the family roof. Celts grew barley, corn, wheat, different types of beans, parsnips, spinach, carrots, garlic, and grains for animal feed (rye, millet, and spelt). They eventually grew flax to make textiles.

Farming Implements

Prior to using metal tools to speed up the farming process, the Celts (and everyone else) made farming tools, like hoes, rakes, and sickles, from animal bones. These tools were effective for a while, but they dulled faster and more easily than metal. Metal tools allowed the Bronze and Iron Age peoples to work faster and more efficiently, as they didn't have to replace their tools constantly. The plowshares farmers used were made of iron, but humans were still the muscle behind tilling the soil; animals were yet to be used as beasts of burden.

In order to acquire farmland in the first place, the Celts had to chop down and clear parts of forests or even huge swathes of trees they encountered in their new land. Since forests were considered a sacred part of their culture and belief system, they did not level all the land, but they still had to make room to cultivate their crops and pasture their animals. The most recognizable Celtic tool today and back then was the axe. Because the heads could be made of bronze or iron instead of stone or bone, felling trees had never been easier. The Celts then used some of the lumber to demarcate their different small fields for farming.

The Celts are known for their mobile colter, which simply yet ingeniously allowed farmers to plow and till their fields at the same time. The colter, a sharp, blade-like tool at the end of the plowshare, cut the soil vertically while the plow itself turned the cut soil with its horizontal bar. This type of colter and plowshare combination was in use for centuries because of its efficiency.

Another amazing Celtic farming invention was the wheeled plow. When we think of ancient peoples plowing and tilling the soil by hand, we often think of the Roman model, which was light enough for a person to carry and push laboriously through the soil. The Celts invented a heavier model, but it was supported on either side by a wheel, which made the extra weight insignificant to the worker but great for churning the soil.

Farming Techniques

Depleting the soil of nutrients has always been an issue ever since farming was invented around twelve thousand years ago. Through the millennia, farmers have been (and still are) discovering new and better ways to grow food and other crops. British and Celtic farmers learned that if the soil was being depleted, they could fertilize the fields with deep chalk pits and loam. Loam is part of the topsoil, and it is made up, depending on where it is found, of various percentages of silt, clay, and sand, meaning that it is found near water or where sources of water used to be. Loam provides much-needed nutrients to the soil, and chalk raises the pH level of the soil. Of course, the ancient Celts had no idea what a pH level was, but certain crops, such as beans, spinach, kale, and asparagus, grow very well in alkaline soils.

When Celtic farmers had a grain surplus, they would use granaries to store the extra produce. Most of these were built underground. Before the farmers would fill them up with dried grain, they would usually place an offering of some sort to the gods at the bottom of the granary.

Animal Husbandry

The Celts kept herds of cattle, from which they procured meat, milk, and clothing. They also kept some form of domesticated pig whose species no longer exists, and they raised sheep for their wool and goats for their milk—both of those were also consumed.

In fact, the Celts kept all the standard farm animals we think of today— chickens, geese, and even rabbits, although those probably more closely resembled wild hares than our fluffy bunnies of today. It has been speculated that the Celts used roosters for gaming cocks, as small, roofless enclosures have been found at their settlements that hardly differ from cock cages used today.

Julius Caesar, perhaps mistakenly, thought the Celts only kept fowl as pets, not for consumption. He made connections between the animals and certain speculated Celtic gods and goddesses, but we must remember that Greek and Roman outside observers were continually wrong about those whom they wrote about. More than likely, the Celts ate all the animals they kept.

Naturally, granaries would attract mice, so it is likely the Celts had close relationships with cats. Arguably, cats domesticated themselves—they are opportunists that realized life alongside humans would offer them food security and shelter. Dogs were used for hunting and were huge parts of Celtic heroic epics, as the hero typically had a canine companion of some sort.

Housebuilding

Like other Bronze Age societies in Europe, the main building method for houses and smaller structures (like roofed animal pens) was the wattle and daub method. This method primarily used wooden posts and bendable sticks collected from nearby woodlands. These posts and sticks would then be woven together like a huge basket. The Celts pounded the posts into the ground for stability, although they sometimes had to dig holes to get started, depending on how hard the ground was.

They then arranged the posts in a circle as large as they wished the home or structure to be. They would weave the twigs and sticks into something skinnier than the main skeletal poles; it was as if their home were a stable basket.

In order to fill the gaps between the weaves, a mixture of mud, clay, and even animal dung was used. Housebuilders made a mixture of these materials to "daub" onto the "wattle" that the house was constructed from. The mud, clay, and dung mixture would harden incredibly, although it did need repairs from time to time, especially after periods of inclement weather.

The floor was flat and made from packed earth. Eventually, this packed earth would become hard and strong after generations of feet walking over it and people sleeping on it. The roofs of these round, rather humble dwellings were thatched. This meant that people would need to dry straw and gather more twigs to layer on top of each other. They then bound these straw and twig bundles together in layers, making the roof waterproof. Some houses had small holes at the top for smoke to escape. Other families preferred not to get wet when it rained, so they made vents in their thatched roofs to allow smoke to escape. They didn't want to have to keep away from the middle of the house every time the sky opened up.

On the issue of privacy, there really wasn't much. Most of these round houses with thatched roofs had one room in which the family did everything: cooking, eating, making and repairing clothing, and watching children. Otherwise, activities were done outside unless it was extremely cold.

It might be surprising to think of whole families, often multi-generational, spending time inside a small one-room house together for hours on end. However, Bronze Age societies were very communal and different from what we are used to today, even for things like growing the family. It is likely that the couple was simply separated from other sleepers by just a curtain. The family would keep warm and chat around the fire, and as we mentioned earlier, they would use the hot stone method to cook stew. Rather than directly hanging a pot over the fire, Celtic chefs would place stones into a yellow-hot fire and then let those stones get hot enough to boil the water of the stew. If the temperature of the meal ran low, they would just add another stone. The Celts also roasted whole carcasses on spits over a fire.

Hunting, Fishing, and Foraging

Although the Celts were prolific farmers, they never stopped hunting wild game. The most popular animals to hunt in the woodlands were deer and wild boar. The Celts' favorite roasted meat was wild boar, which was even better than the domestic pigs they raised. The Celts sometimes consumed bear meat as well. It is unclear whether they purposely hunted bears to consume or whether these kills resulted as an act of self-defense.

The Celts also ate foxes and beavers. These animals were plentiful and, in the eyes of the Celts, edible and useful for their furs, so they were fair game, so to speak. Celts did not hunt on horseback; rather, they used hunting dogs to stalk prey like foxes or deer. They also sometimes split into two groups, with one group of hunters chasing their prey into the waiting spears of the other group. The Celts always hunted on foot, but since they did not hunt alone, they could look out for each other, warning against incoming dangers like the errant bear or irate boar. Typically, spears were the weapons of choice when hunting and fishing.

It's only natural that Celtic settlements developed near freshwater sources, which were typically rivers but sometimes large lakes. This means that a large part of their diet came from fatty freshwater fish, such as salmon, trout, and mackerel. These fish provided much-needed omega-3 fatty acids and vitamin C to the Celts. The Celts also often ate eels. Celtic people caught fish typically one at a time by using spears, but they also developed trapping methods just like ancient societies all over the world. They wove baskets for fish to swim into but could not escape. This was a labor-saving way of catching fish while performing other duties.

The Celts supplemented their meat, fish, and grain diet with sweet things too. They foraged for fruits (not necessarily cultivating them themselves until much later) like many types of berries, including blackberries, gooseberries, and blueberries. They also foraged for mushrooms, ate eggs of wild birds, and apples they could reach or that fell from trees. They even consumed nettles, which can be prickly and dangerous to the touch. Nettles were likely used for medicinal purposes.

Although other societies much older than the Celts, like the ancient Egyptians, Greeks, and some Middle Eastern societies, managed to keep/domesticate bees in manmade beehives, the Celts foraged for honey. Beeswax has always been useful and highly prized, as has honey for its delicious sweetness and medicinal properties. As far as we know, Celts did not keep bees domestically, but they still benefited from their hard work by consuming honey and using beeswax.

A Day in the Life

Now that we've discussed the typical arrangements of diet and housing, what did a normal day look like for a Celtic peasant? Noblemen and noblewomen had household staff and were too busy deciding on the future of the settlement, so let's take a look at what a typical day would look like for a peasant girl in a Bronze Age Celtic village.

- If you were a peasant girl in the Bronze Age, you would first get water from a well or from the river for your morning tasks, like cooking and freshening up. This would also be for your family to use as well.

- Breakfast might consist of some leftover stew from the night before, some fruit, some bread, or even some fresh milk from cows or goats.

- Chances are that even though you're a girl, you and your brothers all know how to make tools from flint and animal bones. You would likely get started for the day by sharpening your bone needles and mending clothing or blankets or perhaps continuing your work tanning animal hides from the day before.

- Feeding the animals is hugely important. The pigs get the scraps, and the cows and sheep are usually fine on their own, although they would appreciate some hay or straw. Chickens can feed on corn and other seeds you give them.

- Lunch likely consists of a meat stew boiled with vegetables, but perhaps you and your family went with salted pork, venison, or fish to sustain you in the middle of your day.

- If it happens to be harvest time, you and your whole family are in the fields harvesting crops that are ready to be used or traded as surplus. It's rough work, but luckily, you had that stew for lunch.

- By the late afternoon or evening, the animals need to be fed again, and the ones in the field need to be brought in from the pasture. Your assistance is probably needed with this.

- Dinner is already roasting over the fire indoors on a spit. Your younger siblings are playing with stick men they've made, making them fierce warriors with spears going after a wild boar. You rinse off with a wet rag before sitting around the fire, and you and your family talk about the different tasks of the day and what you all plan to do with your crops. The roast is done, and everyone eats with their hands, savoring the greasy deliciousness of the meat.

- Once everyone is full, the carcass is buried, and it's time to sleep. You curl up on your pile of blankets and furs that you likely share with your siblings, and then you drift off into a deep sleep, your mind and body craving the rest. It's still early for us modern folks with electricity, but you get up with the sun and labor all day. It's best to sleep early to have enough energy to do it all again.

Celtic Crafters

Apart from being capable hunters, fishers, gatherers, and, most importantly, farmers and animal domesticators, we cannot overlook the Celtic propensity for creating art and even imbuing ordinary objects with gorgeous decorations. The Celts made intricate personal decorations, such as brooches, which they used to hold their cloaks around their shoulders. They also made collars called torcs, like the Broighter Collar. It is the most famous example of Irish goldsmithing in the Irish/Celtic style during the Bronze Age.

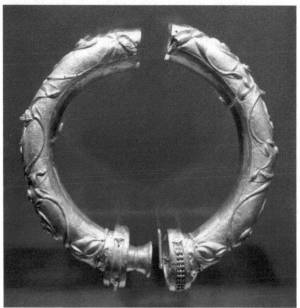

Golden Broighter collar (torc).

The Celts also made ordinary items extraordinary by giving them that extra artistic touch. Spears and swords were engraved with swirling designs and sometimes animals like deer, wolves, bears, and foxes. The handles of swords were also inlaid with semi-precious stones or materials like bone, ivory, and amber and were often intricately carved as well. There are several examples of these painstakingly carved handles on heavy Celtic swords. These featured a human form, and the torso was where the wielder placed their grip, with the arms and legs of the human helping to stabilize the sword during battle. The Celts had a special veneration for the human head (which the Greeks and Romans emphasized in strange ways that may or may not be the truth), and the pommel of the sword was sometimes made into a human head shape. Many of these human head pommels wore fearsome and grotesque expressions, but some were more neutral and blander. It probably depended on what the warrior preferred when commissioning a sword.

Celtic swords were decorated lovingly, but so were their scabbards (the sheath of a sharp weapon). The whole surface could be decorated. Since scabbards were made of a softer material than iron or bronze, like leather or wood, they offered an easier medium to work with when making intricate designs. Swirling and twisting dragons were popular motifs and found on many scabbards. Other popular designs included climbing and curling flowering vines, some of these including animal figures hidden throughout or famous scenes from Celtic mythology.

Horses eventually became extremely important to the Celts, and they would also use them to pull war chariots. As such, horse bridles, saddles, chariot rings, reins, and any other horse-related paraphernalia were decorated for the chieftains and high-ranking Celtic warriors who commissioned them. Designs that adorned these horses and their kits were spirals and knots, the aforementioned floral patterns, and sometimes scenes of a battle.

Gold was an extremely popular material for jewelry, torcs, lock rings (devices used to hold hair back), brooches, and even fancy horse tack for chieftains.

The Celtic artistic style was also evident in woven textiles and even in tools. The Celts decorated their tools, with they then used to decorate other things in their homes. There is something intriguing about making an ordinary item beautiful, whether it is for a spiritual purpose, marking possession, or simply for the sake of beauty.

SECTION TWO:
Myth, Folklore, and Religion

Chapter 4: Pagan Gods and Goddesses

No material on the Celts would be incomplete without coverage of their pantheon of fascinating gods and goddesses. These entities played hugely important roles in the lives of ordinary Celts as they went about their days, interacted with nature, and created implements invoking good luck or reverence to these deities.

The decision-makers, the noble people, and the Druids were even more influenced by this powerful pantheon. Many noble families insisted that their lineage traced back to the supernatural race to which the gods and goddesses belong, the Tuatha Dé Danann—more about them later on. Let's take a look at the most important and interesting deities that make up the main players of Celtic belief and mysticism.

The Dagda

The Dagda is the patriarch of the Celtic pantheon. He is similar to the Norse god Odin in that he is responsible for fathering many, being the god of wisdom, and carrying a staff. But this is where the similarities between the two end.

The Dagda is a typically even-tempered god with an easy-going sense of humor. Humans can joke at his expense, and his mercy allows him to appreciate the joke and not seek vengeance. Epithets for the Dagda used by the Celts include words and phrases that roughly convey the following meanings: the great god, the fertile one, the great father, the all-father, and the lord of great knowledge.

Several powerful objects are associated with the Dagda besides his beard and long, flowing cloak, which are the only defining characteristics of his appearance, along with his enormous size. The most important objects the Dagda possesses are his staff, his cauldron, and his harp.

With the staff, which is extremely long, he can kill many men with just the outer side. But if the Dagda so chooses, he can raise the dead with the inner end of the staff. He literally holds the power of life and death in his hands. The staff is the main reason the Dagda is so powerful and can drive off the Fomorians, a mythological race of ragtag magical creatures that the Druids believed inhabited Ireland before their gods defeated them. It is actually unclear because of translation challenges whether the Dagda actually wields a staff, a club, or a mace. Scholars of Celtic lore all agree that it holds the power of death and life and that it is a weapon matching the size of the Dagda.

The second artifact the Dagda is known to have is a cauldron nicknamed "the un-dry cauldron" since it is always full. No one will walk away with an empty stomach after eating from that cauldron—it is bottomless, and not only that, but it can hold a dozen humans, with the ladle itself comfortably able to fit two inside. The cauldron can be seen as a symbol of the Dagda's rule over agriculture and the seasons. The cauldron never went empty, and so it can be extrapolated from that idea that his wish for the Celts was that there would not be famine but always plenty.

How did the Dagda control the changing of the seasons? He had a harp that was made of oak that he used to keep the seasons in their proper time. Some legends say that the harp stirred men's hearts so that they would be courageous while plunging into battles. The Dagda also had fruit trees that always produced.

Where could one find the Dagda, his power and wisdom, and all this bounty? Newgrange is a Stone Age tomb located in the east of Ireland. This monument, which still hosts a few hundred thousand visitors annually, is said to be the home of the Dagda. It was designed so that at the winter solstice, sunlight shines through the hole built into the roof and illuminates its passageways. It has been a site of pagan significance and worship for more than five thousand years.

The Cailleach

The Cailleach is also simply known as the Hag, and she is the goddess of winter. It is unsurprising that a place with such damp, gloomy, and sometimes prolonged winters as Ireland has its own goddess for that particular season.

The Cailleach.
No restrictions;
https://commons.wikimedia.org/wiki/File:Wonder_tales_from_Scottish_myth_and_legend_(1917)_(14566397697).jpg

Her rule over the winter season begins right after the end of what we now know as Halloween, October 31ˢᵗ, which the Celts started and still call Samhain. The Cailleach actually controls how long the winter is, which is why it was so important for the Celts to stay on her good side. If anything was displeasing to the winter hag, she could make the winds blow harsh and loud over the land and plunge them into a deeper and longer winter.

Despite the fact that she is nicknamed the Hag and has quite an alarming appearance, like the Dagda, she is depicted as a personality on the neutral side of the spectrum; she is neither good nor evil. Those attributes are usually kept for lesser deities, mystical creatures, and humans. The Cailleach has one eye and extremely pale skin, the color of snow, but she is extremely powerful, despite having an odd limping way of leaping and scaling the landscape. She can even carve out valleys and create mountains. This description makes her seem a giantess, the size of even the Dagda. Boulders and landslides can slip right out of her apron, where she holds these structures.

The most important aspect of Cailleach's appearance is her veil. In fact, in Irish and Scottish Gaelic today, her name literally means "hag." However, the etymology of the term is much older, originally meaning "veiled one." The Cailleach is, in fact, also known as the Veiled One and the more flattering Queen of Winter. The ancient Gaelic meaning of "veiled one" is said to have originated from the Latin root *pallium*, meaning woolen cloak.

Like the Dagda, the Cailleach also has a staff, although this one lacks the power to grant instant life and resurrection. It freezes the ground or whatever it touches. In the Scottish tradition, she also carries a hammer for smashing and shaping the landscape. The Cailleach does not have horns herself, as the Dagda sometimes does, but she has control over deer and other horned animals. She herds them and even cares for them during the harsh winter months. This is what cements her as perhaps the second most important deity in the Celtic pantheon. The Dagda is called the father of the gods, and the Cailleach is considered the mother.

The home of the Cailleach is said to be on or near the Beara Peninsula in southern Ireland.

As the Cailleach controls winter, she works together with the goddess Brigid, who rules over the summer. Some legends have it that they are one and the same, with the Cailleach turning her face and Brigid taking over when winter is over and vice versa. Some other legends liken the Cailleach to a much more inhuman deity than Brigid and say she turns to stone each year when her job is finished, allowing the humanoid (and much more aesthetically pleasing) Brigid to rule over the warmer seasons.

Brigid

The Cailleach rules over the winter, and Brigid rules over the summer. Brigid is the daughter of the Dagda, and there is some fuzziness over whether Brigid (or Brigit or Bríg) was one goddess or a triune goddess; however, most of the literature and oral traditions passed down say that this Brigid, the goddess of summer, was also the goddess of wisdom, poets, and protection. Her two sisters, also called Brigid, were called Brigid the physician or healer and Brigid the smith. This is why she is sometimes considered a triune or tripartite goddess, which would be one entity with three different functions.

Brigid, depicted in 1917.
https://commons.wikimedia.org/wiki/File:Thecomingofbrideduncan1917.jpg

However, later literature written by Christians in Ireland suggests that "Brigit" was a title for a goddess, so Brigid may very well have been three separate sisters.

As the Cailleach's season is welcomed at the close of Samhain, the season of Brigid is ushered in at Imbolc on February 1ˢᵗ each year. This is when the Hag lays down her staff and, in many legends, turns to stone until the next Samhain. It is now Brigid's turn to take over.

Brigid's main duties include healing, protection, and looking after domesticated animals. While the Cailleach cares for deer and wild animals, looking after livestock as well during the winter months, Brigid acts as a shepherd for the Celts' domesticated livestock, alerting them if there are any illnesses spreading among them and keeping herds together.

When she is merged together with her two sisters as one entity, she becomes the goddess of healing and smithing, which makes her quite a talented individual. Brigid is associated with spring because Imbolc, which is her annual celebration, venerates fertility and is traditionally the start of the season when ewes begin to give birth. As the patroness of domesticated animals and fertility, Brigid is very busy during the spring months.

Any section about the goddess Brigid would be incomplete without the mention of St. Brigid of Kildare, which the Catholics merged with the Celtic goddess Brigid. There is still some friction between the Catholic and pagan communities, the latter of which still celebrate February 1ˢᵗ as Imbolc rather than the feast day of St. Brigid.

The Morrigan

The Morrigan is another Celtic deity that may actually be three separate goddesses or a single deity with three facets or main aspects. The Morrigan can be compared to the Greek god Ares, the god of war. She meddles and stirs up men's hearts, which then leads to conflict, battles, and ultimately death. She is known as the goddess of war and death. However, because the Morrigan is the Dagda's husband, and they are both powerful warrior deities, their coupling is celebrated on Samhain when the Cailleach is welcomed.

The Morrigan has the power to shapeshift into any living being, including beautiful and terrifying humans, fish, birds, mammals, or even the wind, which, according to the Celts, was arguably living. Her typical appearance is meant to inspire terror and awe, as she is the goddess of war and death. However, she can choose to appear how she wishes to whoever views her, be that as a wolf, a raven, a young woman, a hideous hag, or something else altogether. According to the Táin Bó Regamna, a story that recounts a cattle raid and is part of a whole genre of much later Celtic tales that were written down, describes the Morrigan as a red-haired woman with a red cloak, bringing to mind Melisandre from *Game of Thrones.*

No depictions of the Morrigan survive from the time of her heyday, which, if the terrifying descriptions are anything to go by, might be for the best. Since she can appear any way she chooses, does she really have a true form in the first place?

The Morrigan and the Dagda are the true definition of a power couple, and they had several children together, including Brigid. They have three sons: Aengus, Cermait, and Aed, and another daughter, Bodb Derg. However, just because they are married does not mean that the Dagda and the Morrigan are faithful to each other. The Morrigan had children with others, and she famously attempted to seduce one of the most famous Celtic heroes, Cú Chulainn, but failed.

Legend says that the Dagda wondered how best to win a battle once upon a time, a time that would eventually come to be celebrated as

Samhain. There was a woman bathing in the Unis River in Connacht, which was not far from his home, especially if he was a giant. She was comely, and he was smitten pretty much immediately. The woman told him how to win his battle. He married her, and that woman, the Morrigan, and the Dagda predicted how well the harvest would go each Samhain by performing their marital duties.

This is an interesting juxtaposition—the Dagda is more awed than feared, although he does have control over almost every aspect of life and death. The Morrigan, on the other hand, is more complex yet has less control. She is the goddess of priestesses, spellcasting, divination, war, conflict, bloodshed, and violence. She does not have the power to resurrect, unlike her husband, the lord of agriculture, seasons, time, life, and rebirth.

Cernunnos

Cernunnos is a god from the Celtic religion that seems older and slightly more obscure than the ones we've already discussed. Essentially, his name means "the horned one," and he is known as the god of all wild things. He is often accompanied by a stag; Cernunnos has two horns himself.

Cernunnos.
Nationalmuseet, CC BY-SA 3.0 <https://creativecommons.org/licenses/by-sa/3.0>, via Wikimedia Commons; https://commons.wikimedia.org/wiki/File:Gundestrupkedlen-_00054_(cropped).jpg

This may be confusing, as Brigid takes care of domesticated animals, and the Cailleach cares for animals as well, but Cernunnos does not have a period of inactivity during the year like the goddesses mentioned. He is active all year round.

Cernunnos prefers life with animals, away from humans, deep in the forest. Although Cernunnos seems obscure, he could be even older than the Dagda and the Morrigan, with representations of him in art found from Romania all the way to Ireland. In fact, by the time Christians arrived in Ireland, he had a cult that was going strong. It is not uncommon for people's devotion to particular gods and goddesses to wax and wane over time, and Cernunnos seems to be one of the original gods of the first Celts, as well as one of the more popular ones toward the end of Celtic dominance in Ireland.

He is associated with fertility, the forest, and flora and fauna. He can be likened to the Greek god Dionysus because of his love for the forest, but that is where the comparison abruptly ends. Cernunnos is not concerned with raucous moonlit celebrations in his honor, and he prefers the company of animals to humans. This does not mean that Cernunnos the horned one has not been venerated as much as he deserves—he is one of the most represented figures in Celtic art throughout the whole Bronze Age and the Iron Age. He is easily recognizable by his stag horns.

When Julius Caesar wrote about the "barbarian Celts," he compared Cernunnos to Dis Pater, the Roman father of Jupiter (Zeus). In this way, we can also see that Cernunnos is perhaps even older than the Dagda and is where the main pantheon of Celtic deities originates.

One interesting theory of where the idea of a horned devil in Christian tradition originated is with the Christian monks who came to Ireland. The cult of Cernunnos had been gaining traction for a while, and the Christians even called him the Antichrist and used his horned image as a representation of the devil (a monster with horns is a medieval construct for Lucifer—previously he was just a fallen angel). Several factors likely came together to vilify the Wild One of the Forest, and this is quite possibly a consequence of the slander.

Although Cernunnos is known today as an important Celtic deity due to the backlash from the Christians later on, as well as the persistent depictions of him throughout Celtic history on art pieces, it is possible that he never was a god in the first place. There is almost nothing written about him from Celtic sources. None of the surviving literature or art pieces identify the horned one as a god, so it is possible that this is a huge case of mistaken identity. Cernunnos could simply be a venerated shaman, a Druid with enormous power and wisdom with a cult of his own (including animal sacrifices and sometimes human ones) simply because of his own human achievements, which have been lost in the annals of time. This simply adds to the mystery of the Druids, the Celts, and their ancient pagan religion.

Lugh

Lugh is a god known for his mastery of athletic skills; in fact, one of his nicknames, Samildánach, literally means "equally good at all the skills/arts." The origin of his name, Lugh or Lug, is a confusing one, and no scholar can agree on its origin. Some say it comes from a root meaning "to swear a contract," while some say it comes from a root meaning "flashing light." The cases for each are weak at best—again, this simply adds to the mystery of Celtic theology that we may never discover.

Lugh is often depicted riding a horse and wielding a spear. He is famously good at, well, everything, but throwing spears is a special skill of his and one that he practices daily. Lugh is larger than a human, but he is not considered a giant like the Dagda. In one of the legends of famed Irish hero Cú Chulainn, Lugh is described as young-looking with curly blond hair and wearing a green cloak. Of course, he sits on a horse. He also carries a five-pointed spear and a javelin in the same hand.

Despite the lethality of Lugh's favorite weapons (indeed, these were the preferred hunting weapons of the Celts), he mostly makes games and contests with them rather than causing bloodshed.

Lugh is the son of the god Cian and the goddess Eithne, and this is notable because Eithne is the daughter of Balor. Balor is the ruler of the Fomorians, the nasty little beasts that inhabited Ireland before the deities, the Tuatha Dé Danann, kicked them out. Lugh ends up killing his grandfather Balor. Lugh is also mentioned in some legends as the father of Cú Chulainn, with Cú Chulainn's mother being a mortal woman. This would explain Cú Chulainn's strength, craftiness, cunning, and skill as a warrior, although we will mention that a little later.

Sometimes, Lugh is remembered as a trickster god, a little bit like the Norse god Loki. It is said that when thunderstorms occur, the lightning and thunder are Lugh and Balor battling.

Epona

Simply put, Epona is the goddess of horses. The Gallic (remember, Gallic and Irish Gaelic broke off from a larger Gaelic language group) root *epo-* means horse. The suffix *-ona* means on. She is literally "on a horse."

It might seem silly to us for people to have a goddess fully dedicated to equines (horses, donkeys, and mules), but this makes perfect sense to a Stone and Bronze Age culture during a time when monumental developments in farming, herding, and warfare were being discovered and implemented in everyday life. The horse was central to Celtic life. Eventually, devotion to Epona reached all the way to Rome. The Roman Empire worshiped her, despite the fact that she was originally a Celtic goddess.

The goddess Epona with her horses.
Rosemania, CC BY 2.0 <https://creativecommons.org/licenses/by/2.0>, via Wikimedia Commons; https://commons.wikimedia.org/wiki/File:Epona.jpg

When Epona is depicted, she is typically accompanied by a horse or donkey with her hand resting on its head, seated regally next to the beast.

Epona was revered in Celtic villages, where families had a horse or two and a few donkeys to help with their labor and to check on their land. Epona was called upon when a mare was in labor to ensure the foal would be born healthy and so that the mare would recover swiftly.

Although she was a Celtic goddess, you have to remember that the Gauls and the Celts were one people at one time, and they remained closely related in language and culture. The Gauls relied heavily on their cult of Epona because of their fierce cavalry, which defeated the Roman conquerors time and time again. Thus, Epona became a patron goddess of military cavalries due to their reliance on their noble mounts. When the Romans eventually took over, they adopted Epona into their pantheon and renamed her Augusta.

Goibniu

Many Celtic gods and goddesses were warriors, and the number one thing they were always in need of was metal goods and repairs to their existing weapons. This is where Goibniu comes in. He is the god of metalsmithing, and as such, he was the patron god of human blacksmiths. More importantly, though, he was the smith to the Tuatha Dé Danann. The Celtic pantheon needed weapons, spears, equipment maintenance, and, of course, horseshoes.

Who better to outfit the gods and goddesses with their metal items than a god of smithing? Goibniu is also included in the trio of the gods of art, which also includes a silversmith and a carpenter. This trio was essential for the Tuatha Dé Danann to defeat the Fomorians (which we *will* cover, don't worry).

Apart from his absolutely crucial role as the smith of the gods, Goibniu is also known as a master brewer and for his legendary hospitality. As such, he was the patron god of tavern owners, brewers, and innkeepers. His skill for putting on feasts for the gods and goddesses earns him a drama-free place among the pantheon. One fun fact to make Goibniu even more interesting is that during a battle, one of Brigid's sons stabbed him with a spear. Goibniu simply removed the spear, stabbed Brigid's son with it, and killed him.

Ériu

Ériu's very name is the root of the name of the land of Ireland, which in modern Irish Gaelic is Éire. She is the embodiment of the land of Ireland. The mythical Milesians are said to be the humans who first inhabited Ireland and eventually became the Celts. We know this is all according to legend. Ireland did have normal human inhabitants before the Celts arrived; we just don't have much in the archaeological record to give us a robust picture of who those people really were.

However, according to Celtic mythology, the Tuatha Dé Danann inhabited Ireland before any humans did, and the Milesians were the ones who forced them underground. The gods and goddesses were still present and working, but they weren't the dominant inhabitants of the land. Like the Dagda, the gods and goddesses inhabited burial mounds, sacred groves, and other sites holy to the Celts rather than parading about on land like they did before the Milesians defeated them.

This is important because the last words of Ériu before she was driven underground with the rest of the Tuatha Dé Danann is that the land would be named after her. She scaled a hill called Uisneach, which is now the sacred center of Ireland to pagans. The hill is located in County Westmeath. At the Hill of Uisneach, Ériu demanded the Milesians name the land after her, and it was so. It was known as Éire ever after.

Ériu is the goddess of fertility and abundance. The root of her name means abundance or bounty, which makes perfect sense, with the rolling green hills and fertile farmlands of Ireland lasting to this day. She is also known as the goddess of sovereignty since she was able to get the whole island country named after her. As such, she also has the responsibility and privilege to be the matron goddess of the land of Ireland itself.

Áine

Our last deity on this list deserves a place because she is one of the most revered goddesses in western Ireland. Several places are named after Áine all over County Limerick, including the Hill of Cnoc Áine and at least three other town names. Why is Áine so beloved? She is the goddess of warmth, fertility, and the sun. These three things were extremely important to ancient peoples, especially the Celts. Without these three aspects of the natural world, death would follow.

Midsummer celebrations at the solstice are carried out in Áine's honor, with the last recorded one openly occurring less than two hundred years ago. Áine is not only beloved for the characteristics she represents (abundant harvest, new growth, wealth, and prosperity) but also for her personality. She is said to have been raped by a king, but she bit off his ear so everyone would know what he had done. Many families in Ireland today have family lore that includes the goddess Áine as an ancestor.

Chapter 5: Traditional Celtic Festivals

Like many ancient cultures and traditions, the Celtic festivals and holidays followed the moon rather than the sun. The Gregorian calendar, which we use around the world today, was not adopted until the time of Shakespeare, which is why even as recently as the Middle Ages, specific dates of important events are often disputed (the Julian calendar was the solar calendar in use before the Gregorian calendar was adopted).

The Jews, Muslims, Chinese, and pagans still use the moon to dictate the dates of their important holidays, which means the dates of these festivals change each year. The Celts were no different. Although their feast days and traditional festivals were seasonally based, events like the winter or summer solstices do not fall on the same Gregorian date each year.

It must be stated that the modern celebrations of traditional Celtic festivals do have steady dates (Samhain on November 1st, Imbolc on February 1st, etc.) because of the Christianization of Ireland, as priests and missionaries attempted to be more appealing to the Celts by aligning All Saints' Day and St. Brigid's Feast Day with Samhain and Imbolc. Thus, these two have specific dates in the modern world.

However, since the ancient Celts did not mark time in the same way that we do, instead relying on the sun, the moon, the stars, and seasonal changes to mark a year, these important festivals would fall whenever a significant seasonal event occurred. And because these traditions were so ancient, and the Celts built monuments like Newgrange to mark solstices and equinoxes, they were able to track the year's movements and celebrate accordingly.

We will cover the four essential traditional Celtic festivals here, as well as four minor festivals. These were all important events to mark different aspects of what was happening in nature around the Celts, to honor their deities, and to garner favor for new seasons. The modern pagan community that identifies as modern practicing Druids and witches celebrate these holidays today, albeit much differently (there are fewer sacrifices, for one thing). There are eight main holidays in the wheel of the Celtic year, and an eight-spoked wheel, much like the one in Buddhism, is used by Neopagans to represent the yearly cycle. Let's get into how the ancient Celts celebrated these eight important holidays.

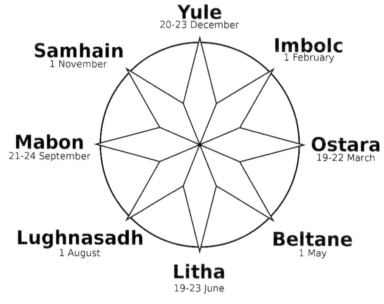

The Wheel of the Year.
https://commons.wikimedia.org/wiki/File:Wheel_of_the_Year.svg

Yule

Yule occurs with the arrival of the winter solstice. Because of the shortening of the days, it represented the rebirth of the sun (and whatever deities the people of the Stone and Bronze Ages associated with the sun) and was a portent hailing the return of new growth and springtime. It was not seen as a barren, empty time but a time of hope for new beginnings, a time for the sun to rest so that it could return in all its glory to revive the land and help all living things flourish.

Eventually, the associations with Yule, the winter solstice, changed. The Celts, no doubt helped along by their portrayal of the winter hag Cailleach, began to associate the beginning of winter with death and the harshness winter brings. They still celebrated Yule at Stone Age sites like Newgrange and Stonehenge, but the idea was more somber and less full of hope than it had been when celebrated in generations past.

If Yule sounds familiar, we sometimes use the term Yuletide to describe the arrival of Christmastime. The association of evergreen plants, holly and its berries, mistletoe, ivy, and wreaths come from this ancient holiday. The Celts made wreaths and bound sprigs of these winter plants together and gave them as offerings. They also used them as decorations for their homes. They also decorated trees—sound familiar?

In order to offset the bleakness of Midwinter, which is another name for Yule and the winter solstice, the Celts held many feasts in their own homes and in the homes of family and friends. They gave gifts as well. If this sounds like Christmas, it is pretty much the same, minus the tradition of hanging stockings. Also, today, we do not typically sacrifice animals to any deities during the Christmas season.

Imbolc (Spring)

This holiday, known in modern times as St. Brigid's Feast Day, aligns with North American Groundhog Day, which is celebrated a day later. Both symbolize the impending arrival of spring, which is how the association began. However, Imbolc is the original celebration of the goddess Brigid, and it is right between the winter solstice and the spring equinox.

Imbolc was celebrated to usher in spring after the long winter. Although the weather may still resemble its icy wintry character, by welcoming in springtime on February 1ˢᵗ, the Celts were optimistically looking forward to warmer and more fertile times ahead. Since Brigid, daughter of the Dagda, is the goddess of wealth, prosperity, domesticated animals, and fertility, she is the perfect patroness for springtime. As we mentioned earlier, there are several different ways to tell the story, but Brigid has control of the light half of the year, taking the weather and season mantle from the Cailleach, who controls the dark half of the year.

Not much literature from the same time as ancient Celtic Imbolc practices survived, but a continuous theme is the pregnancy of ewes and the birth of lambs around this time. We have discussed how important sheep were for the Celts as sources of wool, meat, and sometimes milk. Since sheep give birth earlier in the year than cattle, the arrival of lambs was inextricably linked with the arrival of spring.

Ostara

Although Ostara takes place on the actual vernal equinox (the start of spring), Imbolc is the holiday associated with spring's actual arrival. Because the days began lengthening, Ostara was a celebration that those light days had arrived instead of just a symbol of hope for warmer times to come. Ostara typically arrived during what is now the third week of March on the Gregorian calendar, which would be the time when the green hills of Ireland and all its natural glory were on full display.

This holiday is not as ancient as the others, with records of its celebration appearing around the 8th century. It is a corrupted spelling of the name of the goddess Eostre, which some people say is where we get the name Easter (there are many etymological theories for the name Easter; this is simply the one that comes from Britain and Ireland). Eostre is a Germanic goddess representing spring. Since she is an import, it makes sense that her holiday is a later addition to the Celtic calendar. However, she is associated with rabbits and eggs, symbols of fertility.

Beltane (Summer)

Beltane normally falls on or around May 1st, and it falls between Ostara (the spring equinox) and Litha, one of the major Celtic solar festivals. Its celebration by Celts was largely influenced by Germanic tribes, with even some Roman influence thrown in. The Romans venerated the goddess Flora at the time, and this adoration carried over to Ireland. Instead of having a specific goddess by the name of Flora, the Celts celebrated the concept of fertility in general. Fertility was a key aspect of ancient life in all cultures, and the Celts were no exception.

Celebration and joy were on full display, filled with bonfires for purity. People danced and made music around the fires, encouraging and celebrating fertility. The reason bonfires were so important at Celtic festivals is that they represented the power of the sun, and the Celts believed that fire had cleansing properties. On Beltane, they would light two huge bonfires and walk their cattle between them, cleansing the cattle and ensuring they would produce plenty of milk and calves.

The modern iteration of this pagan holiday involves dancing around maypoles, donning flower crowns, and celebrating summer's arrival. It is known as May Day.

Litha

Litha, or the summer solstice, is the longest day of the year, and the sun is celebrated in all its power and magnificence. It is also called Midsummer and typically falls during the third week of June. The Celts absolutely loved their bonfires, and Litha was a special day for them. The Celts would light bonfires on top of hills so they could be seen for miles, and those daring enough on the summer solstice would attempt to leap through the fires to garner good luck. This seems like a steep price to pay for luck, but ancient peoples were nothing if not thorough when it came to ensuring prosperity.

Some legends say that because this is the longest day of the year, it is a battle between the light and the dark. After all, in ancient Celtic tradition, the year is split in two—the light half and the dark half. But, of course, inevitably, the dark side of the year wins; the longest day of the year eventually comes to a close, and the days shorten from Litha onward. There are records of celebrants lighting huge wheels on fire, then proceeding to roll (and even race) the enflamed wheels down hills to the shores of a nearby river. Fire and light reigned during Litha, which itself means "light."

Lughnasadh (Autumn)

Lughnasadh is one of three harvest festivals celebrated by pagans, but in the Celtic tradition, this festival more recently marked the beginning of the harvest season. This holiday is typically celebrated on August 1ˢᵗ, making it another "halfway holiday," this time in the middle of the summer solstice and the autumnal equinox. However, in ancient Celtic practice, Lughnasadh fell between harvest time and planting season, which means that the largely agricultural Celtic society was at a bit of a standstill. Hence, the festival of Lughnasadh was born.

As you may have surmised already, the festival contains the name of the god Lugh, the master of all skills. The Celts took this time of idleness between harvesting and planting to host games, bringing different villages and communities together for the competitions. These competitions were more ritualistic and religious in nature than they were for the sheer sport of it, from what little we know of them. Scholars believe they involved spear-throwing, perhaps arrow shooting, maybe hunting, and definitely fire in some form. The Celts were wonderful storytellers, and there is evidence that shows they would put on plays honoring Lugh and his defeat of the blight, which eliminates harvests.

These festivities usually took place in high places, such as plateaus or hilltops, which gave participants and spectators ample viewing for the role-playing exercises and the sacrifices, which typically included the first fruits of the village harvest and a bull.

This harvest festival was such a big deal that there were often corresponding traveling markets and fairs to sell and trade surplus crops and to prolong the festivities. Lughnasadh was definitely a festival where one could have a good time, and it took the people's minds off the fact that they could not yet plant new crops in this in-between time.

Mabon

The celebration of the autumnal equinox is a pagan harvest festival, the second of three. The name Mabon was not used until 1970, and the Celts probably did not celebrate this as a major holiday. We mention it here because it is included in the Wheel of the Year, and during the autumnal equinox, there is no doubt that the ancient Celts marked the occasion in some way. However, we do not think that it was a major, bonfire-lighting, feasting occasion. It was simply another way to mark the passing of the days and may have been lightly celebrated with fall fruits and a hearty meal.

Samhain (Winter)

Samhain was arguably the most important ancient Celtic festival. This holiday began on the evening of October 31ˢᵗ but was celebrated all through the day on November 1ˢᵗ until sunset. November 1ˢᵗ was the official start of the winter season, and this is the third pagan harvest festival on the Wheel of the Year.

Samhain is pronounced like *saw-win* or *sah-ween*, and the second pronunciation contributes to our modern word Halloween (All Hallows' Eve, shortened and corrupted with the -*ween* part of Samhain). On this day, the Celts marked the finality of the harvest season and prepared for winter, when the Cailleach would reign again over the land.

The Celts believed that if the Dagda and his wife, the Morrigan, chose to mate over the river where they met and first fell in love on Samhain, then the next harvest would be a bountiful one. Whether or not the gods coupled that year, Samhain was always a raucous and joyous occasion for the Celts, despite the fact that it was a winter-welcoming ceremony.

Many cultures, the Celts not excepted, associated winter with death—crops did not grow at this time, and game was scarce, either because of hibernation or migration. However, this did not stop them from celebrating Samhain. As pagans still believe today, the ancient Celts believed that the veil between the real world and the spirit world was the thinnest on the evening of Samhain (October 31ˢᵗ). They believed that not only could their dead ancestors visit them, wishing them luck and prosperity, but that unsavory ghosts could also trouble them.

This is where the tradition of wearing masks and costumes comes from. If a harmful spirit or entity cannot recognize the costume-wearer, how are they supposed to cause them harm? Later Celtic tradition saw people carving faces into turnips and leaving them to dry like shrunken heads, which was another method to ward off unwholesome spirits. These evolved into our jack-o'-lanterns of today (Irish immigrants used pumpkins in the New World instead of turnips).

Taking a look back at the ancient Celts, many burial mounds from the Stone and Bronze Ages keep time with this ancient celebration that is halfway between the autumnal equinox and the winter solstice. It is likely that the Celts, as they often did, built enormous bonfires around or on top of these burial mounds to welcome the spirits of the dead, as well as to honor the last of the light part of the year while welcoming the dark half of the year. The burial mounds were hugely significant at Samhain because of the belief that the spirits of the departed could come and go during this night.

It is probable that Samhain, like other major Celtic holidays, included sacrifices, mostly animal but possibly human. Records for this holiday were only set down in detail in the early modern age, so some of the practices we associate with the Neopagan Samhain and with Halloween do not have roots tracing all the way back to the Bronze and Iron Ages. It is almost certain the Celts marked this important occasion with fire, and it is almost just as certain that animals like bulls or goats would have been sacrificed and/or purified during this festival. Feasting and merrymaking definitely happened, as it was a time to celebrate, a kind of final hoorah before the land began to freeze.

Samhain and Beltane are at opposite ends of the year and were the most important holidays to the Celts. This is not so much because of crop harvests as it was due to the importance of raising livestock. The Celts had a system of pasturing their animals in summer and winter fields, and this clear delineation between the two halves of the year was mainly due to the need for shepherds and farmers to take care of their livestock. Crop planting and harvesting were essential to each and every holiday, but the reason these two festivals are so important (Samhain, the winter, and Beltane, the summer) was because of livestock, or so 19th-century scholar Sir George Frazer writes.

Chapter 6: Celtic Mythological Beasts and Entities

Each and every culture, modern and ancient, has its own creatures that make up legends, myths, and bedtime stories. Most of the following Celtic creatures and beings are still spoken of today with a hint of discomfort or even fear for those who are skittish. Others love spine-chilling stories of monsters and ghoulies, and whether you love these stories or they creep you out, they're still fascinating.

These creatures aren't all bad. Some are creepy, some are terrifying, and some are simply amusing. Which one is your favorite?

The Banshee

The banshee is likely the best-known mythological export from Ireland besides the leprechaun. She is often depicted as a grotesque hag with thin, long, flowing white hair, claw-like hands, and dressed in black. However, she can sometimes appear as a lady of indeterminate age in a white dress or as a young woman wearing a mourning veil.

Woodcut depiction of the banshee as a crone.
https://commons.wikimedia.org/wiki/File:Banshee.jpg

The most terrifying aspect of the banshee is not how she appears or what she is wearing. It is that she appears at all because the appearance of a banshee and the subsequent wailing she performs are said to predict death. If you see/hear a banshee, either you or someone close to you will die. This is why the banshee is likely the most feared of all Celtic mythical creatures. Her eyes are said to be red-rimmed and bloodshot from constantly crying, and that would admittedly be terrifying to behold in the gaunt face of a woman wearing tattered clothing in a foggy bog.

There is a theory on where the myth of the banshee comes from (although many people today swear that banshees are no myth and that they do wander the moors of Ireland). In ancient Celtic funeral rituals (as in many places in Asia), some women were paid to mourn an important person's death. Their wails became known as keening, and today, we use the word to describe a high-pitched scream or cry that eagles often make, as well as infants or adult humans.

The legend of the banshee is alive and well today in the countryside, although her status as a mythical creature is slowly being supplanted by rational explanations of hearing her keening. Some say the banshee's wail is the scream of a rabbit or a fox, and if you have ever heard either of those sounds, that is a spot-on explanation. Proponents of the existence of banshees ask, how then does one explain a death so close after hearing the "banshee's" wail? Coincidence?

Dearg Due

The Irish vampire comes in both male and female forms, but this particular story concerns the female version.

The story goes that there was once a young woman who was in love with a local boy, but her father did not take her feelings into consideration whatsoever. The father promised his daughter to a powerful chieftain, but this chieftain was not the man the woman loved. He and his family also had a reputation for being brutal and cruel.

The chieftain and the stunningly gorgeous young woman were married, and of course, there was a huge celebration, but the bride and her love were miserable. And family life with the chieftain provided no relief. He would lock his bride up for days or weeks at a time. She starved herself out of misery, and the chieftain remarried quickly, seemingly unconcerned. The father did not care either. The chieftain had provided him with a handsome bride price for the beautiful (now deceased) girl.

The dead girl's grave had only one bereft visitor—her love, the man she was not permitted to marry. According to legend, the spirit of the dead woman simply left the grave because her lust for vengeance and her anger were that strong. One can only hope that the man she loved did not see this terrifying sight.

The spirit of the woman, compelled by her thirst (pardon the pun) for revenge and by her blind rage, made her way to her childhood home and killed her father in his sleep.

Her next step, as you can imagine, was her evil husband's home. According to most stories, as she burst into his chambers, likely looking like a ghostly nightmare, he was in bed with several women, with no care at all for her suffering or her memory.

The woman-spirit disregarded the other people present in the bed, throwing herself onto her husband and killing him almost immediately. Then she proceeded to do what she did not do with her first kill—drink all the blood from the body.

After she drained him of his blood, she began to feel an unquenchable thirst for human blood. She then became known as the Dearg Due or Red Bloodsucker, and she spent her undead existence luring men with her ethereal beauty to dark places to kill them and suck out their life force. She is said to even dress in red, emphasizing her deepest desire.

With every kill, the doomed Dearg Due became more and more ravenous, the hunger and thirst for blood ever more powerful. She was known to be insatiable. One wonders if her lost love, who visited her grave every day, transferred some of his feelings of revenge and retribution to her spirit, feeding her own want of vengeance and prompting her to rise to seek her own form of justice.

The male version of the Irish vampire is similar to the traditional story of the undead monster in only a few respects. There is a relatively modern (so the ancient Celts would not have told this story) tale about an evil dwarf, Abhartach. He terrorized the town of Derry until a hero slew him. However, the hero buried him upright (as one would), and the next day, the dwarf came back even more evil and despotic than he was before. The hero slew him again, but the same happened.

A wise Druid told the hero to slay Abhartach again but to bury him upside down to keep him from rising from the dead once more. This tactic worked.

The vampire connection comes with the idea of rising from the dead, but it also has its place in another legend concerning the vicious, bloodthirsty dwarf. He drinks the blood of those in town, another vampiric trait. Instead of a Druid, a pious Christian tells the hero that in order to slay the "walking dead" blood-drinking dwarf, he must stab the dwarf with a sword made of yew and then bury him upside down. But he must also place a huge stone slab on the grave while surrounding it with thorns—one can only presume as an extra precaution.

One thing that sticks out in the Abhartach legend that parallels the typical vampire story is that the hero was told to kill the dwarf with a yew sword. Yew has been revered for millennia, especially by the Celts and their Druids, for its association with the power of death and its magical properties. Voldemort from the *Harry Potter* series possesses a wand made of yew wood.

The Dullahan

Although across time and many different countries and cultures, the concept of a headless horseman appears, we are, of course, focusing on the Celtic version, the Dullahan. The Dullahan is also not exclusively male, as this magical entity can take on a female form as well; however, it is most commonly portrayed as a male figure.

This imposing, frightening being either rides a black horse or is pulled along in a black carriage by six black horses. This carriage is known as the

Black Coach or the Death Coach. It travels so quickly through the night that nearby branches and bushes will be set alight.

The Dullahan depicted with a headless horse.
https://commons.wikimedia.org/wiki/File:Croker(1834)Fairy_Legends_p0239-dullahan.jpg

As for appearance, the Dullahan dresses in all black and always carries its head with it. This head is said to have supernatural powers of sight, scoping out the land over long distances in search of the cursed people the Dullahan seeks to take the souls of. The head is said to have eyes that roam back and forth, left and right, constantly. The Dullahan can also hold its head high above its shoulders, using it as a periscope to search out its victims. Again, the Dullahan is most commonly depicted as a man, but there's really no strict gender reference.

If you come across the path of the Dullahan as he rides his hell-horse or is pulled along in the Black Coach but are not his intended victim, you still have a price to pay. He will likely spare your life, but he will blind you. His supernatural head will stare into your eyes to complete the deed. If you try to avert your eyes, the Dullahan will either pour a bucket of blood into your face to blind you or whip you across the eyes with his whip made from a human spine. Charming.

If you *are* the one the Dullahan seeks, there is no way you can lock this powerful being out. All doors, gates, windows, trap doors, and anywhere you can hide will fly open at his command, and all he has to do is say your name for your soul to flee from your body.

If this sounds terrifying to you, you are not the only one. The Celtic entity known as the Dullahan is sometimes said to be the embodiment of the Celtic god Crom Dubh, whose name means "the dark one." His followers are said to have employed the use of human sacrifice more than the average group of Druids, and Crom Dubh is said to have a constant battle over light and dark, as well as over the harvest, with the god of skills, Lugh. Crom Dubh, who is depicted as a dark, hooded figure, evolved into the concept and physical manifestation of the Dullahan.

If you carry pure gold with you, you may hold off the Dullahan for a time. If it is a golden necklace or even a gold coin, this may protect you the first time he sees you, but it isn't a talisman that has a permanent effect. Where the banshee's wail provides a warning or an augury of death to someone close to you, the Dullahan's appearance assures it.

Why is the Dullahan depicted as headless? The main theory, besides the fact that a headless being in all black carrying a supernatural, bright-eyed possessed head and a whip made of human spine cantering down the moors on a horse like a bat out of hell is absolutely bloodcurdling, the Celts, as we mentioned in previous chapters, held special beliefs about the human head. The Celts thought the soul resided in the head. That is why sword pommels were often carved into the shape of human heads (for power) and why the Celts are written to have kept the heads of their enemies in Greek and Roman sources. This practice wasn't so much to usurp their enemies' power like some cannibalistic tribes did and still do; it was more a talisman that served as a reminder of the power of their enemies, which they now possessed.

Balor

Known as Balor of the Evil Eye, he is the king of the Fomorians, the demonic race that was eventually defeated by the Tuatha Dé Danann before humans came to inhabit Ireland. We will discuss more about the Fomorians below.

Balor was the chief of the whole race, and he became Balor of the Evil Eye when he looked upon a powerful magic potion his father's Druids (yes, humans were not the only ones to have Druids) were brewing, and the fumes got into his eye. Typically, the tales depict Balor as a giant with only one eye, much like the Greek Cyclops. The difference between Balor and the Cyclops is that Balor's eye constantly shoots a stream of burning, destructive light and heat that destroys everything it falls upon each time he opens his eye.

Some stories say that Balor has two or three eyes, but they all agree that one of the eyes is the "evil" destructive one that he used to bolster the Fomorians in their fight against the god race, the Tuatha Dé Danann. In fact, unless he constantly wishes to burn everything in his path or close his only eye, this interpretation holds the most water. He can use his normal eye or eyes while covering the malignant eye with a leather shield, as is mentioned in one version of the story.

Balor is actually the grandfather of the god Lugh, whom we have mentioned several times. Lugh valiantly kills his own grandfather and beheads him. Another version of the story has Lugh shooting a sling stone through Balor's eye with a blow so powerful that the stone emerges from the other side of Balor's head. When the giant falls, he crushes twenty-seven of his fellow Fomorians.

Fomorians

This is the demonic race that Balor championed. Balor was actually a chieftain, not their king—the Fomorians were led by King Indech. Above, we mentioned that Balor's fallen body crushed more than two dozen of his comrades in arms, and we must remember that most Fomorians were not giants like he was.

Group of Fomorians off to battle.
https://commons.wikimedia.org/wiki/File:The_Fomorians,_Duncan_1912.jpg

They were known as the "demon race," which inhabited the Irish Isle before being defeated by the gods, who subsequently were driven underground by humans. Therefore, the cataclysmic battle between the

Fomorians and the Tuatha Dé Danann took place before humans were said to have come to Ireland.

Describing the appearance of Fomorians is challenging because they did not take on one specific form. There didn't seem to be any uniformity of appearance, and since they were demons or demon-like, perhaps they could choose their appearance at will. Some are described as those who dwell in the underworld or in the depths of the sea, and in the 7th century, the Fomorians took on personas as raucous sea marauders, no doubt due to the Viking invasions of Britain and Ireland. But as for looks, some are completely cloaked; some are small, hairless, long-eared, and wear only loincloths; and some resemble half-baked forms of animals like horses or goats. They often are described as having only one arm or one leg or even one eye, so they were basically all malformed in some way.

However, it should be noted that some of the gods, such as Lugh, are products of deities mating Fomorians. The ones that the gods took as mates were, of course, beautiful. This begs the question raised earlier if the demon race could appear as they wished or if their appearances were something that could not be helped. Besides the more than occasional coupling and even marriages between the Tuatha and the Fomorians, the two races did coexist for ages until the final battle between the two occurred.

It is also said that the Fomorians could have been antagonists against the gods *and* the first humans in Ireland. That is what the Celtic legends say—that the first humans had contact with both the gods and the Fomorians and that they could have seen this epic battle between the races.

Pooka

Changing pace from hell demons, soul-stealing, and battles of epic celestial consequences, we now introduce the Pooka. The Pooka (or *Púca*, in the Irish spelling) is a shapeshifting creature that can bring either good luck or bad luck to households, depending on the treatment it receives.

The Pooka reminds one of the brownies, which are more popular in Scotland and are said to help out with household chores while a family sleeps as long as it is left a bowl of milk at night. The Pooka has several recorded appearances, but it is normally described as brown, small, hairy, and may or may not have a tail. The Pooka usually wears a dark cloak, whether in humanoid or animal form. Even when in humanoid form, the Pooka will have a tail—perhaps that is why it always has a cloak handy.

The Pooka has a proclivity for mischievous behavior more than anything particularly harmful. If it chooses to take the form of a pony or a horse, for example, it can lure a rider onto its back and run as fast as it can through terrifyingly uneven terrain, frightening the rider out of their wits and then dropping them off in the middle of nowhere, technically unharmed, while the Pooka laughs and gallops away. If one were ever to suspect an encounter with this type of Pooka, it is said that it can be controlled if the rider is wearing a pair of sharp spurs. This will disappoint the Pooka but will save the rider from the prankster's plans.

The other side of the Pooka is auspicious and even selfless. One story has it that a Pooka appeared to a young farmer as a bull, and the farmer took the bull in and gave it food and a warm cloak. In return, the Pooka, as a bull, did mill work, plowing, and other heavy labor. In Pooka form, it would clean and organize the barn at night. One night, the boy saw the Pooka in his true form, but unlike most mythical Irish beings, Pookas willingly introduce and show themselves to the humans they interact with. The two became friends and exchanged gifts over their friendship.

Some stories also tell of Pookas, who can see other magical entities otherwise invisible to humans since they are magical themselves, throwing themselves in the way of beings wishing to cause harm to unsuspecting humans, thus saving the humans. The Pooka will then reveal themselves to the human, and the grateful human will likely strike up a friendship with the creature that saved them.

Aos Sí

The Aos Sí is, in simplest terms, the name for the magical race of faeries and otherworldly beings that inhabit Ireland. In fact, the name Aos Sí or Sídhe is synonymous with faerie. This isn't what we typically think of as "fairies," the tiny insect-like humanoid beings that adorn themselves with flowers and live in tiny houses in the woods. Although those beings are part of the faerie race in Ireland, Aos Sí is an umbrella term that includes all magical beings, whether they choose to reveal themselves to humans or not, hence the spelling we use here, faerie.

Depiction of Aos Si riders in 1911.
https://commons.wikimedia.org/wiki/File:Riders_of_th_Sidhe_(big).jpg

Even the dreadful Dullahan is said to belong to this race of faeries or Fey in Ireland. The origin of the name Aos Sí is typically traced back to a phrase meaning "people of the mounds" or "people of the fairy mounds." This goes back to the gods going underground after being defeated by the Milesians, the legends discussed in Chapter 4 in Ériu's section.

Celtic tribes were very careful not to offend the people of the mounds. Burial mounds were considered sacred places where festivals could be held, some specifically built to light up during certain solstices and equinoxes, but before and after festivals, during ordinary days, these places were treated with respect and caution.

Many legends in Ireland state that if a human becomes entranced by any being of the Aos Sí or if they eat any of their food, the human will become trapped in their world and not be able to return to the world above ground. They will never be seen again by any of their kind.

As for not offending the faerie race, they are often not referred to directly by name—euphemisms like the Fair Folk, the Folk, or the Good Neighbors, along with Sídhe or Aos Sí, are used even today. The Celts would set out offerings of milk, fruit, or sometimes bread to appease these beings.

Some sources say that the Aos Sí were the remnants of the Tuatha Dé Danann, the race of the gods, after the humans pushed them underground. The Aos Sí live in a liminal space between the two worlds, which is why humans can see them if they reveal themselves and can interact with humans if they choose. Banshees, Pookas, or leprechauns would be included in this designation.

Sluagh

One of the more intimidating creatures on our list is the Sluagh, or the "host of the dead." These fearsome faeries-gone-bad are said to fly in the air in a crescent formation, much like birds, and swoop down to take the souls of those they prey upon.

Before Samhain and Imbolc and the other major fire festivals of the ancient Celts, some origin stories of the Sluagh say the Celts were forbidden from lighting fires on these occasions because the space between worlds was so thin. The Druids warned that fire would attract the Sluagh. However, at some point, that practice was abandoned in favor of huge bonfires and offerings to the dead and other spirits.

The unforgiven souls, the Sluagh.
https://commons.wikimedia.org/w/index.php?curid=93481

The Sluagh typically travel in large groups, hence their name, and they are said to be the souls of unforgiven dead people. We've already mentioned two versions of the Sluagh—the ancient Celts thought they were part of the Aos Sí, the Fey Folk who had been corrupted in some way, seeking to make humans as miserable and lost as they had become. After Christianity was introduced to Ireland, the belief in the Sluagh persisted, but the lens from which they were viewed changed. They were seen as unforgiven sinners bent on dragging happy, thriving souls down to hell with them when they swept down over the earth.

Although there are so many more mythical beings to cover, we will end on a whimsical note rather than a creepy one. We hope this chapter has encouraged you to check out Irish folklore for yourself to explore the enchanting and often terrifying world of the Fey.

Glas Gaibhnenn

Glas Gaibhnenn is the cow of plenty and fertility. Said to be owned by a smith, this cow is light green in color or has green spots, making it easy to pick out. This cow never runs out of milk, so for a culture dependent on the favor of good weather for its harvests and to feed its domesticated livestock, Glas Gaibhnenn was a symbol of plenty and of comfort because of its consistent ability to provide.

Balor in disguise stealing the enchanted cow.

No restrictions;
https://commons.wikimedia.org/wiki/File:Myths_and_legends;_the_Celtic_race_(1910)_(14596782139).jpg

One interesting legend Glas Gaibhnenn is involved in is one in which Balor of the Evil Eye steals the cow and takes it to a glass tower. This tower also holds his daughter, whom he never lets leave because it is prophesized that she will give birth to a son who kills Balor (Lugh, as mentioned before). The hero Cian must take back the cow from Balor of the Evil Eye, and he ends up becoming the father of Lugh. Lugh is conceived, and the cow is returned to its rightful owner. All is well until the major battle between the Fomorians and the Tuatha Dé Danann.

Chapter 7: Celtic Legends and Stories

In this chapter, we will be covering some essential Celtic tales that sometimes get overlooked in today's retellings of famous Celtic legends. The famous stories that every Irish person is somewhat familiar with will be covered in Chapter 8.

The Sons of Tuireann

Sometimes, this tale is known as the "Tragedy of the Sons of Tuireann." Tuireann does not feature in this story other than his part as the father of three sons: Brian, Iuchar, and Iucharba. Tuireann has another three sons, but this is not their story. The previous three sons' mother is Danu.

As for Brian, Iuchar, and Iucharba, their mother is Tuireann's own daughter, Danand. During the great battle, the Mag Tuired, in which the Fomorians are overcome by the Tuatha Dé Danann, the same battle in which Lugh kills Balor of the Evil Eye, Tuireann's sons, Brian, Iuchar, and Iucharba, actually kill Lugh's father.

In short, Lugh kills Balor, his own grandfather. Tuireann's sons kill Cian, Balor's son and the father of Lugh. This is where the "Tragedy of the Sons of Tuireann" begins, a tale that is heavily influenced by Greek mythology and takes place in far-flung foreign empires.

Because they have killed his father, the god Lugh exacts a blood price, known in Irish as *eric,* and he requires the brothers to accomplish incredible feats and retrieve various magical items. Retrieving those magical items requires massive strength, cleverness, and fortitude. The items Lugh demands for the blood price include the following:

- Three golden apples from the Greek garden that the Hesperides cultivate. The Hesperides were akin to forest nymphs, and the brothers had to get past them, as well as the giant serpent guarding this mystical garden.

- A magical pigskin from King Tuis in Greece. This pigskin had the power to turn water into wine and cure disease.

- A poisoned spear from the king of Persia.

- Two horses from the king of Sicily, Dobar, who were able to pull chariots across water and land.

- Seven pigs that were the property of the King of the Golden Pillars that, if eaten at night, would reappear in the morning.

- The mythical dog Failinis as a puppy, which was known as Lugh's companion (after the brothers get the puppy from the king of Iruaith).

- The cooking spit that belonged to the women of Inis Fionnchuire, which was located much closer to home than the first few items. The significance of this cooking spit is that these women were of the faerie race, and they lived underwater. The brothers also return to Ireland with the previous items before setting out again to retrieve the cooking spit. The faerie women laugh because they could easily overpower any of them and let the brother who dives down to retrieve the spit take it because of his audacity.

There is one final task. Unlike the other tasks, which required feats of cunning and strength to capture or acquire items, the final requirement is something the three brothers must do.

This last task takes place atop the Irish hill of Miodhchaoin, or it is meant to. The three brothers must shout at the top of this specific hill to complete the *eric* and be free from Lugh's obligatory enchantment. However, this hill is occupied by the sons of Miodhchaoin, and he and his three sons stab Brian, Iuchar, and Iucharba with spears.

The sons of Tuireann manage to kill Miodhchaoin and his three sons (their trials made them formidable warriors), but the three sons of

Tuireann are all mortally wounded. Brian lifts his brothers' heads, and the three of them complete the task as best they can, using the last air in their lungs to weakly cry out so that the final task is fulfilled.

Iuchar and Iucharba die soon after, and although Brian still lives, he barely has any life left in him. He does have enough to entreat Lugh to use the enchanted pigskin they retrieved to heal his brothers (and one can presume himself), but despite all that they have done to fulfill the *eric*, Lugh refuses to use the pigskin to heal any of them. Tuireann buries his sons, dying himself soon after, one can say perhaps of a broken heart.

The ultimate winner of this story is the god Lugh, whom some may say cruelly denied mercy to the men who killed his father. He profited immensely through the acquisition of these magical objects, with the spear becoming his famed weapon and Failinis his faithful canine companion. In a way, the "Sons of Tuireann" is as much about Brian, Iuchar, and Iucharba as it is an origin story of sorts for Lugh, who is celebrated during the Lughnasadh festival.

The Faerie Folk

Where does the story of the faeries come from? They are ubiquitous throughout Celtic and Irish stories, and many people still believe that their existence is possible in forested areas far away from human civilization.

The short answer is that the Fey Folk or the faeries, which can appear as beastly creatures, evil apparitions, deities, or beautiful, magical beings, originate with the godly race of the Tuatha Dé Danann. The race of the gods was the predecessor of sorts of the Fey Folk, and the faeries remained behind in the spaces between this world and the other.

The origin story of the Tuatha Dé Danann, the race of the goddess Danu, the ever-living ones, may have seemed clear-cut from our other stories about them, but things began to get cloudy when Christianity arrived in Ireland and histories began to be written down.

Before this, oral tradition was the only way that lore survived besides artistic depictions. The Druids famously never wrote any of their knowledge down because they were so protective over it. It was only in the 9th, 10th, and 11th centuries that visitors to Ireland began describing the Tuatha Dé Danann as deities from the clouds rather than simply shapeshifting, mischievous or benevolent beings. This idea was an attempt to say that the Christian God was greater than any other gods, and it changed Celtic pagan practice to honor the Tuatha Dé Danann through the lens of godhood rather than simply beings to be honored and feared.

The bottom line is that the boundary between the race of the gods and the race of faeries is very blurred, and they have similar abilities. Faerie folk essentially remained at the edges of the human world while the gods went underground to be revered without being directly viewed.

The Origin of the Harp

The harp has been an enduring symbol of Irishness for as long as anyone can remember. The Dagda's enchanted harp has the power to change the seasons. Ireland has had the harp on various currencies for centuries, and today, Irish euro coins still bear the harp on the obverse side.

The origin story of the harp begins with Cana Cludhmor, who is sometimes referred to as Canola, a corruption of her Irish moniker. Cana Cludhmor is said to be the Celtic goddess of inspiration, dreams, and, of course, music, likely due to this story. One evening, she had a fight with her husband, and Cana Cludhmor chose to take a walk along the beach to calm herself down. She ends up reclining and falling asleep, and she hears delightful music in her dreams.

When she awakes in the morning on the beach, she realizes that the music she was hearing was not only in her dreams; it was being created by the wind, which was gently and steadily blowing through the sinew stretched across the ribcage of a rotting whale carcass. The tale is charming up to that representation. But the ultimate takeaway is that Cana Cludhmor becomes inspired to create the harp based on this example made by chance in nature. It's a good thing she and her husband had that disagreement!

Chapter 8: Famous Stories: The Children of Lir, Cú Chulainn, and Tír na nÓg

These are some of the most beloved and well-known stories in Ireland today, and they all stem from Celtic tradition and mythology. These stories have enchanted and amazed legions of people from all generations stemming back centuries, and they've been the inspiration for countless modern pop culture references and world-building. Why did these stories, particularly these three, stand the test of time to the point that there are even several variations of each? We will answer this below, and we will also stick with the most traditional and widely accepted version of each.

The Children of Lir

The Children of Lir, also sometimes referenced as "The Fate of the Children of Lir," is a tragedy told over and over and even studied in Irish schools.

After the death of the great Dagda, there was a need for a new ruler of the Tuatha Dé Danann. Lir wanted to be elected king, but he was passed over for Bodb Dearg, who was elected the new ruler of the Tuatha Dé Danann. Lir was understandably upset, as he had missed out on the role, but in order to get Lir's loyalty and appease him, Bodb offered Lir his daughter Aoibh's hand in marriage. Lir accepted, and he pledged his fealty to Bodb as the new ruler.

Lir and Aoibh's marriage was a happy one, and they had four children together. These children were the light of their lives, but after the birth of the set of twins, Aoibh died, and Lir was distraught, as were the children. Bodb Dearg was heartbroken, but he did send another one of his daughters, Aoife, to Lir to wed.

Because both her father and her new husband doted on her four stepchildren, Aoife became jealous. It only took about a year for her to cultivate feelings of unworthiness and anger against them. She even pretended to be sick during this year of mental anguish and perceived slights, thinking that she had lost Lir's love because of his obvious love for his children. Aoife even went as far as to plan to kill them outright. She got her entourage together and promised them riches beyond compare if they would slay the four children. Her entourage, of course, refused, so Aoife, in her hurt and rage, took up a sword herself. But she could not go through with the bloody deed.

It was then that she forced the children into a lake to bathe, and once they were in the water, she transformed them into swans. However, these were no ordinary swans—they kept their personalities, intellect, reason, and speech. They also had the ability to sing songs of incomparable beauty.

Aoife set a time limit (albeit a ridiculously long one) on their curse, with some versions saying at the eldest child's request. The four children were to remain as swans for three hundred years in the lake in which they were transformed, then spend three hundred years in the cold north of Ireland, and then a final three hundred years as swans on a lonely, desolate island.

Instead of returning to the castle of her husband, Aoife returned to her father's castle. Bodb asked her why the children weren't with her, and she made up a story about how Lir did not trust Bodb with his own grandchildren. Bodb did not believe this nonsense for an instant, and he sent a message to Lir, saying that his four precious children were missing.

When Lir received this message, he searched for his children, eventually coming to the lake where they were bound to remain for the next three hundred years. Four gorgeous white swans came to him and revealed themselves to be his lovely children. Lir wept at what Aoife had done. The eldest informed him that they were to be cursed like this for the next nine hundred years. To ease his pain and lull him into a restful sleep, the children sang their lovely swan songs to their beloved father, and he fell into a deep, dreamless sleep.

Lir discovering his children, now swans.
https://commons.wikimedia.org/wiki/File:Ler_swans_Millar.jpg

When he awoke, Lir headed to his father-in-law's castle and informed him of what his daughter Aoife had done to the children. Bodb's anger and grief filled the castle, and he immediately said that Aoife's suffering and torment would be even greater than the children's could ever be. Bodb asked his daughter what the worst being was that she could imagine turning into, and she answered that it was a demon of the air. So, she became one forever. Bodb turned Aoife into a demon of the air, and she is cursed so to this day.

During the first three hundred years of the children's curse, people, gods, and Milesians alike came to hear their heart-stirring and unbelievably beautiful music. However, the time eventually came for them to move north to the cold rivers and lakes at the Maoilé, where they had to spend the next three hundred years singing. It was at this time that killing swans became outlawed throughout Ireland. Their time at the Maoilé was trying and full of suffering. A severe storm once separated the siblings, and although they were eventually reunited, the end of the second three hundred years could not come soon enough. They were all ready to get out of the north.

Finally, when the time came, the children flew to Iorrus Domhnann in the northwest of Ireland to complete their last three hundred years as swans. Here's where certain versions of the story differ. Some versions say that it was so cold in Iorrus that one night, the waters froze, and the poor swans' feet stuck fast to the ice. They then prayed to the one true God and professed their faith in him, which freed them from the ice. Other parts of the story leave this out, and the swans are simply said to endure their time in the northwest for the next three hundred years. What is normally told in all the versions of the Children of Lir is that during their time in Iorrus Domhnann, there was a young man they met who recorded an account of their story.

When their full nine hundred years of being cursed were over, they flew back, still in swan form, to the home of their father, Lir.

When they reached their homeland, the children were distraught to find that the lands of Lir were abandoned, appearing as if there hadn't been any inhabitants for long enough that everything appeared overgrown and lay in ruins. Dismayed, they traveled to the island of Inis Gluairé, where many birds congregated. They could at least live in peace with other birds and with each other.

After St. Patrick Christianized much of Ireland, there were still many who remembered the children of Lir, including a holy man ringing a bell for prayers. When the children heard the bell, they were frightened, but the eldest said that perhaps they should listen to the bell calling out the time for prayer, as it could break the curse. When they had all finished listening to the bell, they sang an otherworldly, enchanting song. When the holy man came to the shore of the lake to hear their song, he asked them if they were indeed the Children of Lir, for he had heard of their ancient plight and was actually in the area to track them down.

The four swan children put their trust in the monk, allowing him to put silver chains on them and lead them away from the lake. The king of Connacht's wife heard of these swans being the tragically cursed famed children of Lir, and she demanded that the monk bring them to her at once. The monk refused, and so the king went to take the swan children by force. As soon as he touched them, the curse was broken—all their feathers fell off to reveal four extremely aged and bony people, three men and a woman, the nine hundred years taking their toll instantly. Apparently, this disturbed the king of Connacht so much that he left immediately.

The legends line up here to say that the children knew they were close to death and asked the monk to baptize them. He did as they requested, and he buried them soon after.

So, what does this story teach us, and why is it so popular even to this day? The Celtic symbolism in the story and the connection to the mystical and magical Tuatha Dé Danann is one reason. Another reason this story is so popular in post-Christian Ireland is that it shows that accepting God brings peace and freedom. This is, after all, one interpretation. There is even a statue of the four children in their swan form in Dublin. The Fate of the Children of Lir is just a part of Irish cultural heritage as the harp, Irish Gaelic, and the rolling green hills.

The statue of the Children of Lir in Dublin.
https://commons.wikimedia.org/wiki/File:Children_of_Lir.jpg

The Great Cú Chulainn

Every Irish person knows the story of Cú Chulainn, the great warrior who was half mortal and half immortal. Cú Chulainn is likened to Hercules, Ireland's version of Achilles, and other great warriors from other mythologies, but the similarities end when their birth origins and enormous strength are discussed.

Even from a very young age (some sources say seven years old), Cú Chulainn possessed massive strength, which he achieved by essentially turning himself inside out. This was frightening enough to those who would harm him, but his rage gave him enough strength to singlehandedly hold back armies. The mental image this evokes is quite disturbing, but it is how the legends talk about his unbelievable strength and power.

Cú Chulainn was not always the name of this young, powerful legendary figure in Irish mythology. He was born to a mortal mother who named him Sétanta. He was given the name Cú Chulainn, literally meaning "Hound of Chulainn," when he was a young boy. Chulainn was a blacksmith with a fearsome guard dog, and the child Sétanta killed the dog while defending himself, to everyone's shock. Chulainn was understandably distraught that this superhuman child had killed his dog, but Sétanta offered himself up as Chulainn's security guard until he could find and train another guard dog for the man. Whether or not he succeeded in finding Chulainn another hound is up for debate since the stories differ, but Sétanta was forever known as the Hound of Chulainn.

Sétanta kills Chulainn's hound.
https://commons.wikimedia.org/wiki/File:Cuslayshound.jpg

There are multitudes of stories and legends involving this son of a mortal woman and Lugh, the god who is master of all skills. Cú Chulainn's prowess in battle and his good looks (when he wasn't raging out) make sense when one realizes he was the son of the great Lugh.

As a young child, Cú Chulainn was trained in martial arts by Scáthach, the warrior woman of Scottish legend. She gave him his spear and taught him to fight, although when he went into his rage fits, he really had no control and would trash anyone and anything in his way. During the time of Cú Chulainn's training, it was prophesized that he would be enormously famous but that he would have an early death, much to the dismay of those who loved him.

One of the most famous stories involving him is when Queen Maeve from Connacht attempted to take over the territories of Ulster. Cú Chulainn is with a woman in the forest when that happens. As the Ulster troops struggle to hold off Queen Maeve's forces, Cú Chulainn joins the fray pretty much when the last Ulster man falls. He goes into rage mode and singlehandedly beats hundreds of men in Queen Maeve's army, becoming the hero of Ulster.

As prophesized, Cú Chulainn died young, with most sources saying at the age of twenty-seven (he was seventeen when he defeated Queen Maeve of Connacht). Maeve conspired with several noblemen to draw out the Hound of Chulainn so that they could slay him. In Celtic culture, there were grave taboos that must never be broken. If they were, the person who broke them would become not only weak physically but also spiritually and emotionally. The two taboos that Cú Chulainn were faced with were eating dog meat or refusing hospitality. One day, he comes across an old crone who offers him dog meat that she is roasting on a spit. Trapped between these two taboos, he accepts a sliver of dog meat and eats it.

Thus, Cú Chulainn has broken one of the most severe taboos of his culture, and he is in a weakened state for the upcoming attack. Lugaid, one of Maeve's conspirators, has three magical spears made, each designed to kill a king. The first spear is used to kill Cú Chulainn's chariot driver, the king of drivers. The second spear is used to kill Cú Chulainn's horse, the king of horses. And we all know for whom the third spear is intended.

After Lugaid mortally wounds Cú Chulainn with the third spear, Cú Chulainn pulls all the strength he has left to tie himself to a tall stone so that he can die facing his enemies on his feet rather than on his knees. A beam of light is said to have shone on Cú Chulainn, and when his sword arm drops, it cuts Lugaid's hand off. A raven then lands on the hero's shoulder, signaling that his breath has left his body.

The stories of Cú Chulainn could fill many more pages; this is simply an introduction to the famed Irish hero, whose only weakness was that he broke Irish taboos, which could happen to anyone. Nowadays, the Hound of Chulainn is a symbol of Irish nationalism and identity. He is not so much a mascot as a legendary figure that the Irish take pride in, and the town of Dundalk's motto is "I gave birth to brave Cú Chulainn." This is because the stone that Cú Chulainn tied himself to so he could die with dignity is said to be in Dundalk.

Cú Chulainn's image has been placed on Irish coins and military medals, made into bronze statues, and depicted on flags and other Irish nationalist materials. There is no way the Irish people will forget about Cú Chulainn, his bravery, or his many exploits any time soon.

Tír na nÓg, the Land of the Young

This tale is truly one of the most provocative, beautiful, and heartbreaking tales that have been handed down through the centuries on the isle of Éire. When listeners hear the story of Tír na nÓg, it is almost impossible not to be moved in some way. This is why stories about this enchanting land free of aging and pain are told today.

We will focus our story of Tír na nÓg on a princess from the Land of the Young, the beautiful Niamh (pronounced niav) of the Golden Hair. This is the story of how Niamh from Tír na nÓg and Oisín of Ireland met and fell in love. There is one variation to the story, which we will get to at the end, so make sure to pay attention to the first telling and then see how the alternate story changes things.

Oisín, his father Finn MacCool, who is a hallowed Irish hero in his own right, much like Cú Chulainn, and the Fianna, the hunter-warriors with whom they travel, behold a gorgeous maiden on one of their many adventures. She has long flowing hair, full lips, and bright, shining eyes. None of the men have ever seen any living being so beautiful in all their years.

The maiden introduces herself as Niamh to the band, and she looks upon Oisín (pronounced a bit like "ocean"), informing him that she has heard tales of the Fianna and the famed young Oisín MacCool and that she had left her land specifically to find and marry him.

All present are a bit confused and stunned, especially when Niamh tells them that she comes from Tír na nÓg. They all know the meaning of the place's name—the Land of the Young, of the Unageing, the Land of Eternal Youth. They never consider that Tír na nÓg is an actual place, so naturally, they react with disbelief. Niamh continues to describe her homeland with such detail that the band cannot help but conclude that there must be some truth to what she is saying.

Niamh explains that her land is the most beautiful place imaginable and unimaginable. There is no death, no sickness, no pain, and no aging. Whatever one's age is when one arrives in Tír na nÓg becomes their eternal age. Niamh says they must not tarry long, though, as the effects of leaving Tír na nÓg will begin to affect her, although much more slowly than any mortal who comes to the Land of Youth and then leaves.

She professes her love to Oisín (whom she has just met, so this may seem odd to us, but it is a story, and she is extremely beautiful). Niamh begs him to come away to her home, where they will both stay young forever and live to their hearts' content, with all the jewels and gold they could ever imagine and all the delicious feasts they could ever consume. Oisín is almost convinced, but he agrees to go on one condition: that he is eventually permitted to return to Ireland to visit his beloved father. Niamh, of course, agrees to this sensible request, and father and son have a tearful, heartfelt goodbye. The Fianna are sobered by the loss of their second-in-command.

Oisín and Niamh traveling to Tír na nÓg.
https://commons.wikimedia.org/wiki/File:15_They_rode_up_to_a_stately_palace.jpg

So off Oisín and Niamh travel on her silver horse, over and through oceans, viewing spectacles unseen and hearing songs unheard by any mortal for centuries except for Oisín. He is amazed at the fantastic plants and animals he has never seen. He sees a gorgeous grove of trees laden with shining fruits and says to Niamh, "Is this your home?"

She then laughs and replies, "This place cannot even hold a single candle to my homeland. You will know when we reach Tír na nÓg."

On and on the horse canters, through valleys and mountain ranges of gold, through more verdant forests, even through the sky and seas, and eventually, they reach Tír na nÓg. Oisín realizes Niamh was right. He has never felt happier, lighter, or more relaxed than he does when they cross into Niamh's native land. Not even his greatest battle victories can compare to the elation he feels in Tír na nÓg.

Oisín and Niamh quickly marry and have many children together, and the couple never ages. They only grow to love each other more and more as they live, never getting sick and never knowing any strife or unhappiness. Their children grow and prosper but stay forever youthful. Everyone has as much to eat as they need and more. The plants and animals are sources of endless joy for the family and the other inhabitants of Tír na nÓg.

One day, as if awakening from a dream, Oisín remembers the promise that he made to his father to come back to Ireland and visit. For the first time since he entered the Land of the Young, he is troubled. For several days, his brow is furrowed, and he wonders what he should do or even how he could reach Ireland. Niamh notices something is off with her husband.

"My dear love," she addresses him after a few days of observing him like this, "unhappiness is unheard of here in Tír na nÓg. However, I can see distress playing on your features. What could be troubling you so?"

"Niamh, my darling," responds Oisín, "these years with you here have been the happiest I could have ever asked for. It's just I've remembered the promise I made to my father, Finn MacCool, and to the Fianna. I miss my father terribly, and I wish to visit Ireland to fulfill my promise."

Niamh provides her love with a horse that can make the journey, but she cautions, "Dear husband, on your journey, you must stay in the saddle. If your feet touch the ground of Ireland, you may never ever return to me, to Tír na nÓg. Please return to me, dear Oisín. That's all I ask of you."

Oisín kisses his dear Niamh and promises to return to their home in Tír na nÓg right after he has seen his dear father in Ireland. So, he rides off on the faithful horse, and in what seems like no time at all, he returns to Ireland, the vibrant green hills dotted with buildings he does not recognize. These turn out to be monasteries and churches spread across the countryside. He sees a passing old man, and he hails him.

"Ho, kind traveler! What have you heard about Finn MacCool and the Fianna? I am his son Oisín, come back to embrace my father."

The old man looks up at Oisín on the horse first with surprise, then amazement, then a bit of sorrow. "I'm so sorry," the old man answers, "but Finn MacCool has been dead these past three hundred years. The Fianna are tales of legends and fireside stories now, but we remember their glorious deeds."

Overcome with sorrow that his father has passed, Oisín unsurprisingly wobbles in the saddle, but he soon composes himself, remembering Niamh's warning. *Truly, three hundred years have passed in my beloved homeland? It only felt like a few...*

Some stories go on to say that Oisín sees a group of men attempting to lift a beam out of the mud and stick it vertically on some construction project in the vicinity. Seeking a distraction and knowing he can solve their problem instantly, he rides over and leans to the side, heaving the beam up alone with ease. Suddenly, the girth of the saddle snaps, and Oisín and the saddle both fall off the horse and onto the ground. Three hundred years catch up with Oisín instantly, and he dies soon afterward, unable to return to his love in Tír na nÓg.

Before we discuss the significance of this enduring story, let's look at some alternative details that crop up in some versions. Sometimes, storytellers insert a mini-story alongside Oisín and Niamh's first journey together to Tír na nÓg. He sees a stunningly beautiful marble castle after they've passed through a sparkling sea, and he says, "Niamh! That is beautiful! Is that where you live?"

She answers, "No, this is not yet Tír na nÓg, but a horrendous ogre of a man lives there and keeps a princess as his prisoner. He is forbidden to wed her until he defeats another in battle, but no one dares to fight him, so they remain unmarried, and she remains a prisoner in that marble castle."

Her story moves Oisín, and he asks that they stop because he wishes to challenge the ogre to battle. Niamh readily agrees; after all, his bravery and strength were so legendary that she heard about him all the way in the Land of Youth. Oisín defeats the ogre jailer, and the princess is now free to do as she pleases. This makes Niamh fall in love with the young MacCool even more.

Another important variant has to do more with Tír na nÓg and the way that some stories say they select their ruler. Every seven years, there is a contest to determine the king. All contestants must run up a certain hill, and the winner becomes king. The current king has won for many years, although doubts are starting to creep in that make him worry about how many more times he can win the competition. He consults a Druid about the future of his rulership of Tír na nÓg, and the Druid assures him that he will remain ruler of the Land of Youth unless his son-in-law competes.

The king is relieved by this news since his daughter is still unmarried. He orders the Druid to turn his daughter's head into that of a pig. However, the Druid also tells the daughter, Niamh, that if she marries a son of Finn MacCool, her curse will be broken, and she will be herself again. This is why Niamh sets out to find Finn MacCool and the Fianna, and she chooses Oisín to be her husband. She tells them all about the curse and everything that happened and about her origins, and then they are wed. Then the journey of Niamh and Oisín back to Tír na nÓg begins. Once they return, the competition for kingship is held. Oisín obviously wins, and no one dares to run against him again.

Why does the story of Tír na nÓg persist today? There is even a scene in the movie *Titanic* where an Irish mother tries to lull her frightened children to sleep with stories of Tír na nÓg, a place where there is no fear, pain, suffering, and death, as the ship is sinking. Knowing the story of the Land of Youth makes the scene all the more poignant, as the children desperately cling to the words their mother tells them, all while she knows the truth.

A land without any sort of disease, suffering, and aging sounds appealing to a people who were subjected to rulers of various sorts for centuries, especially after English colonization. Tír na nÓg becomes a dreamland, an escape, and something inherently Irish to hold onto. However, many arguments have been made that a person cannot truly appreciate life in a place devoid of suffering. How can one recognize victory, justice, or joy if they have never experienced failure, despotism, or negativity?

Chapter 9: Origins of the Irish Language

The origins of languages starting back to when humans began to speak are almost impossible to detangle, although many scholars, linguists, historians, and scientists throughout the ages have attempted. It would seem that the most widely accepted theory is that there was a first language from which all others stemmed. There is a story in the Bible about how languages were created, which is likely where this idea came from initially (the Tower of Babel in Genesis, Chapter 11). However, after centuries of tracing languages, their families, resemblances to other languages, and how people have migrated across the globe through the ages, the (at least working) theory is that the "first language" did exist and is referred to as Proto-Indo-European.

With that being said, we wish to point out how complicated tracing linguistic roots can be. With changes in lifestyle, practices, ceremonies, clan relationships, and location, people change, and so does their language. The language spoken by the Celts prior to the Early Middle Ages would be entirely unrecognizable to Irish Gaelic speakers today.

We call this language Goidelic. If you recall in our earlier chapters, the Celts used to inhabit the Iberian Peninsula, parts of eastern Europe, and perhaps all the way down to Turkey. The language these far-flung Gallic and Celtic peoples spoke can be referred to as Proto-Celtic—the grandmother of the Goidelic language.

Proto-Celtic split into three "children" of sorts: Celtiberian, Insular Celtic, and Gallic. These three languages became distinctive because Celtiberian was used by those who remained in Spain, Portugal, and what is now the Basque area between Spain and France. Those Celts we know and love who sailed the seas and ended up changing Ireland forever are the originators of Insular Celtic. Finally, the third child, Gallic, was the Celtic-rooted language spoken by the tribes inhabiting modern France and Austria that gave the Romans a good fight before being conquered along with the Germanic "barbarians."

Insular Celtic is the language child we wish to focus on because the Goidelic that Celts in Ireland used developed out of this language, as well as another sibling that we call Brythonic. This is what was used in Britain, and it later evolved into the Cornish, Welsh, and Breton that are still spoken and written today. Goidelic evolved into modern Irish Gaelic (Gaeilge), Scottish Gaelic (Gàidhlig), and Manx.

We are concerned with Goidelic and its development. Its writing system, *ogham*, which we've touched upon, is normally considered to have been first used in the 3rd and 4th centuries. Scant examples remain because *ogham* was likely mostly written upon organic materials like wood that have not survived. The examples that do survive show us that Goidelic and Brythonic differed in which sounds were present. For example, Goidelic has the "qu" sound, which seems to have changed to a "p" sound in modern Gaelic, whereas the Brythonic languages did not seem to have the "qu" sound but did possess the "p" sound.

Popular Gaelic Words & Phrases

- *Uisce beatha*: This is where we get the word whiskey from! It means "water of life," and its roots are from two Proto-Celtic words preceding Goidelic. *Uisce* comes from *udenskyos*, meaning "water," and *biwotos*, meaning "life." We can assume the Goidelic versions of these words were some in-between versions.

- *Dia duit*: This simple phrase means "hello." This is a modern greeting, especially when compared to how the ancient Celts would have greeted each other. Most of that is a mystery, but it is likely they would have met with a strong handshake with a forearm grip just to make sure the other party wasn't stashing a weapon. *Dia duit* is modern Gaelic for "hello," but it means "God be with you." They're not talking about the Dagda.

- *Sláinte!*: Cheers! This literally translates to "health," as many toasts around the world do.

- *Céad míle fáilte*: This charming phrase is found all over Ireland even today, and we can imagine a version of it existed in Goidelic because of the immense importance the ancient Celts placed on hospitality. It means "one hundred thousand welcomes."

- *Go raibh maith agat*: The Irish version of "thank you" literally means may you go with goodness. This is especially poignant when one thinks of the situation in which you would use this phrase, mostly upon saying goodbye, which is *slán*, meaning "safe." The Bronze and Iron Ages were not easy times to live in, but as we can see, the Celts did more than survive—they thrived.

- *Is fearr Gaeilge briste, na Bearla cliste*: This is a saying with a powerful meaning. It translates to "Broken Irish is better than clever English." This is a favorite phrase of proud freedom-loving Irish who resent English domination. It is just tongue-in-cheek enough to make its statement without being overbearing.

- *Gaeltacht*: This is a word that refers to a place or region that mainly speaks Irish Gaelic. It is often notated on maps or guides, and one can often see blatant Celtic influence in the area when it comes to historical sites and museums.

Why did we include modern Irish Gaelic words in our list instead of those the Celts would have spoken? Well, it's almost impossible to track down the Goidelic language in its spoken form, at least for concepts and ideas that would be familiar to us. Instead, Celtic thoughts and ideas remain with us through the artifacts they left behind, their burial mounds and monuments, and, most importantly, their descendants. Even though all Celtic languages are considered endangered by UNESCO today, they have undergone revival movements throughout the 18th, 19th, and 20th centuries by various groups attempting to preserve Irish and Celtic culture. Many of these groups do this for political reasons, and many simply understand that with the loss of a language comes the loss of rich history and cultural heritage.

Ogham, Again

Ogham (pronounced owam) was written from right to left, contrary to modern Celtic. It had twenty regularly used letters, but later on, an extra five letters were added on, but it is unclear when the use of these letters began. *Ogham* has all the sounds of English because the letter "q" did not have its own solitary symbol—it was written as the sound "qu."

Although when you compare *ogham* and Norse runes side by side, similarities seem to pop up at first, but upon closer inspection, it would seem that the similarities end when the realization hits that in order to carve symbols into hard surfaces, they, of course, have to be straight, rigid shapes. Some scholars still see a resemblance and thus a relationship between the two writing systems, and this is understandable since the two cultures definitely interacted with one another, with Vikings landing on Irish shores and eventually founding Dublin.

However, another theory, perhaps one that makes more sense since the presence of similar letter counts lines up, is that *ogham* is simply the Celtic way of representing the Latin alphabet. This might be more plausible since Celts, as far back as the Hallstatt and Gallic cultures, would have known the Roman Empire intimately. The Greeks and Romans visited and wrote about the Celts in Ireland, as we've established, and there may have been an exchange of language and ideas, that is if the eastern visitors deigned to speak with those whom they wrote about as barbarians.

Many Irish people and those with Irish heritage outside of Ireland (think the US and Canada) have begun to reclaim their ancient Celtic roots and craft *ogham* pieces or wear jewelry with *ogham* writing on it. They also create or purchase art pieces, jewelry, clothing, or other items with ancient Celtic motifs, which we will describe in detail in the next chapter.

Chapter 10: Celtic Art

Spirals and swirling depictions of humans and animals, intricate, knotted designs, golden brooches, and expertly designed torcs (collars) meant to fasten cloaks and denote wealth and status—these are just a few of the ways ancient Celts used art to express themselves in their daily lives.

During the Bronze Age, smiths produced untold amounts of bronze alloyed from copper reserves in Ireland and tin in Cornwall, England. Bronze was then created and expertly transformed into items that were not only useful but also beautiful. These included items like drinking vessels, horse tack, weapons, and farming implements, and they were exported all throughout Europe during the Bronze Age.

This was also when the Celts in Ireland produced a veritable fortune of gold products because of the gold deposits throughout the Emerald Isle. These golden objects have been found in abundance throughout Ireland, Britain, and continental Europe, meaning these objects were prized and sought after because of their quality, craftsmanship, and assigned value.

Tara Brooch

One of the best-surviving pieces of Celtic workmanship is the Tara Brooch. It is made from cast silver, and archaeologists date the brooch to be from around the 8th century. It is decorated in the La Tène style of art, which we will discuss in greater detail below. This art style influenced artisans from the time of the Hallstatt civilization all the way through to the Christianization of Ireland.

The Tara Brooch.

The Tara Brooch gets its name from the legendary seat of the High Kings of Ireland, the Hill of Tara. This seems a fitting name for a piece that is so quintessentially Irish Celtic. The brooch has nothing to do with Tara or any legendary kings—it was simply called that by a salesman thinking to aggrandize his ware, which he purchased from a farmer woman in the mid-1800s who found it in one of her fields. The brooch is in a recognizable shape even to modern eyes because it has a round outer side and a pin that goes through that circle, like an ancient safety pin.

This is also the shape and size that Roman brooches were made, and they were not as delicate as the Tara Brooch, which leads historians to conclude that the Tara Brooch had a purely ornamental function rather than actually binding cloaks to the wearer. It would not be strong enough for a brooch's traditional purpose.

Muiredach's High Cross

This massive, towering stone cross found at the Boice Monastery (Monasterboice) is part of a group of three similar crosses, but this particular piece is known to be the most exquisite.

Muiredach's cross is over five meters tall (more than fifteen feet), and it is made of sandstone, which is easier for artisans to carve than other types of stone. Sandstone is also plentiful in Ireland. Although this cross is not the tallest of the three (the West Cross is seven meters tall), it is the most intricate and detailed.

This standing cross is full of Christian iconography, but interestingly, it is all done in the traditional Celtic art style, covered with knots and twisting vines. It even includes the sun and the moon, which are represented by two soldiers. These may be references to the ocean and to the earth goddess Gaia. Celtic art, especially the art exemplified in this cross, retains its characteristics and style no matter the subject matter. This cross was commissioned to show various scenes from the Bible, such as the crucifixion of Christ, possibly Christ's seizure and arrest by Roman soldiers, and Christ giving the key of heaven to Peter.

The western face of Muiredach's cross.
Adriao, CC BY-SA 4.0 <https://creativecommons.org/licenses/by-sa/4.0>, via Wikimedia Commons; https://commons.wikimedia.org/wiki/File:Mainistir_Bhuithe_cross_Muiredach.jpg

Charmingly, there are other symbols throughout the cross. For instance, the bottom of the cross on each side features two cats, animals long associated with magic. There is a ridiculous amount of ornamentation, including men's heads surrounded by winding snakes, centaurs, wrestlers, and abundant horsemen, along with about a dozen other biblical scenes.

Muiredach's High Cross is an essential part of Celtic history because it shows how Celtic culture and Christianity blended in Ireland, and it preserves the artistic style used about 1,200 years ago for viewers and scholars today.

Battersea Shield

This stunning piece dates from the Iron Age and also emanates the La Tène style of art that was prominent in most Celtic art pieces during the Iron Age, Bronze Age, and after. Even though it is only part of a shield, its purpose is obvious.

The Battersea Shield piece that survives today is the bronze outer plating for a shield that would ordinarily have a wooden backing and perhaps some sort of strapping or padding for the user. These materials have long since degraded, but the bronze plate is stunning.

Battersea Shield.
British Museum, CC0, via Wikimedia Commons;
https://commons.wikimedia.org/wiki/File:British_Museum_Battersea_Shield.jpg. Image has been flipped

The Battersea Shield, now located in the British Museum, is an important example of ancient Celtic craftsmanship because there are four structural bronze pieces and three decorative bronze pieces all fused together seemingly by magic. The smith was able to hide where they attached the pieces into its overall design, so the pieces are held together seamlessly. This gorgeous shield is decorated with red glass ornamental studs. The museum insists that the shield was made in Britain, but the La Tène style and Celtic design contradict this.

What Made Celtic Shields So Important?

Shield-making in the Iron and Bronze Ages contributed new techniques that made shields more useful in actually protecting the wielder from attacks. Celtic broadswords were huge and fearsome, and the shields had to be made to withstand these attacks.

In Celtic culture, weapons, armor, and shields seemed to take on personalities and attributes of their own, and Celtic warriors often thought of their weapons and gear as partners in battle rather than mindless implements. There was a famed shield called Ochain, which is said to have screamed whenever its owner was in danger. Its scream caused all other shields in Ulster to shriek out along with it.

The predominant shield design in the ancient Mediterranean and hence most of Europe was rounded. But the Celts preferred to make their shields tall and flat, like rectangles, with a protruding bump bulging out from the center. This was simply for the benefit of the user because it added more room for their arm, thus giving the person greater maneuverability. Of course, it took time to get the design right; nails holding the shield together would often pierce the wearer's arm on impact, so the design needed tweaking.

There were shields specifically made for battle, and these may have a central adornment where the protrusion was but little else in the way of ornamentation. And then there were shields like the Battersea Shield specifically made for ornamental and/or ceremonial purposes. For those of high status, like royalty and chieftains, decorative shields were often made to be buried with them. Archaeologists have uncovered many shields from the Celts in great condition because they had a habit of sacrificing them to the gods by tossing them into rivers and lakes, which has kept them in excellent condition.

Let's Talk About La Tène

After the rather utilitarian and geometric Hallstatt and Urnfield styles came the La Tène style, which is named after the site, La Tène village in Switzerland, where thousands of artifacts in this distinctive style were found.

What makes this style unique and prevailing throughout Celtic civilizations both on the islands and the European continent is the maturity of stylistic thought during the creation process and the idea of beauty and functionality. So much of this artistic style survives because around the time when La Tène was developing, between 480 and 190 BCE, these ancient civilizations switched from cremation to burial as the preferred method of interring the dead. This is why so many of these artifacts survived.

La Tène art is responsible for the gorgeous golden torcs, the intricate brooches, and the carefully carved and decorated weapons and everyday objects (plates, drinkware, knives, hair accessories, etc.) the Celts were famous for. This period is when Celtic design and expression flourished.

This period is where we see the familiar S-scrolls intertwined, the curving foliage patterns, and other knotted motifs, which survive until even today. This is similar to Norse patterns on shields and their own art and metalworking. Some animals included in these famous Celtic designs were wolves, owls, snakes, and ferocious wild boars. The Celts even included human forms and sometimes figures from their pantheon and mythological stories on their chariots and weapons.

It is important to note that the La Tène style, which is intrinsically insular Celtic (despite the prevailing thought by historians that the "stylistic maturity" of the age is from contact with the Greeks and Romans), is found in textiles, metalwork, and even surviving stone and wood carvings. However, there are almost no paintings, sculptures, or pottery examples of this style. This is interesting because it shows us which objects the Celts placed particular reverence on and respect for—which items to show off and which to create simply for utility's sake.

Chapter 11: Celtic Rituals

It may surprise you to learn that some normal, everyday activities people in Ireland and even around the world do today have some root or origin in rituals practiced two thousand years ago.

One main tradition that carries over is storytelling. When the Celtic civilization arose, spread, and then flourished, everything was still passed down orally. Even the Druidic rites and knowledge were never written down—all Druids and their acolytes had to memorize the entire canon of Druidic knowledge. The Druids were so secretive that modern Neopagan Druids can only guess what their ancient predecessors truly believed and practiced.

No, storytelling, a pastime still very much alive in Ireland and one the Irish are quite adept at, stems from the Celts having a rich tradition of passing down their tales and their real histories through oral tradition. It wasn't until monks came to Ireland that these tales and histories began to be recorded.

One reason storytelling and ancient histories have survived is because the bards, the story keepers, worked alongside the monks, as long as they were permitted to, in order to keep Celtic culture alive, at least in story form if not practice. With the arrival of St. Patrick, the bards' and Druids' offerings to demons were banned, as was animal sacrifice.

The Importance of Fire

The Celts believed fire to be cleansing, which is why giant bonfires were lit at nearly all of their annual festivals. Fire represents light, the sun, warmth, and fertility. Celtic societies cremated their dead until the 5th century BCE, as did many other ancient peoples—many around the world still do.

Fire is said to keep evil spirits away, and it's easy to make this jump. There were many dangers to Bronze Age peoples, not the least of which were wild animals and other people who may wish them harm. Fire helped provide a sense of community and security, as the fireside is often where storytelling took place. Humans have always had a close relationship with fire, and even today, sitting around a fire and looking into the flames, we can remember our ancestors who did the same.

Animals were often sacrificed to the Celtic pantheon on bonfires during festival days, although this was later outlawed by the Christian monks and St. Patrick.

Life Cycle Events in Celtic Society

Nature

In general, the Celts held natural places of great beauty to be sacred, like forest groves, trickling streams, or mighty waterfalls or rivers. These sites were often unmarked for ritual use, but they were just as often marked with little shrines and sites where offerings were given.

At these shrines, the Druids would take offerings from the communities they served, such as grains, jewelry, fresh meat, honey, choice fruits, and other valuable goods, and give them to the gods they served in these sacred places of nature. If a good like a weapon, shield, piece of pottery, or artwork was offered, it was often broken before being offered to the gods.

The tradition of leaving milk out for Pookas or Fey Folk, which is practiced even today by some superstitious people, may have had its origins in ritual offerings to the Celtic gods of old.

Many people still burn sage as a cleansing agent after a bad experience or to make sure an area is safe from harmful spirits. This was a practice the Druids often employed. The combination of sage's powerful smell and the cleansing properties of fire joined to sanctify places and people. In order to cleanse a person, the ashes of the burnt sage were smudged onto them, usually on their forehead.

Holidays

In Chapter 5, we mentioned the main festivals Celts would have celebrated throughout the year. Many of these are still celebrated today, although under the guise of Christian celebrations (St. Brigid's Day on Imbolc/February 1ˢᵗ and Christmas/Yule). Halloween and All Saints' Day on November 1ˢᵗ is the most notable change; originally, this was the Samhain celebration. However, Wiccans and Neopagans around the world still celebrate Samhain without human or animal sacrifices.

Children

Celtic beliefs concerning children line up with the thoughts the whole Western world had about them up until the Industrial Revolution. Children weren't considered fully formed humans until they could speak, which would be between two and three years old. However, if a child died, there was quite a juxtaposition between how they were perceived while they were alive and how they were buried. Children's graves from Celtic burial sites were positively festooned with jewels and valuable objects. In death, it seems families overcompensated for the way they thought of their children in life.

Weddings

Incense is lit to purify the air, and ritual handwashing is performed at several stages throughout the ceremony. These rituals are still performed at Celtic weddings today. Three candles, which represent unity, are lit by the spouses. One candle represents the families of each of the spouses, and the third and final candle they light represents the creation of a new family.

There is also a tradition that comes from Scotland but is Celtic in origin, and that is the Stone of the Jury. The couple holds a stone where they are holding the wedding ceremony, which is always outdoors. The stone represents the ancestors and the earth, and as the couple makes promises to each other, they hold the stone together. This is also a way to ask the ancestors and nature to bless their union. After the wedding vows, this stone is then plopped into a river. Sometimes, the couple keeps the stone after the ceremony.

One meaningful ritual often present in a Celtic wedding is the prayer of protection. A circle is drawn around the couple to protect them in their own separate dimension, as the Druids did with standing stones and circular shrines. These circles can be made with stones, flowers, or pieces of wood.

Marriage and Divorce

Men and women were shockingly equal in Celtic society two thousand years ago. It is unclear whether women could become Druids or bards, but they could hold other positions of authority and had the freedom to marry whom they chose under Celtic tribal law. This is not how things always played out, but men and women had similar, if not the same, rights under the law. The Druids were the keepers of the law, and if a particular chieftain gained the loyalty of a certain corrupt Druid, he could bend the law to his own desires.

There were actually *nine* types of marriages that could take place in Celtic Ireland.

1) The man and the woman each take equal financial responsibility during their union.
2) The man contributes more financially.
3) The woman contributes more financially.

In these three, which were the most common, no dowry was required, but a bride did take her valuables with her, and they stayed in her possession. In case of divorce, she had her own possessions and would not be dependent on other parties. When we say financial contribution, we mean possessions coming into the marriage since working within marriage was typically farming and regular household chores. These three marriage arrangements were a precursor to the modern prenuptial agreement.

4) A man simply moves in with a woman.
5) The couple elopes without getting the bride's family's permission.
6) Involuntary abduction, meaning no consent from the families.
7) "Secret rendezvous," which can be interpreted to mean that the couple meets without either of their families' knowledge and eventually either elopes or makes their relationship public.
8) Marriage by rape.
9) Marriage of two insane people. This one is up for interpretation.

Polygyny, or having two or more wives, was permitted, but women could not have more than one husband, at least under the law. However, both parties were not required to be monogamous.

Circumstances in which a woman could divorce her husband include if he seduced her or lied to her in order to get her to agree to marry him, if he is impotent or too obese to have sex with, if he leaves her to have sex with men exclusively, if he beats her to the point of leaving visible marks, if he fails to provide for her, and if he leaves her for another woman. A woman could even divorce her husband if she found out he was telling tales about their sex life.

Grounds for a husband divorcing his wife included if she mistreated him physically and/or verbally, if she ran off with another man, or if she was sterile. But women asking for divorce was much more common, if divorce was common at all.

Death

In most cases, it is unclear how the deceased were dressed prior to burial, but we do know from extensive archaeological evidence that feasts were held near the gravesites to honor the deceased, and we know they were buried with pottery filled with foodstuffs. If the dead was a warrior, they were buried with their armor, weapon, and shield. If the deceased was a weaver, they would be buried with the tools of their profession— spindle, loom, perhaps even spinning wheel, needles, and other textile-making materials.

The dead were buried with their jewelry and valuables unless some were set aside as heirlooms to be passed down. Objects that were buried with the dead were often ritually broken before being interred, just like the offerings to the gods we mentioned earlier.

SECTION THREE:
Patterns of Change (430– 600 CE)

Chapter 12: Here Comes St. Patrick, 432 CE

Palladius

Patrick is credited with bringing Catholicism to Ireland, which has heavily shaped its national identity. However, there is reason to suspect, based on papal correspondence and records that exist from the 430s, that St. Patrick was not the first Catholic missionary to the Emerald Isle.

That title belongs to Palladius, a freshly ordained bishop whose family was from Gaul. He was sent by the pope to the believers who already existed in Ireland at the time. Since St. Patrick is regarded to have landed in Ireland in 432, Palladius's journey is estimated to have taken place just a year before.

One thing to note is that there were two purposes for which missionaries were sent to far-flung locales. One was to bring Christianity to people who had never heard of Jesus and where there was no established church or monastery. The other purpose was to bolster the believers who were already there and to make sure they were following the orthodoxy laid down by the Roman Catholic Church (remember, that was the only branch of Christianity that existed at the time). From time to time, sects would pop up that had different (unorthodox) ideas from what was professed by the church.

At the time Palladius was ordained, the pope wished for him to check on the people of Britain and make sure that if they were engaged in some sort of heresy that he put them back on the orthodox track, so to speak.

The main threat at the time was Pelagianism, which emphasized the human nature of Christ and suggested that the divine and human aspects of Jesus loosely existed together in one entity. Pelagius also attested humans were born good, so babies were born without sin (rather than the prevailing idea of original sin). Pelagius believed that Christians could essentially achieve their own salvation. Once they accepted Jesus as Christ, then that would preclude them from even wanting to sin, and they would simply live a righteous, ascetic life. Pelagius was branded as a heretic, and bishops were dispatched to the European continent and Asia Minor to ensure his followers stopped their errant beliefs.

Palladius was sent on a mission to the believers in Britain and Ireland. It is unclear whether he was meant to visit the Scots or the Celts, but he likely went to Ireland first. This is because when he arrived in Wicklow, he was soon banished by the king of Leinster. He then went to visit the Scots in Britain. Therefore, he is pretty much forgotten as the first bishop to Ireland, and this is for several reasons.

One reason that Palladius and his mission are overlooked is that historically, the record blurred the lines between him and Patrick. Since Patrick likely landed back in Ireland as a bishop (we will tell his story shortly—this was not the first time he went to Ireland) the year after Palladius's failed mission, records do conflate the two, including the dates of their death.

However, we have enough evidence to conclude that Palladius did make his mission to Ireland, was there very briefly, and then went back to where he felt most comfortable. Most reports that we have now say that he and his companions were banished almost as soon as they arrived in Wicklow. Some accounts say that Palladius was then killed, but this is not the majority opinion. Most historians now and then stick with the story that Palladius went to the Scots in Britain and to monasteries and congregations that had already been established. And now St. Patrick enters the story.

Saint Patrick, the Patron Saint of Ireland

If you are unfamiliar with the story of St. Patrick, this should be a fascinating look at a famous missionary. We do not know the name that Patrick was born with; he most likely took the name Padraig (Irish) after his ordination and return to Ireland. Sources from half a millennium later suggest several names he may have been called as a youngster, but there is no way to know for sure.

Stained glass portrayal of St. Patrick.

In fact, the date of his arrival is also shady. We mentioned that St. Patrick returned to Irish shores in 432. However, this date may have been chosen to maximize the veneration of Patrick and minimize any information about Palladius's mission, which happened the year before. This is because the earliest dating of Patrick's landing was from a century after it supposedly happened. This is an example of writing history backward because you favor a certain person over another.

Patrick was not actually Irish. He grew up as a Roman citizen in Britain, but he was stolen by Irish pirates when he was young. He worked as a shepherd in Ireland for about six years. In his famous *Confessio*, Patrick writes that he was not yet a Christian at the time of his abduction, despite the fact that his father was a deacon and his grandfather a priest. However, time in captivity amongst his sheep provided him with ample opportunity for reflection and prayer, and it was during his time as a slave that the young Patrick embraced Christianity.

After six years as a shepherd, Patrick writes that he heard a voice telling him to flee to a ship, that he was going home. Patrick then traveled more than two hundred miles to a port, and he eventually convinced the captain of one of the ships to let him board.

Once the captain was finally convinced to let this scruffy escaped slave join the voyage, they sailed for three days and landed in Britain. The crew wandered around through the country for about a month. The story goes that they were weary, hungry, grouchy, and bedraggled when Patrick prayed for sustenance for the crew. They then came upon several wild boar, and the captain began to see Patrick in a new light.

Eventually, Patrick made it back to his family, and he became ordained as a bishop. He wrote that he had a vision of a saint bringing him a letter from the people of Ireland, welcoming him back and saying they had a great need for him. Strangely, Patrick also landed in Wicklow, just like Palladius, and just like Palladius, he was chased out. However, unlike his predecessor, which he likely knew nothing of, Patrick simply traveled farther north until he found a place where he was welcome.

Now, why was Patrick so successful in changing the face of Ireland forever, planting and sowing the seeds of Catholicism that still grow today? Many say it was because Patrick had lived and worked among the Irish, and although he was taken as a slave by an Irish master, he held no ill will toward them at all. He loved the Irish people, and unlike many missionaries before him in other places, he respected their pagan practices. Because he reached out with love and a bit of compromise, his mission was a resounding success.

Patrick was able to explain difficult concepts, like the Trinity (Father, Son, and Holy Spirit), to the Celts by using the three-leaf shamrock that grew all over Ireland. It is one plant, but it has three essential parts that come together to form it. He also had a hand in merging Celtic holidays, such as Imbolc and Samhain, with Christian festivals and feast days. St. Patrick is one reason we have such beautiful standing crosses and other pieces that meld Celtic artistry and Christian iconography because they were allowed to coexist to a degree. Patrick condemned animal and especially human sacrifice, but he often used the Celts' existing ideologies to explain concepts about the Christian God, such as the Celts' veneration for nature (God created it).

This doesn't mean that Patrick's time amongst the Irish was easy. In fact, it resembled his time as a slave. Because he refused to accept gifts from prominent members of society, he offended them and, in turn, had no one to protect him. He was beaten and robbed plenty of times, even spending two months as a slave again at one point.

Yes, Patrick did use the shamrock to spread the notion of the Holy Trinity across Ireland. Yes, he changed some of the Celtic practices that were repugnant to the church and melded Christian celebrations with other practices. No, he did not banish the snakes from Ireland. Ireland has never had snakes, so this story is just one of the many fanciful apocryphal stories that are associated with someone whose life history does not have that many contemporaneous sources. We do have Patrick's own writings, the *Confessio* and the *Epistola*, the latter being a letter to the soldiers of a man who was excommunicated for enslaving some of Patrick's converts. But they are short and lack detail.

Patrick mostly won over the Irish people because he concentrated his efforts on prominent figures in society. Once kings were converted, their subjects usually followed. He also converted many wealthy women to Christianity. If these women's families objected to their choice, the women would simply leave with their money and join nunneries, sponsoring their nunnery and the construction of others. There was a huge wave of monasteries and nunneries built in the century after Patrick's death, and this can be traced back to him and his followers. He preached in Ireland tirelessly for forty years, becoming the most venerated saint in Irish history. His feast day, March 17th, is fairly calm even in Ireland—its raucous bender-like celebration overseas would likely give St. Patrick quite the shock.

Chapter 13: Paganism versus Christianity

We hope that the previous chapters about the Celts and their culture and practices have given you some type of an outline of their beliefs, which in modern times we simply refer to as paganism. Each culture around the world has ancestors that practiced (and some still do practice) forms of paganism or animism, which are religions that are specific to that region or country and usually involve nature and/or ancestor worship. For our purposes, we are referring to Celtic paganism in this chapter.

Side by Side

Paganism	Christianity
Many gods, some more powerful than others, different personalities, some vengeful and some benign, all to be revered.	One God, manifested on Earth in the form of Jesus of Nazareth. The Holy Spirit is the third part of the triune God, explained later.
Gods appeased and pleased with offerings, festivals, and sacrifices. The gods and goddesses are also revered and pleased with retelling their flattering exploits and legends.	God simply wishes that everyone love one another. Jesus was the sacrifice who rose again after three days. When he left Earth for heaven, he gave his followers the Holy Spirit, God's representative on Earth.

Paganism	Christianity
Festivals include Samhain, Yule, Imbolc, Ostara, Beltane, Litha, Lughnasadh, and Mabon. These are all seasonally based on the changes of the year and equinoxes/solstices. The Wheel of the Year essentially revolves around nature and the harvest.	Major festivals include saints' feast days, which may or may not replace pagan celebrations; Christmas, which was placed during Yule to celebrate Jesus' birth; and Easter, taking the place of Ostara in the spring.
Nature is holy, especially when it comes to sacred groves, majestic waterfalls, stunning mountaintops, or flowing rivers and deep lakes.	Holy places are sites where saints performed miracles; monasteries and churches are where believers gather to pray.
No central authority; each household can observe certain practices differently. However, if there is a serious issue, the Druids may be called upon to settle it.	Congregations made up of families from the same village listen to their priest; larger areas have bishops. These are representatives of the pope, and they are his mouthpieces.
The Druids hold all the wisdom and knowledge associated with the veneration of nature, divination, interpreting the will of the gods, and advising civil leaders. There is no written canon—everything is passed down orally for secrecy.	Local monks are the reason we have so much information about Celtic paganism. They wrote down *everything*, and the 5th century is when we began to see an explosion of writing and illuminated manuscripts in Ireland.
The dead were cremated at first, but this practice eventually fell away as people buried their dead in burial mounds with many personal items.	Community cemeteries in villages held the dead grouped together.

Paganism	Christianity
Nature is the absolute final authority. The waters, forests, and mountains are all to be looked at with awe and adoration. Fire is purifying and essential.	God is to be revered for creating nature; nature is never to be worshiped for its own sake.
Spells, amulets, special charms, and daily practices like candle lighting and paying tribute in the form of votive offerings play huge parts in the daily practice of the veneration of the gods.	There is only one God, and he is venerated through prayer. In the 5th century, it was still uncommon for people other than the clergy and monks to be able to read, but listening to the Bible was another way to venerate God.
Witchcraft (the practices mentioned above) were part and parcel of daily life, especially during important festivals like Samhain and Lughnasadh.	Witchcraft was forbidden. St. Patrick was so successful in his missionary endeavors because he used pagan practices to explain Christian ideas and practices. He patterned much of his converts' thoughts using what they were already familiar with.
Ultimate values: strength, reverence for nature, attuned to the seasons, virtuous, hospitable, fierce in battle	Ultimate values: one God to be worshiped, love one's neighbor as oneself, spread the message of Jesus Christ

Both paganism and Christianity have frameworks for life after death, although they are different. It is obvious that the Celts believed in the afterlife because even before they began burying their dead rather than cremating them, the deceased were buried with all that they would need for their next life. Unlike the concept of Valhalla for the Norse, it's difficult to peg down what Celts thought the afterworld would be like. Evidently, they thought it would be much the same as this world since their dead were sent away with edibles, potables, weapons, weaving materials, and sometimes even pets.

Christianity's concept of death and the afterlife was still quite new at this time; it was only four centuries after Jesus of Nazareth's death, and although the religion was making headway in Europe and Asia Minor, Christianity still had a long way to go. Christians of the time did think that believers in Christ would join him in heaven, and it was common for them to get buried in cemeteries that housed both pagans and Christians in villages or towns. Being buried on monastic grounds was reserved for clerics and those who held powerful community positions.

There is a story of St. Patrick in which he prays to God to help him make the pagans of Ireland believe in God, and God gives him a vision of purgatory. God says to Patrick that showing this vision to the people will convince them. It was meant to be a powerful picture of how awful the fires of hell were and the glories and joy of heaven. The Catholic concept of purgatory, heaven, and hell was well formed by this point, informed by various popes and church leaders.

One thing that was ingenious or enraging, depending on your perspective, was that Christian leaders like St. Patrick used existing holidays the Celts already celebrated and appropriated them as holidays in the Christian calendar. This is a phenomenon employed by many clerics and missionaries throughout the Western world when converting pagans to Christianity. It was very successfully done in Ireland. However, even to this day, Christians celebrate the Christian version of the holiday, and modern-day pagans (Neopagans) do their best to recreate pagan holidays in a way they find respectful and authentic of their ancestors' practices.

Both Irish Catholicism and Celtic paganism represent national identities that are sometimes at odds with each other but sometimes work together for common goals. For example, the monks worked closely with the Druids to record common daily practices of the Celts for posterity's sake, as well as other knowledge the Druids felt like sharing with them. These were learned men speaking respectfully with each other. Although violence and anger did erupt between the old and the new, Catholicism and paganism in Ireland had lived fairly peacefully for at least a century. Catholics fought much more heartily and viciously with Protestants than they ever did with pagans.

After all, paganism is a peaceful belief, only seldom invoking the gods for warfare and using human sacrifice. Christianity definitely has a much bloodier history, with its leaders eschewing the teachings followed by the early church (loving, helping, and healing) and following whatever paths they wanted. The Crusades are an excellent example, as are pogroms against Jews and infighting between Catholics and Protestants. Paganism was never responsible for levels of violence like those historical tragedies.

Chapter 14: The Decline of the Celts and Paganism

The Rise of Christianity

The 5th and 6th centuries in Ireland saw the rise of Catholicism and the decline of Celtic paganism. Despite the fact that St. Patrick and other clergymen on the island ingeniously appropriated pagan holidays and rebranded them as Christian ones, used Celtic iconography to explain their new message, and worked closely with the Druids to write down recent history, paganism still fell into the fringes while Catholicism took over.

In many countries and regions around the world, Catholicism exists beside native pagan practices like animism and ancestor worship, and there was a certain flavor of that in Ireland as well. Laypeople (people not part of the church leadership) often blended practices they had grown up with and the new ideas they had accepted about there being one God in the form of the Holy Trinity. Technically, Christianity itself expressly forbids this and demands devotion to Jesus only; however, policing villagers in far-flung rural areas has always been a challenge.

Even though the Irish Celts were able to keep some of their ancient practices alive, most of Ireland turned to Catholicism over the next three centuries after St. Patrick's ministry. Ireland became known and is still nicknamed the "Land of Saints and Scholars" for the virtual explosion of monasteries and churches founded in the 5th and 6th centuries and onward.

Why was this flourishing of monasteries and nunneries so successful in 5th-century Ireland? This question must first be answered by looking at St. Patrick's main mission model, which was to travel to each of the many smaller kingships that made up the whole of Ireland and preach his message to the king there. This was four decades of work, as Ireland had many of these little kingships, but if Patrick was successful in converting the king, the nobility and the commoners would eventually follow. Of course, St. Patrick spent plenty of time with rural villagers, but his main plan of action was to start with those in power and work downward.

Because Ireland was split into so many kingships and pockets of different authority, the decentralized nature of monasteries and nunneries fit right into this culture of independence and self-reliance. Indeed, most of these institutions had their own farms, animals, weavers, smiths, horses, and anything else they might need. The monks spent their days illuminating manuscripts, collecting Celtic oral tradition, and putting that information down on paper. There was much less attachment in monastic life to the whims or authority of the pope, which suited the Irish just fine. That does not mean that the clergy or monks went against the pope—they were simply used to governing themselves, and the model that the many kingships had already set out was adapted quickly and easily for the Christianization of Ireland.

Illuminated page of the Book of Matthew.
https://en.wikipedia.org/wiki/File:LindisfarneFol27rIncipitMatt.jpg

Appropriation of Holidays

Samhain is easily the most recognizable of the pagan holidays that the Catholic Church adopted and changed to fit its agenda. Even today, when we learn about Halloween, we know that it is a tradition that came with Irish immigrants to the United States during the Great Potato Famine. What is sometimes also discussed is Halloween's pagan roots, which date much further back than the 19th century.

October 31st began to be known as All Hallows' Eve and was eventually shortened to Halloween. In Christian Ireland, practices began to evolve that were at once familiar (dressing in costume, making protective charms, eating special treats, etc.) and new. Some of the new explanations for the holiday is that instead of dressing in special costumes and masks so as not to anger dark spirits, people would wear this protection to ward off Satan himself. The concept of a devil was foreign to the Celts, but the concept of malevolent spiritual beings was not. Each Samhain, every household would make a charm to protect them from these beings and hang them over their doors. It resembles St. Brigid's cross, which was no doubt adapted from these charms, not the other way around.

St. Brigid's cross, probably appropriated from the goddess Brigid.
Culnacreann, CC BY 3.0 <https://creativecommons.org/licenses/by/3.0>, via Wikimedia Commons; https://commons.wikimedia.org/wiki/File:Saint_Brigid%27s_cross.jpg

Jack-o'-lanterns, as they eventually became known, were either used as lanterns for those who walked from house to house, or they were set on stoops or porches to ward off evil spirits. These practices were recorded as early as five hundred years ago, and combined, we can recognize the modern practices of trick-or-treating and carving pumpkins. There were some differences, though. Trick-or-treating probably originated from the aforementioned practice of disguising oneself, in which folks would put on costumes and go from home to home asking for food (sometimes soul cakes, a special Samhain treat), fuel for the bonfires, or even offerings to the Fey Folk for the holiday. This was accompanied by the practice of carving monstrous faces into turnips and either using them to light the way as they went or as protective totems outside the home. The modern reader can easily see the traditions leading to our practice of Halloween festivities today.

Plaster cast of turnip jack-o'-lantern.
Rannpháirtí anaithnid at English Wikipedia, CC BY-SA 3.0
<https://creativecommons.org/licenses/by-sa/3.0>, via Wikimedia Commons;
https://commons.wikimedia.org/wiki/File:Traditional_Irish_halloween_Jack-o%27-lantern.jpg

Keep in mind that all of those activities were still practiced long after Ireland was Christianized. Those practices evolved and changed, but most of the Samhain practices stayed around in some form until church authorities forbade them relatively recently, like in the 18th and 19th centuries. These include making wine offerings to the sea and using stones for divination around the bonfires to see who around the fire would live another year. Some Irish never forgot these practices and simply kept doing them, mixing Samhain traditions with their Christian religion.

All Saints' Day eventually "replaced" Samhain, as the day after October 31st was the official celebration of the halfway point between the autumnal equinox and the winter solstice. November 1st was appropriated by the church as a day to venerate the saints, but many of those rituals and practices to do so, such as lighting candles, mimic the lighting of bonfires, which was so integral to Samhain. By the year 800, Irish Christians were celebrating all the saints and martyrs of the faith on November 1st, which became known as All Hallows' Day. All Hallows' Eve was, of course, October 31st, but there was a third day added called All Souls' Day on November 2nd. This three-day festival was known as Allhallowtide. This term is a bit unfamiliar to those who live outside of Europe, but it is still practiced in many Catholic communities today. Rather than making sure angry ghosts don't disrupt the harvest or harm people in the community, the saints and martyrs are remembered for their sacrifices and commemorated on these days.

The clever rebranding of celebrations that already existed was key in the rise of Christianity and the decline of paganism all over the world, but it is extremely obvious in Ireland.

Monks and Monasteries

Irish monks are often credited with recording and preserving historical records, and we know a lot more about medieval Ireland than we ever would without their dutiful studies and recording. These monks knew Latin and Greek, and they helped to disseminate spiritual teachings and guidance to each village. It was not uncommon for there to be small monastic communities on the borders of small kingships. The villagers would help the monks with farming, and the monks, in turn, would teach the villagers and help them with their problems. However, the drawback to this mostly peaceful and mutually beneficial arrangement was that if the kingships ever decided to go to battle, the monks were expected to join in. That was likely a surprise to these peaceful men the first time they had to hold a sword and shield.

Besides the many tiny monasteries, many of which do not survive today because of perishable building materials, there were great monasteries that do survive today. The largest of the Aran Islands off the coast of Galway, Inis Mór, is home to Ireland's oldest surviving monastery and likely the first one, St. Enda's Monastery. There is no longer a roof, but the structure of the building is clearly laid out, and it is a hugely popular site to visit because of its gorgeous location and the solemn history it represents.

Glendalough in Wicklow is home to the "Monastic City." This complex of religious buildings and monuments was founded by St. Kevin in the 6th century and receives between 500,000 and 750,000 visitors each year. Visitors can see the remains of the Round Tower, the monastery itself, and gorgeous decorated crosses, as well as some medieval churches in various conditions.

Chapter 15: Celtic and Pagan Influence in Modern Ireland

Through the Celts' long and storied history, we have witnessed their early start in Austria and Switzerland, watched them spread eastward and even south toward Turkey, and finally saw them settle in Éire, the land of the harp, epic myths, saints and scholars, where some of the most amazing stories, legends, and traditions the world has ever seen have come to life. The decline of the Celts and their traditional, nature-related practices did not mean the end of their culture entirely; it was simply an evolution.

Of course, chieftains made way for kings, who made way for the church, although they did enjoy autonomy for a while, especially against the English, who held Ireland in bondage for so long. One reason Celtic art, language, and stories are kept alive today is that they provided a binding agent for Irish nationalism, which became especially important in the 20th century as the battle for Irish independence from Britain became vehement and bloody.

One important reason for the survival of stories like those of Cú Chulainn, Tír na nÓg, and the legends of the Tuatha Dé Danann is because the Druids and chieftains told these stories to the monks, who then preserved them in manuscripts so that they survived for generations. The reasons for the differences between versions of the same legends have to do with who told them and where they were recorded, as each tribe likely had its own version.

Nowadays, in Irish schools, these stories, like the Children of Lir, the origin of the harp, and Celtic folklore, are taught. Why do schools bother with dusting off these ancient stories? What are they meant to convey? The easiest answer is that the Celts, through the different iterations of Celtic history (Bronze Age, Iron Age, and Middle Ages), managed to keep some cohesiveness of their culture, no matter what tribe they belonged to. For example, it took Germanic tribes much longer to unite than it did for the tribes of Ireland, who always considered themselves part of the same people. This is why, despite Roman rule coming to Britain and remaining there for centuries, Ireland was a much more difficult land to conquer politically. Religiously, though, the country submitted much more easily. This has a lot to do with the conviction of the missionaries and saints to the Emerald Isle, most notably Patrick.

The most obvious remnants of Celtic paganism are the celebration of festivals traditionally held between and on equinoxes and solstices, such as Samhain and Lughnasadh. These festivals are still held today, just with different names and no animal sacrifices. Candle lighting has been a prominent practice throughout history, both to honor the dead and to protect against the forces of darkness, and Catholics still do this, just like their pagan ancestors.

In the early 20th century, the harp became the national symbol of Ireland, a banner to unite separatists who were fighting the English for their freedom. The harp was on Irish money and is even still on euro coins. These freedom fighters (or terrorists, depending on your point of view) told stories about Finn MacCool, Cú Chulainn, the chieftainess Boudica, and all the gods and goddesses of the Celtic pantheon to bolster their courage and to stir nationalist fire within their hearts so that they could continue to fight for their land. Much like Native Americans, the Irish have always had a deep connection to the earth, and after centuries of building revered pagan holy sites and fighting for the land taken by conquerors, that connection does not easily leave. These sites, like Newgrange and other burial mounds, sacred mountaintops, and famous sites like the fabled stone where Cú Chulainn perished, became rallying points, physical, tangible things worth uniting over and fighting for.

Paganism and Christianity cross over in other ways. Often, Irish churches and Bibles are decorated with symbols like St. Brigid's cross (originally a pagan symbol for the goddess of the same name), Dara knots, shamrocks, and even the tree of life, a widely known and used symbol throughout many religious and cultural traditions. The trinity knot, or triquetra, is actually known to predate Christianity's arrival and has even been found in Norwegian churches dating from one thousand years ago. It is said to be one of the oldest surviving religious symbols. Although there are a few more popular persisting symbols, one of the most ancient is the triskele, the triple spiral, symbolizing things in groups of three. You have the choice of its meaning. The Christians use this ancient Celtic pagan symbol to represent the Father, Son, and Holy Spirit. The triskele can also be used to represent the earth, sea, and sky; past, present, and future; life, death, and rebirth; or any other triple element one can think of.

Triquetra.
https://commons.wikimedia.org/wiki/File:Triquetra-circle-interlaced.svg

In the 21st century, Celtic reconstructionist pagans, or Neopagans, are starting to revive their ancestral practices. Although the Republic of Ireland has long been known for its staunch conservative politics, even within the last few decades, it has really loosened up on a lot of its conservative politics and viewpoints (healthcare, abortion, marriage, immigration, etc.). There has also been a religious shift. Today, more than ever, modern Irish citizens either identify with atheism or have no religious affiliation at all. The Catholic population is still the majority, but those without religious affiliations are on the rise, as are those who wish to reclaim their heritage in the form of Celtic pagan practices.

Triskele.
https://commons.wikimedia.org/wiki/File:Triple-Spiral-Symbol.svg

Modern Irish pagans practice Samhain as similarly as they can to what their ancestors did, lighting two bonfires and walking between them to purify themselves. They also use the bonfires to toss in offerings of produce to the Dagda and the Morrigan. It is easier than it ever was to practice these traditions openly without fear of reprisal from oppressive authorities. Many Irish today practice the wedding traditions we mentioned in Chapter 11, holding ceremonies in sacred groves and having pagan shamans conduct these ceremonies, which are deeply connected with nature.

Conclusion

Simply walking around in Ireland, whether in a city, national park, or in nature, especially along the Cliffs of Moher, Newgrange, or the Giant's Causeway, one can feel its ancient traditions and beauty. It is easy to understand the connection the Druids and the ancient Celts felt to nature and the land, and it is understandable that the Irish fought tooth and nail to take back their beloved homeland.

The Celts of Ireland were proud warriors, but that does not mean they were ruthless and without compassion. Women had unprecedented rights during the Bronze Age and the Middle Ages. Despite their agricultural lifestyle, which did involve felling forests to make way for fields and pastures, the Celts held a deep respect for the environment around them and used sustainable farming practices and field demarcation that are used in Britain and Ireland to this day. They were healthy and robust people because of their varied and plentiful diet, which is one reason they thrived on Irish soil, despite the desolate and barren winter months on the island.

Legends and stories of creatures like the Dullahan, the Pooka, and the infamous banshee still abound in schools and homes. The Irish are still famed storytellers with a gift to weave great tales, and they have honed their skills with these legends all their lives. Every Irish child can recite tales about the Fair Folk and the Tuatha Dé Danann and its most famous members. Most Irish adults know the origin of the harp, the story of the Land of the Young, and the Tragedy of the Sons of Tuireann. These stories are not just stories—they give a voice and a picture of the national identity of those with fierce pride. This pride is justified, as it comes from a long line of warriors, sages, bishops, saints, scholars, freedom fighters, revolutionaries, poets, authors, historians, activists, musicians, and artists.

Although Irish Gaelic is definitely not the same language the Celts spoke, it is its grandchild. Through tracing the origins of words in Irish Gaelic, we can see the fingerprints of the Celts, and we can see through their eyes. Language often reveals the way that people see the world, and that is no less true when it comes to the Celts. This is also true for religious practices. By looking at Celtic art, we can see that they venerated plants and animals as essential to life, and they honored their gods by honoring nature with artwork they presented as offerings. The Celts believed their loved ones went on to an afterlife and that they would see them again, so they were sure to laden their graves with as many needed and beloved objects as they could. They also believed that Samhain was a special liminal time when the dead could visit them, and they cared for their dead by laying out food offerings for them in much the same way that people celebrate Día de los Muertos today.

Christianity has had a profound and lasting effect on Ireland and the people who called it home in the 5th century. There were some Christians there before, but they were likely slaves taken from other lands; they had no established community that early on. In spite of the clash of beliefs, the Celts managed to keep quite a few of their traditions when converting to Catholicism, which is another testament to Celtic and later Irish resilience and adaptability.

Why are the Celts so important? They ruled Ireland for about two millennia. Their belief system, marriage and death rituals, and festivals shaped the very land on which they chose to settle. The Celts are inseparable from Ireland, even though Gauls (who mixed with Franks and Normans, among others, to become the French) and Basque people are descendants of Celts. Scottish, Welsh, and Manx are all descendants of Celtic peoples as well, but it is the Irish Celts the world remembers the most clearly. This is partly because of the La Tène art that is so enduring and captivating. It is also because Celtic history and mythology were kept alive in writing, although we have lost quite a bit of it. And it is partly because the Celts managed to live on through what they left behind, archaeologically, artistically, poetically, and linguistically. They have left their indelible mark on the world, which is more than many ancient peoples can say. Who knows how many ancient cultures have vanished without a trace? But the Celts, whether they realized it or not, made their mark on the world.

By learning about the Celts and Irish history, we can learn about how Ireland became what it is today, and we can learn about how ancient people in western Europe conducted their lives. By learning about their traditions, we can see where many of our modern traditions originated. After all, more Irish people live in a diaspora overseas than in Ireland itself, and these are the Celts' descendants. They have kept the Celtic tradition alive in poetry, song, and family traditions they may not even be consciously aware of.

We hope you enjoyed this introduction to Celtic history, and we also hope that it has inspired you to delve deeper into whichever aspects spoke to you. There is so much more to know and discover about these mysterious and fascinating people.

Part 2: Celtic Mythology

An Enthralling Overview of Celtic Myths, Gods and Goddesses

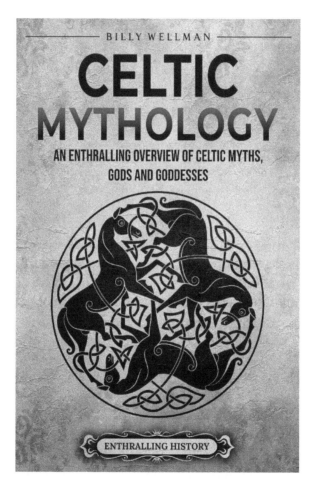

Introduction

The word myth conjures up different images for everyone. Many people think of the well-known Greek and Roman gods and goddesses. Others may envision worlds that differ from planet Earth. The word myth might bring forth images of creatures with supernatural powers that are used for good and evil.

Myth is often associated with falsehoods or untruths. Dictionary definitions of the word vary from narrative to traditional stories created by early peoples to fabricated tales. From research and what we can infer today, myths were orally shared stories with a purpose.

The purpose of myths could be to entertain, similar to narratives and fictional stories today. Some myths were meant to explain. Back then, people didn't fully understand how Earth was formed, what caused thunder, or what happened when people died. These myths are akin to today's grouping of explanatory or informative pieces. Other myths told by our ancient ancestors shared tales of people's behaviors. Through these stories and examples, social norms and mores were established. These would loosely fall into today's categories of persuasion or self-help book.

However myths are categorized, these timeless tales continue to explain possibilities about the beginning and end of time, life after death, natural disasters, and what motivates people.

Following the exploits of characters in myths provides role models for what to do and what not to do. Finding the strength to grow and transform and face challenges can be experienced just by reading the myths of the Celtic people. The momentous battles fought by heroes who stood up for their beliefs continue to inspire awe in readers.

The importance of myths when it comes to understanding history cannot be overstated. To better understand a culture, sometimes the best place to start is with what the people told each. We hope you enjoy your journey into Celtic mythology and learn something new about this fascinating people group!

SECTION ONE:
Gods, Goddesses, and Mythology:
An Overview

Chapter 1: What is Mythology?

Myth is a frequently used term. When someone tells an outlandish story, listeners respond, "That sounds like a myth." If someone wants to dispel a notion or belief, they will say, "It's only a myth." Stories about unusual events today are labeled as urban myths, such as frequent sightings of Elvis Presley. These connotations lead many to believe myths are falsehoods or works of fiction.

Categorizing myths as fiction is actually a myth. Myths were never intended to be fiction or nonfiction. Instead, the early storytellers who told myths were telling universal truths. Across the globe, people have used myths to explain human nature and the physical world around them. All cultures have their own myths that have been told and retold from one generation to the next.

Since myths are neither fiction nor nonfiction, what are they? Myths have many layers of meaning. They are meant to be more than a story and contain truths for each listener. Timeless yet essential questions about life are answered by exploring myths.

Though cultures can be separated by thousands of miles, all cultures developed myths surrounding common themes or to answer similar questions, even though there were no good means to share their stories. Exploration about the origins of the universe can be found in primal or creation myths. Explaining phenomena that occurs in the world can be discovered in nature myths. Guides to living a good life are shown in myths about people through a plethora of beings. The question of eternity and what happens when we die are investigated in myths about the afterlife.

Since myths were stories from the earliest days of humans, the first ones were never written down. They were shared through oral storytelling tradition and evolved from storyteller to storyteller and generation to generation. These stories were accepted as universal truths on which societies continued to develop.

Early Celts had no written records. Celts were suspicious of written records when other tribes and cultures began to write. So, by the time their traditional stories were written, there were vast differences in the stories and details from the original stories. When reading myths today, one can discover multiple iterations of the same story.

Myths about the beginning of the world or universe are often called creation or primal myths. In these stories, possible answers to questions about how the origins of the universe, people, and creatures are provided. In this grouping of myths, a topic still discussed today is explored: How did we and the universe appear? Ancient peoples were trying to understand the world they inhabited, just as we do today.

Creation and primal myths create order from chaos and serve as the foundation for other myths. Since this category of myths explains how the world and all that is in it came to be, they are considered the most sacred.

Similar motifs are used in many cultures to illustrate how the gods formed Earth from disorder. Water and floods are often used in myths to create or recreate the physical world from the empty space of the cosmos. In stories, gods have been known to flood the world as a punishment for its inhabitants' unwanted behaviors. Flooding also allows the gods to recreate the world if they are not pleased with their first attempts. From the watery abyss, a new world emerges.

Most cultures have creation myths. In Celtic mythology, there is not one cohesive story that illuminates the origins of the world, though. Since they did not write their own stories at the beginning, written records are not available for their earliest myths. However, it is believed the Celts viewed the preliminary stages of Heaven and Earth as two giants. From these two massive beings, numerous offspring were created.

Heaven and Earth had descendants that were either beings of light or beings of darkness. The beings of light were also called sons of Heaven. The beings of darkness were considered sons of Earth and referred to as Titans because of their massive size. The children were complete opposites to each other.

In their world, there was extraordinarily little space. Heaven laid upon Earth, and the children were confined between the two parents. The confines of their living situation caused growing hostility between the groups of offspring. One of the sons of Earth murdered his father and declared himself Titan, becoming the leader of both groups.

However, the beings of light refused to acknowledge the Titan king as their leader and fought against him. The Titan king lost the battle and was relegated to a nomadic existence. The sky was created with Earth's skull. The blood that poured from their father's dead body caused massive flooding.

After the flooding subsided, a new king was named: Father Sky. However, the king of the Titans returned from his wandering. He had reigned over creation during the darkness and cold. He battled Father

Sky, who brought the light. Despite the Titan king's fierce attempts, Father Sky always successfully wins the battles. That is why darkness fades to lightness and why winter emerges after summer.

Creation myths, such as this one, provide a basis for all other gods to emerge. Additionally, out of this grouping of traditional stories, other myths provide a rationale for the early people to understand how other elements in the world appeared or worked. Explanations of natural phenomena, including the emergence of human beings, build upon creation myths.

Human life and nature are intertwined in their stories and how each came to be. Myths portray the extremes of nature. Forces within nature can be unstable and brutally destructive. However, nature also nurtures. From nature, life is sustained, and the wonders of nature give hope and wonder. The cycles of myths that explain the human condition mirror the cycles of nature. Extended metaphors of the cycle of life and that of the seasons are often woven into myths.

The stories of nature's power involve many of the gods. Through the roles and examples of the higher powers, early peoples received the message of honoring nature and treating her with respect.

Myths from many cultures include a powerful flood or deluge of water. These stories demonstrate nature's power. Gods used flooding or the threat of flooding as punishment. If the inhabitants of Earth were not behaving in a manner that pleased the gods, the cleansing power of water gave the gods a way to start anew.

One well-known story of flooding and rebirth is from the Hebrews. In the story of Noah's ark, the people were punished, although a few were selected to survive to continue the cycle of life. The destructive forces of nature led to the restoration of life. These myths show the curative powers alongside the detrimental forces of nature.

It is from the story of Noah's ark that the first people came to inhabit Ireland. Noah's granddaughter, Cessair, led the first people to Ireland to escape the impending flood. As with many Celtic myths, there are numerous variations. Some people claim this story Christianizes an earlier myth, but the story is interesting and comes to us from the *Lebor* Gabála Érenn, which combines Christianity with pagan traditions.

Folio 53 from the Book of Leinster, which contains Lebor Gabála Érenn ("The Book of the Taking of Ireland")

https://en.wikipedia.org/wiki/File:Book_of_Leinster,_folio_53.jpg

Cessair's father, Bith, was not permitted passage on Noah's ark. Knowing the devasting deluge was approaching, Cessair needed guidance. She sought advice from an idol, which told Cessair and her father that their only means of escape would be to build a boat. After building three ships, Cessair selected women with different skills to join them on their journey.

Other versions tell of Bith having to ask Cessair for passage on her ships. She only agrees to let him join if he acknowledges that she is the leader.

Since there were not any people living in present-day Ireland (at least, according to the story), Cessair led her three ships toward safety. Without any people inhabiting Ireland, they could not have occurred the wrath of the gods.

After a lengthy journey, they finally arrived. However, only one ship landed safely land. Along with Cessair, forty-nine women and three men survived the voyage (some versions note that Bith survived, although he died after impregnating sixteen women). The women are shared equally with the men to populate the land. These settlers are seen as the original ancestors of the Irish.

Myths explaining natural phenomena and creation build upon each other. Their interconnectedness leads to another significant role of myths. In ancient societies, myths were shared to assist in the structuring of society itself. Important traits and expectations of society were learned through the adventures of gods, goddesses, and tricksters. All cultures have a number of gods and goddesses that represent different values.

Additionally, gods and goddesses ruled or oversaw different realms of the world. These roles impacted the daily life of everyone in society, as these divine beings provided guidance to the inhabitants. Their realms ranged from growing seasons to raising a family to battles in war. Worshiping the gods was a way to ensure a bountiful harvest, have healthy children, and wage successful battles. Paying respect to the gods was viewed as necessary for survival, so rituals and prayers were part of everyday life in past societies.

Through myths, societies were shown traits to emulate. Some gods and goddesses were shown as heroes or heroines and often had unusual powers or strengths. Stories frequently involve the lead character's journey to outmaneuver or fight a monster or demon. Their triumphs made them heroes to praise, and the personality traits that led to their success were to be mimicked by the people.

Heroes are revealed as someone who is courageous, ingenious, or powerful. They provide an important attribute that society needs. They might supply fertility, peace, or music. As a hero, he or she is a role model and behaves according to the expectations of society. Their unique skills are demonstrated when they are challenged by a negative force. Though they might have a weakness, they are able to overcome all obstacles and emerge victorious.

Another figure seen in many myths is tricksters. Tricksters serve several different purposes. For instance, they can show the many opposing traits within people. The contrast between doing what is expected in society and following whims and breaking the rules is seen through the actions of tricksters. These characters enjoy life by playing tricks on people and the gods. They can change shape and transform into both humans and animals.

Tricksters act on impulses and urges that humans are taught to control. Through tales of tricksters, people see the results of human folly. The tricksters' misdeeds are shown to reinforce socially correct behaviors.

Tricksters are cunning creatures but also demonstrate the need for self-reflection and societal introspection. These wily characters are willing to challenge authority, and in this capacity, their role is to challenge the people to question societal norms. When a trickster breaks a rule, he shows that some rules should be questioned and not just automatically obeyed.

One of the tricksters in Celtic mythology is Gwydion. His stories and exploits appear in *The Four Branches of the Mabinogi*. Gwydion can change his shape and transform others into different animals. His use of his magical abilities varies between vindictive and benevolent.

With his uncle Math, Gwydion creates Blodeuwedd. This young woman was made to wed Lleu Llaw Gyffes, as Lleu's mother had condemned her son to life without a human wife. From flowers and an oak tree, Math and Gwydion formed the lovely Blodeuwedd. However, she ends up being unfaithful to Lleu. As her penance, Gwydion turns Blodeuwedd into an owl.

Besides tales demonstrating a trickster's ability to punish people for wronging a family member, the purpose of other myths is to explain the ending of life and the afterlife. A question that has been asked throughout time is, what happens when people die? This category of myths, eschatology, explains endings, not just of death but also the end of the world.

In addition to explaining death, there is a body of myths that prepare people for the end of the world. Myths complete the full cycle, explaining the creation of the world to its catastrophic end. Some myths warn of potential disasters as consequences for negative behaviors; others show a cycle of renewal in which the world will recreate itself. Still, other myths explain that mortal death occurs as a punishment.

To lessen fears about the unknown, excursions by gods and goddesses to the underworld let mortals see and experience glimpses of the world beyond. In some beliefs and myths, after death, the soul or spirit of a human will continue to live. In some cultures, only certain people's spirits will continue to live after death. In that case, the gods determine whose soul is permitted to traverse from this life to the next.

In Celtic mythology, the world after this one is frequently referred to as the Otherworld. As with other topics in mythology, the Otherworld can vary from a place of wonder to a place to fear.

In some versions of the Otherworld, mortals join deities since the gods reside there. Other accounts transport a spirit to a land of eternal youth. "The Land of the Young" tells the story of Oisín. He fell in love with Niamh of the Golden Hair. She was the daughter of the king of the Land of the Young, also known as Tír na nÓg. Happily married, Oisín and Niamh lived in her father's kingdom for years.

Oisín and Niamh on their way to Tír na nÓg by Thomas Wentworth Higginson from Tales of the Enchanted Islands of the Atlantic.
https://commons.wikimedia.org/wiki/File:Frontispiece--Tales_of_the_Enchanted_Islands_of_the_Atlantic_1899.jpg

Wishing to visit his homeland, Oisín traveled back to Ireland. Niamh warned Oisín not to alight from his horse. If he dismounted, he would never be able to return to Tír na nÓg. While Oisín was riding through Ireland, he realized that he had been away for hundreds of years.

He continued to explore his old homeland. While traveling, a group of men asked Oisín for assistance. They needed help lifting slabs of marble. Oisín bent over from his horse and slipped off. Once Oisín landed on the ground, he immediately began to age. His chance at a youthful existence was gone.

The Celtic Otherworld was an indefinable space. It could be located anywhere. The Otherworld might be part of this world, drifting in the clouds, or a place that floated between all realms. Most Celts believed there was an afterlife.

Questions about life after death and other uncertainties that the ancient peoples wondered about are still thought about today. People want their lives to have meaning and purpose. Mythology continues to hold answers to timeless questions. Myths provide us with a connection to the past and other cultures. They also connect people as one large family with similar concerns and needs.

Myths do not provide a prescriptive answer to any questions about life, death, and understanding people. Instead, they let people develop their own interpretations and explanations based on characters and events that everyone can relate to. Letting people develop their own truth based on a common thread that has lasted for thousands of years allows us to be more connected to the past than one might have previously thought.

Originally, myths established a belief system or religion for people of long ago. The stories provided a basis to create meaning from chaos. Gods, goddesses, and other supernatural powers established expectations of their followers' behavior. The myths acknowledge that there is a greater force than people can explain and provide a sense of direction in a sometimes-tumultuous world.

Chapter 2: Paganism and the Belief in Multiple Gods

Pagans and paganism have varying definitions depending upon the time. When Christianity was initially spreading throughout the world, paganism was considered a religion or belief system that was non-Christian. That definition also includes descriptors of paganism as a pre-Christian religion. A pagan is someone whose religious beliefs do not follow those of the key religions of the world, such as Christianity, Hinduism, Islam, or Judaism.

Paganism is a religion from the earliest peoples. This ancient religion worships many gods and goddesses, which classifies it as a polytheistic belief system. Furthermore, paganism views the divine in all aspects of the universe. Pagans deify nature since the gods are in everything.

Ancient Celts practiced paganism, and their religion was a significant component of their lives. As with other contemporaries of the Celts, their reliance on nature made the natural world extremely important. Therefore, many of their spiritual beliefs were connected to the physical world. The Celts' earthly realm encompassed present-day Ireland, Scotland, Wales, Cornwall, Isle of Man, and Brittany.

It is believed the Celts inhabited these areas from about 1000 BCE through the Iron Age, Roman Age, and post-Roman Age. The word "Celt" is derived from the Greek word for barbarian. Ancient Celts were fierce warriors, which led to their "barbaric" reputation. Much has been pieced together about the Celts from what Roman historians have written. As aliterate peoples, the Celts chose not to write down their history. The

Celts also spoke a group of related languages. Although there were several Celtic tribes, they were similar in many ways, including their culture.

Map of Celts in Europe.
QuartierLatin1968, CC BY-SA 3.0 <http://creativecommons.org/licenses/by-sa/3.0/>, via Wikimedia Commons; https://en.wikipedia.org/wiki/File:Celts_in_Europe.png

Religion was also a unifying factor for the Celts. However, depending on the area, there were variations in the gods that were worshiped and their belief systems.

The gods who were worshiped the most affected the daily lives of the Celts. For instance, since finding sources of food was unpredictable, deities connected to hunting and harvests were venerated. Different local and regional gods provided protection during battles with other tribes. Other gods and goddesses who provided direction and strength reigned over medicinal needs, family concerns, and tribal matters.

In addition to the importance of gods and goddesses in their lives, the ancient Celts viewed animals as sacred. These revered spirits were often incorporated into the design of armaments. Going into battle with esteemed forces of nature provided the warriors with protection and the support of spirits. Talismans, which had a variety of shapes and meanings, were believed to keep away dangers and negativity. These amulets provided a connection between heaven and Earth.

Transitioning from this life to the Otherworld was part of the Celtic beliefs. The Otherworld was thought to be similar to this world but more positive. The Celts buried leaders and brave soldiers with different possessions to prepare them for the next life. Ordinary people were also sometimes buried with items, but many were cremated. Difficult and challenging aspects of this world were eliminated in the afterlife. For example, disease, warfare, and sadness did not exist in the next world. Therefore, the ancient Celts did not fear death when their souls departed to the Otherworld.

Though the Celts had commonalities in their religion, paganism was and is a broad and varied system of beliefs. Its worship can take many forms. Groups might gather to worship and honor gods and goddesses together, or individuals might pray on their own. Pagans did not need buildings in which to congregate for ceremonies, although some temples were built later on. Pagans believe in a strong connection between nature and its deities. Thus, observances of deities occur outside in nature.

Ancient Celtic pagan beliefs are based on the natural world. They did not have a set liturgy for their services. Instead, during their rituals, pagans wanted everyone to experience a connection with nature, their supreme being.

Since nature is everywhere, so are the pagans' gods and deities. People were not superior to any element of nature. However, through their rituals, a joining of the people and deities occurred. By honoring all that nature provides, pagans immersed their bodies, minds, and spirits in their worship. A prescribed set of beliefs or doctrines would not have allowed believers to access their spiritual truths.

Pagans believed that all components of nature contained a spirit. Nature itself was viewed as the physical expression of divinity because nature came from a supernatural power. Pagans explored and studied natural phenomena to understand the cause of events. Nature provided ancient believers with signs sent by the gods. Conversely, in pagan societies, diviners asked deities for information. In the practice of divination, seers would read the signs from the gods to foretell future events.

Since paganism permeated every aspect of daily life, many of the gods and goddesses symbolized elements of everyday living. Their deities were depicted as male, female, or without a specified gender. They were viewed as having human forms with the same weaknesses as people. Though the deities were not flawless, they were revered for their insights and power.

Another aspect of paganism is pantheism. This principle expresses the interconnectedness of the universe. Gods and goddesses are separate forces from the universe, but deities and the universe are a combined force. Gods are ingrained in the universe, which makes the universe a living entity.

From records that can be pieced together, the ancient Celtic pagans had over four hundred gods and goddesses. Not all deities were worshiped by all Celtic tribes. There were many regionalized gods. For instance, a tribe's local river or stream would have had its own god. Therefore, a god of a river could have numerous names, with each being specific to a river near where a tribe was located. Out of the over four hundred gods in the ancient Celtic pantheon, only about one hundred names were used in multiple areas. The remaining three hundred names were often used only once.

Pagan worship was communal and individual. Gods in ancient Celtic societies were celebrated individually or were linked to ancestors and the home. Ancestors could be those celebrated for their lives and the recently deceased. Household memorials were frequently erected in their memory. By combining a connection to ancestors with the worship of domesticity, pagans sought to link the past, present, and future. Thus, the continuity of a family's belief system was protected from generation to generation.

More collectively celebrated deities represented different aspects of nature, handiwork, warfare, and animals. There were gods of thunder, the sun, rivers, etc. Gods who assisted with healing utilized forces within nature. Crafting was an important part of daily life, so there were gods for the arts, handicrafts, and poetry. Part of survival was the ability to fight, so gods of weaponry and warfare were called upon for assistance. Another significant group of deities was the gods of animals. These gods represented animals or their traits and could transform into them.

The gods and goddesses of the ancient Celtic pagans illustrate their strong belief in nature. Ceremonies and rituals were held to celebrate their beliefs or honor the deities. Frequently, observances commenced with a ritual circle. Symbolic of eternity and the cycle of life, circles have no beginning and no end. Additionally, the pagans' ritual circle denoted inclusiveness; all were equal within it.

The solar calendar tracks the equinox and solstice. On the days of the spring and autumnal equinox, the night and day are equal in length. The winter and summer solstice celebrates the shortest and longest days of the year. These days and their corresponding festivals were used for reflection on the changes that had occurred during the last cycle of the year. Ancient

Celts believed that balancing thankfulness for all the gods who had provided through the year with ungratefulness for what had been lost was important to prevent the sin of self-pity.

It is believed that the cycle of the year began at the end of summer. The festival is known as Samhain, which is thought to mean "summer's end." With the passing of the summer season, which saw the sun shine for most of the day, people were transitioning into a darker season. It was believed that for humans to renew themselves each year, they needed to connect with the darkness.

On Samhain, the space or line between this world and the Otherworld became transparent. Spirits returned to provide guidance to leaders about the future. Deceased ancestors could travel back from the Otherworld to visit. Often, the living made their departed family members' favorite food and left it out to welcome them home. But while loving family members could visit during this day, spirits who held grudges could also return. Those in the living realm would wear masks so the deceased spirits would not recognize them.

Part of the Samhain celebration was the building of bonfires. These sacred fires were initially called "bone fires." Part of the festivities was the sharing of sacrificed animals and food from the fall harvest. The animals' bones and internal organs were set ablaze. The bonfires and hearth fires were meant to show that light will triumph over the darker days ahead.

Next in the seasonal cycle was the winter solstice or Yule. As part of the Yule festivities, an evergreen tree was decorated. Pagans believed trees were holy, and the evergreen represented the ability to survive throughout all the seasons. The Yule tree celebrated the birth of the sun god to whom gifts were presented. It was believed that the sun was a tremendous wheel of fire, and the word "Yule" has its origins in the Norse word for "wheel."

In addition to the Yule tree, there was a bonfire. Part of the bonfire ceremony was the Yule log. To discard difficulties from the previous year, participants in the celebration threw holly into the flames to burn away the past and light new beginnings. Part of the Yule log was kept every year. This piece was used to start the fire for the next winter solstice, signifying the cycle of the year.

To mark the beginning of spring, Celts celebrated Imbolc. Thought to have originated from "in the belly," Imbolc referred to pregnant ewes and the upcoming lambing season. Brigid, the Celtic goddess of fertility, fire, and healing, reigned over this holy day. The people made devotions to

Brigid to ensure the fertility of farm animals and a productive spring birthing season.

One of the worries of the winter season was having enough food to last the year. The people used rituals to call upon gods and goddesses for enough food from early February until the fall harvest. Divine support for a strong planting season was requested during these observations as well. Celebrations focused on lighting fires in support of the increasing hours of sunlight.

Ostara was (and still is) celebrated on the day of the spring equinox, which has equal hours of daylight and darkness. As the mother of dawn, it was believed that Ostara arose from the soil where she had been dormant during the winter months. Rebirth and renewal were the focus of Ostara celebrations, and eggs were used to represent new life. Labyrinths were also created. The maze separates light from the darkness of winter, signifying a new stage of life.

To commemorate the beginning of summer, the Celts celebrated Beltane, or fires of Bel, which marked the start of the growing season. Dwellings were decorated with early spring flowers, and rituals were performed to seek a productive year for crops, animals, and families. Bonfires were lit as part of the festivals. The fires represented purification and fertility. Livestock were herded through two fires to ward off evil and ensure the fertility of the herd. Other bonfires were lit to ignite passion and were part of summer courting rituals for the young women and men of the tribe.

Beltane bonfire.

Bonfires were also ignited for the celebration of Litha (or Midsummer), which took place on the summer solstice. When the sun was at its zenith, bonfires were lit to recognize the power of the sun. Pagans celebrated the victory of light over darkness. Though it was realized the light would eventually recede, they recognized the impermanent state of the growing hours of darkness.

The summer solstice indicated the joining of gods and goddesses. These alliances created the upcoming harvests in the fall. Earthly unions between young men and women were also plentiful during the summer solstice, as it was believed the ties that began during the Beltane festivities would result in fertile unions.

Lughnasadh, named after the god Lugh, was celebrated in August. The festival marked the first day of the harvest season and the transition from summer to fall. Gods and goddesses were offered the first foods from the harvest in an act of thanksgiving and for bountiful crops. It was thought that Lugh sacrificed himself by using a goddess's sickle. The god's blood flowed onto the fields, which made the lands productive.

A time for thanksgiving was recognized during Mabon or the autumnal equinox. Rituals centered on the god who entered the Otherworld during that time. She was thought to return in the spring, bringing new life with her. Devotions to the deities for a bountiful harvest were made, and food was prepared and stored to sustain the tribes through the long winter months.

Providing leadership in some Celtic tribes were the Druids. The Druids were priests and liaisons between this world and that of the gods and goddesses. Druids performed the religious rituals in which the ancient Celts believed. Additionally, Druids were called upon to explain natural phenomena. Due to their wisdom, Druids were considered seers. Many other ancient societies had someone who could offer medicinal cures, and for the ancient Celts, the Druids served in this capacity.

While there is no scholarly agreement on the etymology of the word "druid," many follow the traditional opinion that the word is a combination of the words "oak" and "knowledge." This explanation of the word's origin relates to the Druids' role as holders of the tribe's historical information.

Due to the amount of knowledge a Druid needed to retain, the path to becoming a Master Druid took years. To go from novice to master took twenty years. And all of the amassed knowledge that was shared in training was done orally, meaning there was no reference book to look at when one got lost. Because of the Druids' experience and understanding of the community and its history, they had an elevated status in Celtic societies. They advised tribal rulers, officiated on issues regarding the law, and administered warriors' oaths of allegiance.

The Druids performed all the religious ceremonies in ancient Celtic communities. They acted as emissaries to the gods, so offerings to deities were managed by them. Sacrifices were frequently made at special sites of nature. The rivers, lakes, and other waterways along revered groves of trees were sacred locations because they were where the physical and spiritual worlds connected.

Natural phenomena were explained to the Celts by the Druids. They were also expected to use their knowledge to control mystical elements of nature. Druids would clarify omens and use that information to foresee future events. This information would be shared with rulers, who then used it when making decisions.

Picture of Druid temple.

Chris Gunns / Druids Temple, near Ilton;
https://commons.wikimedia.org/wiki/File:Druids_Temple,_near_Ilton_-_geograph.org.uk_-_440563.jpg

The Druids led services after battles, to celebrate the cycle of nature, and to prepare for death. Anyone who did not follow their rulings could be excluded from the ceremonies, which made that person an outsider. Restrictions were levied on people who disregarded Druids' judgments.

Sacrifices to the gods were sometimes made after a battle or significant natural event. Both animal and human sacrifices were performed. The sacrifices were meant as a gift, a way to placate the gods, or to foretell the future. Captured fighters from other tribes were sometimes the source of human sacrifices, although criminals were the most often to be sacrificed. However, animals were by far the most sacrificed. Druids scrutinized the dying process of the victims, whether they were human or animal. From their observations of the final stages of life, they could make predictions of the future.

Since connecting to nature was so important to the Druids and ancient Celts, many of their practices followed the cycle of the seasons and the moon. Ritualistic offerings were made to the gods as part of these ceremonies. Offerings ranged from weaponry taken from enemies to jewelry and food. It was believed these offerings would entice the gods to protect the tribe from future unwanted events, such as pestilence and warfare. People gathered at sacred sites to participate in the services led by the Druids and said chants and prayers in thanksgiving to the gods.

Modern pagans seek a strong connection with nature. Many of the ancient Celts' holy days and seasonal commemorations are still important elements in pagan beliefs.

Chapter 3: Myth, Legend, and Folklore: The Differences

Before the printed or written word, all cultures recited and shared stories. Each generation told and retold the same stories, passing them on to the next generation. Tales were told to share the values and traditions of a group of people. The universality and the timeless nature of these stories cause them to continue to be shared today.

Oftentimes, there was not one originator of the tale. Instead, a story came together over time, with many voices adding to it to fully form the narrative. After the story was modified to meet its purpose, subtle changes were made, adapting it for their audience. Storytellers and their audiences interacted, which added further depth and meaning to the stories.

Some of the most important people in the world of the ancient Celts were the bards. Committing many ballads, poems, and other stories to memory, bards traveled from location to location. At each town they stopped in, they shared and performed the stories they had memorized. Since some of the tales included pieces of history, bards were valued for their knowledge.

Over time, bards developed into *seanchaithe* (singular *seanchaí*). Wandering from village to village, *seanchaithe* recounted myths, legends, and folklore to their audiences. Since there was no written Celtic language, *seanchaithe* shared news from tribe to tribe as well. They also memorized history and family lineages.

For hundreds of years, none of the Celtic history, lore, or tales were written down. *Seanchaithe* tracked tribal information for their clan, making them key people in the community. After all, they were the tribe's holders of memories and traditions.

Oral storytelling created a genre that is now referred to as traditional literature. In published texts today, the author might make note that they are presenting an adaptation of a story told long ago. Plotlines in these tales are usually straightforward since they were originally shared by word of mouth. Also, the tales were intended to instruct, so the listeners (and now readers) could clearly understand the message.

Relatable characters in traditional literature provided role models for ancient listeners. Creatures and people in the tales represented good and evil elements in the world. The settings were often nebulous, which added to a story's collective appeal.

Traditional literature has a few subgenres, although many of the terms are used synonymously. However, there are differences between each of the categories. Most importantly, though, they have a shared history through oral storytelling. All are timeless and still speak to us today. Commonly referred-to classifications include myths, legends and tall tales, and folklore, the latter of which encompasses fairy tales, folk tales, and fables. Within these works, readers and listeners learn about the sun and the moon, Robin Hood, and the Tortoise and the Hare.

Myths tell the origins of people, the world, and nature. Oftentimes in myths, there are gods, goddesses, and other supernatural beings. The ancient peoples revered myths, as they were part of their belief system. The characteristics of divinity and humanity and the similarities of both were explained through myths. These stories were and are truths about us, our ancestors, and our future.

Layers of meanings are woven throughout myths, such as the complexity of people, their relationships with each other, and people's search for meaning in life. While the stories told in myths were (and still are) entertaining, their purpose was greater than just providing an interesting tale. A myth's higher purpose elevates it to a more sacred level. Myths were told as though the story actually occurred, which added credence to the activities of the gods, goddesses, and other supernatural powers.

Myths are often grouped when they are studied to understand the connections between them better. There are several different groupings, but the four categories that capture the most significant reasons for myths are etiological, chthonic, historical, and psychological myths.

Also classified as origin or creation myths, etiological myths clarified the cause of life and the whys of the world to ancient people. The first beings are explained in etiological myths, as well as the sun, moon, stars, and how nature came to be.

For instance, Norse mythology told the people why there was thunder. Thor's chariot bolting across the heavens caused the roaring sound. The Oneida tribe of North America learned why and how chipmunks had stripes down their backs. A bear once bragged that he could do anything. When the chipmunk heard the story, he asked the bear to stop the sun from rising. Every day, the bear tried and tried to keep the sun from appearing. The chipmunk poked fun at the bear, which made the bear angry. So, the bear held the chipmunk down with one of his huge paws. The chipmunk squirmed and squirmed and finally freed himself. But the bear's paw left a set of stripes on his back.

Ancient people also needed help understanding devastation, death, and diseases. Chthonic myths explore death and the afterlife. They answer the questions of why people die, what happens afterward, whether the world will end, what causes illnesses, and what causes natural disasters. In many cultures, there are stories of life after death, which ease the fears of the unknowns associated with dying.

Many cultures have myths involving the phoenix. Many tales about this legendary bird describe it as multicolored, with feathers of reds, oranges, and yellows. After the phoenix has lived its life, which frequently lasts hundreds of years, it readies itself for death, making its own funeral pyre. When the phoenix knows its time on Earth is done, fire consumes the bird, and a new one arises from the ashes. In other versions, the beautiful plumage of the phoenix ignites when its time on Earth is done. That fire devours the old phoenix, giving birth to a new one.

Retellings of past events occur in historical myths. Hyperbolic elements are infused with details from the event, which may or may not have happened. By infusing and elevating the particulars of the story, the myth and the event increased in importance to the ancient people, with larger-than-life heroes emerging from the story's retelling.

Myths surrounding the Trojan War, which are told in the *Iliad* and *Odyssey*, fall under the category of historical myths. We can also find historical myths in ancient India. The Battle of Kurukshetra is told in the

Mahabharata. The *Mahabharata* is seven times longer than the *Iliad* and *Odyssey* combined, and it recounts the battle between two ruling families. After King Pandu of Bharata died, his sons, the Pandavas, to whom he left the kingdom, were challenged by one hundred of their cousins, the Kauravas. Indian gods are involved in the epic tale, whose powerful message transcends the recounting of the battle.

The last category of myths is psychological. These myths provided ancient listeners with ways to understand their emotions and feelings. Through the reactions and decisions of characters in these tales, audiences learned about traits to admire and attributes to be wary of. Often in psychological myths, the hero embarks on a journey or mission. During this adventure, they are faced with multiple challenges. How they address these challenges provided guidance for listeners.

One example of a psychological myth is illustrated in Achilles' story, which the ancient Greeks shared. Achilles' mother, Nereid, wanted him to live forever. In her efforts to provide her son with immortality, she immersed him in the river Styx. Nereid held Achilles by his heel so he would not fall into the river and drown. However, since this part of his body was not submerged, he was vulnerable there. Achilles grew up to be a great hero and leader. In the Trojan War, Paris killed Achilles with an arrow to his only weak spot.

Myths are not the only type of traditional literature. Legends are also set in the past, have larger-than-life characters, and were originally performed in person. Unlike myths, legends were based on actual events and/or real-life people. While the details were often exaggerated to create the legend, there was a basis of historical truth that propelled the story forward.

Legends link myths, which were sacred beliefs, with secular or historical events. The word "legend" is from the Latin *legere*, which means "to read." Legends were originally spread orally. When these stories were first classified, many had a foundation in religion, as tales of saints and miracles were shared at religious ceremonies. While most legends do not have a religious significance, they do have regional, national, or cultural importance.

While some myths may or may not have happened, such as those told in the *Mahabharata*, legends have elements of historical accuracy in them. Mention pirates and the name Blackbeard usually comes to mind for many. Stories of Blackbeard's exploits grew to legendary status, with stories of him lighting his beard on fire being a popular tale.

Gods and goddesses do not intervene in legends as they did in many myths, such as in the Trojan War. Legendary figures like King Arthur relied on their courage, cunning, and sense of right and wrong to set standards of expected behavior. If King Arthur was an actual person, it is thought he lived around 500 CE. Due to time and the many retellings of his story, his feats are usually set after 1400 CE. However, his chivalrous ways are still emulated today. Similar to myths, people learned about human traits to replicate and those to rebuff from legends.

Another popular legendary hero was Robin Hero. The common people saw him as a hero due to his mantra of stealing from the rich to give to the poor. His legacy has lived for hundreds of years. It is believed that the source for the legendary Robin Hood was a man who was born in either Loxley or Wakefield. Most agree that the person or compilation of people at the root of Robin Hood was from North County. Another detail on which many concur is Robin Hood's popular haunt, Sherwood Forest.

Robin Hood's disdain and distrust of the sheriff of Nottingham made him a local and legendary hero. Along with other outlaws, Robin Hood and his gang wandered Sherwood Forest in probably the late 14th to early 15th century. A skilled archer, Robin Hood was known for his quick temper. His anti-establishment beliefs and actions against the local rulers continue to enthrall listeners today. Robin Hood's story is a legend because he might have existed yet fought with unusual powers against his perceived enemy, the sheriff.

A subcategory of legends is tall tales. This is, relatively speaking, a newer category of stories. Most tales in this subgenre are from the exploration of the American frontier. When they were first shared, tall tales were told aloud, often around campfires. Men exploring the American West would tell tales at the end of the long workday while gathered around the fire. Like legends, tall tales are based on actual or true stories and include a tremendous amount of exaggeration. Some tall tales were considered as expansive as the American frontier.

Timeless stories of characters and beliefs in 19th-century America include the adventures of Pecos Bill, a legendary cowboy; Davy Crockett, who claimed to kill a bear at the tender age of three; and John Henry, whose strength propelled the building of the railroads.

Paul Bunyan is another famous tall tale. He was a lumberjack of incredible strength and probably based on Canadian lumberjack Fabian

Fournier. Paul Bunyan was almost always accompanied by Babe the Blue Ox, his trusty companion. Bunyan is credited with forming the Grand Canyon with one swing of his mighty ax. Babe was so huge that his footprints created the ten thousand lakes of Minnesota. Bunyan's energy and powerful physique were attributes that drove America westward.

Myths provided ancient people with an explanation of their origins. Many myths were considered sacred because they formed a belief system. Legends transitioned from a divine element to a secular one. Gods and goddesses were not needed to set the moral tone for society; legendary humans could establish a system of right and wrong instead. This leads us to our third category of traditional literature stemming from oral storytelling: folklore.

Folklore contains compilations of fictional narratives. Beliefs and traditions were shared through these stories, as well as superstitions and fantasies. Folklore could be about one single episode or incident. As the story was shared, that single scene might evolve into a longer, more complex story. Under the umbrella of folklore are fairy tales, folk tales, and fables.

Typical formats for fairy tales include settings of a distant past with an opening phrase of "once upon a time." These tales are dotted with beings like fairies, dragons, elves, dwarfs, and giants. There are clearly delineated villains who work against likable protagonists. Some aspect of royalty is often woven into the tale, either through characters or settings. There are also elements of the supernatural, such as talking animals who make friends with the hero and help them with their conflict.

The conflict has to be resolved before the end of the story. This often leads to people living "happily ever after." When the good characters solve their problem, a clear lesson is demonstrated. Good triumphing over evil gives fairy tales their universal appeal.

There are hundreds of versions of Cinderella throughout cultures and throughout the years. Cinderella is an excellent example of a fairy tale, as it has the classic elements of the genre. She is the likable protagonist who finds herself in an awful situation, as she has an endless list of chores. Her evil stepmother and stepsisters make her life terrible. So, she finds friends with the animals who share the castle with her.

Hope appears when Cinderella receives an invitation to the prince's ball. However, her stepmother thwarts her plans to attend. Magically, a fairy godmother appears. With a flick of her wand, mice and pumpkins are transformed to transport Cinderella to the palace.

However, she can't stay all night, for the magic will fade at midnight. After meeting the prince and having a lovely time, Cinderella flees the ball at the stroke of midnight, losing her glass slipper in the process. The prince searches throughout the kingdom for his love. After trying on the shoe, Cinderella and the prince live happily ever after. Good triumphs over evil. Remakes and adaptations of fairy tales continue today. Movies and books enchant and transport us to worlds where happy endings do happen.

Also within the category of folklore are folk tales, which were originally shared orally. Folk tales are similar to fairy tales, as they both share clear good guys and bad guys and see the protagonists' actions rewarded. However, magic and royalty are not usually present. Folk tales are adaptable to time and place, which makes them different from myths and legends. Their stories are fluid, but their messages are timeless.

Folk tales exist in all cultures. Many stories contain comparable meanings to each other. Characters in folk tales are not usually well-developed. Their one-dimensional nature makes them different from myths, legends, and fairy tales. In other traditional literature, characters are shown with more personality traits, which allows people to easily identify with them.

However, folk tales entertained and provided a message to listeners. Everyday occurrences were shared in folk tales, so the tales showed how characters confronted a problem. For example, in the "Three Billy Goats Gruff," the billy goats had to be creative to outwit the mean troll blocking the bridge.

"The Three Little Pigs" has been told and retold for a long time. The pigs' mother tells her three children that it is time for them to embark on their own. Each of the pigs represents a different character trait, while the wolf embodies the dangers that one can encounter after ones leaves the protection of home. Only the third pig, which demonstrates that hard work and planning are the keys to success, could survive in the world.

Fables were intended to instruct and provide a lesson. The most well-known fables are attributed to Aesop. In ancient Greek society, these tales served several purposes. Fables were often written down during a time of repressive rulers, so they were a vehicle to share disparaging comments about the government. They provided the oppressed with tales of hope that the powerless in society could have a voice against the powerful.

Animals and insects are the main characters in fables. They represent various personality traits and situations that humans face almost every day. In an entertaining way, important life lessons were shared. Fables were written to appeal to all ages and used to entertain and educate.

In the often-told fable of "The Tortoise and the Hare," we see human traits of overconfidence in Hare, while Tortoise is comfortable in his own skin. Tortoise appreciates life and takes time to immerse himself in it. Hare rushes through life and acts capriciously. In the end, the message is that the slow and steady win the race.

Before the internet, social media, books, and newspapers, people had access to an incredible number of stories. Though many could not read or write, they were not uneducated or ignorant. Through the experience of stories, beliefs were created and shared. Moral codes were established and agreed upon. Myths provided beautiful explanations of the world and its origins. Legends began with telling the lives of saints to talking about everyday heroes. Folklore provided entertainment and guidance.

Chapter 4: The Role of Myth in the Modern World

Myths have been told for thousands of years. Gods, goddesses, and other deities have guided people since these stories were first told. Today, people read myths for enjoyment, but these ageless stories still provide insight today. Reading about the heroes, heroines, and tricksters from thousands of years ago offers mirrors how we seek to understand people and various belief systems.

Layered with understated meanings, myths can be read through various lenses that provide enigmatic interpretations. After all, humans are complex beings. The intricacies in myths assist in our understanding of who we are and who we can be. These stories also clarify the obstacles society presents and what prevents us from achieving great things.

Whether it is purposeful or not, mythical threads have been woven into the arts since myths were first told. Traits and actions of gods and goddesses from thousands of years ago are part of today's pop culture. Movies, television, graphic novels, video games, and more are influenced by stories told long ago.

From Celtic stories, readers and listeners experienced human suffering and death. As magical and mythical characters battle evil, goodness and courage provide inspiration. Even in the Celtic tales that end in death and destruction, there is hope, for life in the Otherworld provides a kind of rebirth.

Some movies weave in a surface-level connection to Celtic and Irish myths. There are a number of movies that include leprechauns who are magical, evil, and/or generous. Movies range from horror, like *Leprechaun* starring Jennifer Aniston from 1993, to romantic musicals, like *Pot 'O Gold* starring James Stewart from 1941.

Other movies weaving tales based on Celtic and Irish legends include *The Luck of the Irish*. The original film is from 1948. A reporter from New York City, played by Tyrone Powers, travels to Ireland. While there, Powers encounters a leprechaun who guides him in his decisions. Disney Channel's 2001 movie of the same title stars Ryan Merriman as a high school basketball player who relied on a gold coin for luck. After the lucky coin is lost, Merriman is challenged by an evil leprechaun for control of it.

Continuing with the experiences of mischief and magic is *Finian's Rainbow*, a musical delight starring Fred Astaire. As with many other movies, a leprechaun and a pot of gold feature in this film. Other movies that include leprechauns and the mystery and hope of the rainbow are *Darby O'Gill and the Little People* and *The Magical Legend of the Leprechauns*.

Leprechauns are known to be mischievous tricksters. Legend has it that if you capture a leprechaun, he will offer you three wishes for his release. However, these tricksters cannot be relied on. Movies that base their stories on leprechauns demonstrate how life can be transformed with belief and hope in another realm.

Another mystical figure in Celtic mythology is the selkies. Also referred to as sea people or mermaids, selkies are half-fish and half-human. While in water, selkies are seals. However, once on land, they shed their skin and transform into humans. After selkies shed their skin, humans might hide it from them. If selkies cannot find their skin, they cannot return to the sea.

In the movie *Ondine*, an Irish fisherman catches an intriguing woman, for whom the film is named, in his nets. Once Ondine, a selkie, is on board, the fisherman's catches are dramatically improved, demonstrating her power. The mystical Ondine stays on land, helping the fisherman and his daughter. Love triumphs, and the movie ends with the three characters facing a bright new beginning.

The Secret of Roan Inish talks about the selkies and their ability to care for humans. A young Irish girl named Fiona visits her grandparents, who live on the coast. Fiona begins to uncover her family's history and the story of her brother, Jamie. Family lore tells of Jaime being swept into the sea as an infant. While Fiona is on Roan Inish, she believes she sees Jaime living with the selkies. It is indeed her brother, who has flourished from living with the selkies. In the end, Fiona is able to reunite her family.

Three related movies, *The Secret of Kells*, *Song of the Sea*, and *Wolfwalkers*, were directed by Tomm Moore. All three are drawn from Celtic and Irish myths and folklore. The first to be produced was *The Secret of Kells*, which features fairies, a Celtic deity, and a magical book. In the movie, the protagonist, Brendan, is on a journey to complete an ancient manuscript. The antagonist, Crom Cruach, a Celtic deity, possesses a special eye that Brendan needs to complete his quest. Needing to make ink for his illustrations, Brendan enters the forest. There, he encounters Aisling, a woodland fairy. Aisling can shapeshift between a girl and a wolf, and she assists Brendan on his travels to obtain materials needed to complete the secret Book of Kells.

Inspired by Celtic and Irish mythology, the *Song of the Sea* includes shapeshifting selkies. The lead character, Ben, learns that his sister, who cannot speak, is actually a selkie. He has long blamed his sister, Saoirse, for their mother's death. To taunt his sister, Ben retells the story of Mac Lir and Macha the Owl Witch to frighten her.

After Saoirse realizes that she is a selkie, she and Ben shift between the world of the land and sea. The fairies encounter Saoirse and Ben while they are in the sea. They need Saoirse's help to return to Tír na nÓg and escape the goddess Macha. As the duo continues searching for their way back home, Saoirse finds her voice to free the creatures they encounter. Toward the end of their travels, they reunite with their mother, who is also a selkie. Their mother must remain with the sea creatures, but Saoirse chooses to live in the human world with her brother.

Wolfwalkers is Moore's latest film and the last of what is referred to as the "Irish Trilogy." The main character, Robyn, an apprentice wolf hunter, is in Ireland working to eliminate wolves. While completing her mission, she befriends Mebh, whose spirit transforms into a wolf while she sleeps. Robyn joins Mebh in her search for her mother. But Robyn becomes torn between two worlds: one with her father as a wolf hunter and the other in Mebh's mysterious realm.

Building upon stories from myths of old, *Wolfwalkers* can be connected to the daughters of Airitech. These sisters changed into wolves every time Samhain searched for food. Their weakness was music, which others used to trick them into transforming back into humans. Shapeshifters play a significant role in Celtic mythology. Transferring between multiple domains allowed deities and other creatures to control humans with their trickery and deception.

We can see the influence of Celtic mythology outside of movies as well. Many novels have been inspired by characters and beliefs from the ancient Celts. Research now suggests that the legendary novel *Dracula* was inspired by the Irish vampire Abhartach. In this tale, after Abhartach is killed by the local chieftain, he returns to stalk the living. His dark magic lets him continually return from death as the walking dead or *neamh-mairbh*. Abhartach demands blood from his subjects, much like Dracula.

C. S. Lewis's classic novel, *The Lion, the Witch, and the Wardrobe*, also weaves in creatures from Celtic mythology. The portal the children pass through to enter Narnia is reminiscent of shapeshifters, who can easily transcend the physical world to another dimension. In addition, the story and others in the series contain hags, boggles (goblin-like creatures), and werewolves. All three were evil beings found in the land of Narnia.

Another classic novel is Lloyd Alexander's *The Book of Three*, the first in the *Chronicles of Prydain*. During World War II, Alexander was stationed in Wales for training. While there, he immersed himself in Wales and its myths and legends. Alexander's *The Book of Three* and his subsequent series contain scenes of Wales and an infusion of the Welsh stories of the *Mabinogion*.

Originating from the word *mab*, *mabinogi* initially suggested youth. Over time, the term became synonymous with tales of childhood. Stories that were a part of *mabinogi* were mythical accounts of the early training of heroes. In the *Mabinogion*, Pryderi's story has parallels to that of Taran in *The Book of Three*. Pryderi's tale connects the four branches of the *Mabinogion* just as Taran's connects the *Chronicles of Prydain*.

Taran's youth provides him with the training that he will need for his adventures off the farm. Once Taran follows Hen Wen, the oracular pig, Taran is drawn into a battle for Prydain. Magical swords and enchanters assist Taran in his quest. After Taran defeats Arawn, the Lord of Death, he is crowned High King, an honor he earns through his many feats.

Evangeline Walton spins a story similar to Lloyd Alexander's in another retelling of the *Mabinogion*. Walton's novels—The Island of the Mighty, The Children of Llyr, The Song of Rhiannon, and Prince of Annwn together are called *The Mabinogion Tetralogy*. She weaves all twelve branches of the *Mabinogion* into these four novels. Princes, lords, gods, goddesses, and magical interceptions bring to life the story of Prince Pwyll.

Traveling across the Atlantic, all the way to the US state of Arizona, we can find another series of novels, *The Iron Druid Chronicles*, that have their basis in Celtic mythology. Kevin Hearne's first book of the series, *Hounded*, introduces readers to Atticus O'Sullivan. The unassuming O'Sullivan owns a bookshop and appears to be a twenty-something Irishman. However, Atticus is actually the last of the Druids and is twenty-something centuries old.

Since he is a Druid, he has powers from the earth. Along with those abilities, O'Sullivan has Fragarach, a magical sword. However, some Irish gods do not believe that Atticus should have the sword, as they felt he had stolen the sword from them in a 1ˢᵗ-century battle. Aenghus Óg, the irate deity, leads the battle against O'Sullivan for Fragarach.

Working with Atticus is Oberon, his Irish wolfhound; the Morrígan, goddess of war and retribution; and Brigid, goddess of the fire and the forge. Vampires, witches, and werewolves complete the casting, although a number of other figures from Celtic mythology are included throughout the series.

Graphic novels and comic books also contain characters with similarities to gods and goddesses from the past. The iconic Conan the Barbarian was first seen in the publication of *Weird Tales* told by Robert Howard. Eventually, eighteen stories brought Conan's adventures to life. Marvel Comics then picked up the Conan character, continuing his story. In the 1980s, many were able to visualize the depiction of Conan in two films starring Arnold Schwarzenegger.

Conan is based on Irish mythology. The Fianna was a group of warriors. Conán mac Morna, also known as Conán Maol ("bald"), was part of the Fianna, which was led by Fionn mac Cumhaill. The Fianna and their escapades are documented in the Fenian Cycle of Irish mythology. The creation of the Giant's Causeway in Ireland is attributed to this fierce clan of warriors. Conan the Barbarian is based on Conán mac Morna. A warrior by the age of fifteen, Conan heroically and successfully battles evil.

Let's continue with Marvel Comics and look at its series of Thor. There, we can find other Celtic gods. The Tuatha Dé Danann battles Thor in issue #386. These godlike people come from Celtic mythology and use magic and the occult. Their leader, Dagda, was a wise god known for his two treasured possessions: a vast cauldron and an enormous club. Over time and after a series of battles, Thor joins forces with the Tuatha Dé Danann.

The impact of Celtic mythology influences many graphic novels as well. *Celtic Warrior: The Legend of Cú Chulainn*, written by Will Sliney, retells the story of Cú Chulainn. In the myth "The Hound of Ulster," Cú Chulainn (also spelled as Cuhullin) has magical powers. His head radiated light, and his legendary strength led him to go out of control when he fought. Cú Chulainn's howling greatly frightened his foes.

In Sliney's adaptation, Queen Maeve sends an army of ten thousand men to capture Emain Macha, a land in the northern region of Ireland. Cú Chulainn is the lone protector of the land, as all the other warriors are asleep because of a curse. Cú Chulainn's mythical bravery and skills allow him to challenge the approaching army anyway.

Also loosely based on Cú Chulainn is *Slaine: The Horned God* by Pat Mills. Slaine is a Celtic warrior who leads the Sessair tribe, which protects the people of Tír na nÓg. For years, those living in the Land of the Young had been controlled by unusual Druids. With support from the earth goddess, Slaine learns about his fate. His destiny is to unite the four kings of Tír na nÓg. The future of the world is in Slaine's hands as he launches his battles against the Drune Lords, the Druids who have poisoned the land.

Another avenue for people to experience Celtic mythology is video games. Many games have elements from myths around the world that are blended together to create something unique. Different worlds and landscapes see characters with magical and supernatural powers battle for good.

Games can also be played that transport players virtually to the lands of the Celts. *Assassin's Creed* lets participants plunge into the woodlands and haunted forests of Ireland. Depending upon how you play the game, you encounter Celtic kings or Viking clan leaders. The Giant's Causeway is one of the landscapes included in *Assassin's Creed Valhalla*, and you can see the Fianna being led in battle by Fionn mac Cumhaill (Finn McCool). Mythological creatures and ancient festivals are also part of the game.

Mythology guided and shaped our ancestors' thoughts and beliefs thousands of years ago. However, they continue to influence our culture today. Through the characters we meet and experience in our reading and viewing, we grow as we learn more about human nature and what motivates people.

SECTION TWO:
Irish Myths

Chapter 5: The Children of Lir

It was not until the 7th century CE that the Irish began writing down their history and stories. Ogham was the first Irish Gaelic written language. Most believe Ogham was named for the Irish warrior Ogma. He was the god of eloquence, which is fitting for how vital a role the oral tradition played in early Irish and ancient Celtic societies.

Numerous myths and legends that still impact today's culture were first told years ago in Ireland. The Irish took great pleasure in listening to the spoken word. The Irish blarney, or gift of gab, is a product of the unique poetic oral tradition of the country.

Since stories were shared for years orally, we have different versions of the same tale. The varying iterations add to their mysterious origins. The *Children of Lir* is one such story that was often shared and illustrates the vivid Irish imagination.

Irish mythology is frequently discussed in four main cycles. Each of the four cycles has its own characteristics, stories, personalities, and realms of reality. Within the cycles, societal norms and values are explored through the actions of the characters. To list the cycles from the oldest to the most recent, we have the Mythological Cycle, the Ulster Cycle, the Fenian Cycle, and the Historical or King Cycle.

As the oldest cycle, the Mythological Cycle tells the stories of the founding of Ireland. Tales of gods and other supernatural events are the hallmarks of these tales. Stories within the Ulster Cycle occurred around the 1st century CE. These stories wove together elements of the mystical with the world of warriors. In the Fenian or Ossianic Cycle, escapades of courageous warriors, such as Oisín, were shared. Superheroes were depicted as role models for audiences. Lastly, the Historical or King Cycle regaled its listeners with narratives that blended some actual kings with mythological elements. The stories were shaped to illustrate how effective kings should behave.

Thousands of years ago, during the Mythological Cycle, the people of Ireland worshiped many different gods and goddesses. These deities were descended from several races. One group of celestial beings with supernatural powers was the Tuatha Dé Danann. It is believed they were descendants of the goddess Danu, as stories about the Tuatha Dé Danann refer to the goddess Danu as their mother.

There is no agreement on how the Tuatha Dé Danann arrived in Ireland. Some traditions tell of the Tuatha Dé Danann flying through the air in ships and landing in Ireland. Others claim they traveled in the shape of fog, while another variation is that they came on dark clouds. Where they originated from is also debated, as people cannot agree on whether they are from heaven, Earth, or another world.

Some sources believe the Tuatha Dé Danann brought four island cities to Ireland with them, that they originated in the four cities, or that they located themselves in these cities. There is agreement that the four cities or areas connected to the Tuatha Dé Danann were Falias, Gorias, Finias (Findias), and Murias.

Wise men in each of these cities taught the Tuatha Dé Danann magical skills. Murias was the wise man of Falias. In Gorias, Urias assisted the Tuatha Dé Danann. Arias taught wisdom in the city of Finias. Lastly, the Tuatha Dé Danann discovered their enchanting talents with the aid of Senias in the city of Murias.

In addition, the Tuatha Dé Danann obtained four treasures from each city that would impact Ireland and become the component of many Celtic myths. Each valuable possession provided the Tuatha Dé Danann with tremendous capabilities, which made them a formidable tribe in Celtic mythology.

From Falias, they obtained the Stone of Fal (Lia Fáil), which proclaimed the High King of Ireland. Gorias's treasure was the Spear of Lugh. When the spear was drawn, no one could elude it, and no one who possessed it could be defeated. The Sword of Light came from the city of Finias. Once it was removed from its sheath, no one could resist its glow, and no one could anyone defeat it. Dagda's Cauldron, which had the incredible ability to feed an entire army, was the fourth magical treasure.

With their fantastical powers, the Tuatha Dé Danann battle others who want to assume their power and invade their lands. Details of these battles are found in many Celtic myths. However, other myths also emanate from events that result from the conflicts. One such myth is the *Children of Lir*.

The Second Battle of Moytura was a fierce conflict between the Tuatha Dé Danann and Fomorians. During the battle, the Dagda Mór is wounded; he eventually succumbs to his injuries. A new leader must now be selected to head the Tuatha Dé Danann: Bodb Dearg, the Dagda's eldest son. Since the main reason he was selected was because of his lineage, there were many who did not support the new leader. Lir arose as a strong opponent of Bodb Dearg's new role.

Lir thought he should have been selected as the next king of Tuatha Dé Danann. After the announcement of Bodb Dearg as king, Lir angrily stomped out of the council meeting. He refused to swear his allegiance. Bodb Dearg's supporters wanted him to eliminate Lir. Instead, Bodb Dearg knew that Lir's wife had recently and unexpectedly died. To appease Lir and obtain his support, Bodb Dearg arranged a marriage between Lir and his eldest daughter, Eva or Aoibh. This marriage forms the basis for the *Children of Lir*.

Lir and Aoibh's marriage was filled with love and children. The couple had a daughter, Fionnuala; a son, Aodh; and twins, Fiachra and Conn. But their love did not last forever, at least in the physical realm. Some versions tell of Aoibh's death occurring as a result of the twins' birth; others say her death was from an illness when the children were young. Regardless of the cause, Lir was grief-stricken.

Attempting to fill the void in Lir's and his grandchildren's lives, Bodb Dearg came up with a solution. The king offered another one of his daughters to be Lir's wife and the stepmother to Lir's four children. Lir agreed to the plan because he wanted a caring mother for his children. So, Aoibh's sister, Aoife, married Lir.

At the outset, the new marriage thrived. Aoife was a loving stepmother and wife. However, as time passed, Aoife grew jealous of Lir's relationship with his children. Lir spent most of his time playing with the children, leaving little to no time for a relationship with Aoife. She plotted different means to gain Lir's attention, but none of her ploys were effective.

Next, Aoife worked on eliminating the children, who she now viewed as her rivals. Aoife wanted Lir all to herself. However, she chose not to kill them because she feared their ghosts would eternally haunt her. There are different versions of the steps Aoife took to cast her spell. In one tale, Aoife tells Lir that she wants to take the children to visit their grandfather, King Bodb Dearg. Unbeknownst to Lir, Aoife had ulterior motives for the trip.

Due to a dream the night before, Fionnuala was suspicious of her stepmother. However, Fionnuala was powerless to stop the journey. Aoife summoned the chariot and took the four children with her, stopping along the way at a lake. Aoife ordered the children out of the chariot and into the lake. Once the children did as she had bid, she cast her spell and transformed the children into swans.

Perhaps at Fionnuala's urging or on her own accord, Aoife permitted her sister's children to keep their ability to speak. The children were given the power to sing the music of the *sidhe*. (*Sidhe* is also a reference to the Tuatha Dé Danann.) When the children sang, their songs were calming and pleasant to hear.

Aoife with the children at the lake.

Leaving the children on the lake, Aoife continued her journey to King Bodb Dearg's castle. Upon her arrival, the king looked for the children, eager to greet them. Aoife lied to him, telling him that Lir would not let her bring the children to see him. Not trusting her, the king sought the truth from Lir.

Lir knew the children had left, so with his staff in hand, he headed for the king's castle. On his way, he passed the lake and heard voices. Fearing the worst, Lir and his men followed the voices where they discovered the transformed children. Lir's children spoke to him and sang for his entourage. Grief-stricken, Lir continued to the castle, where he informed Bodb Dearg of the terrible news.

Enraged, Bodb Dearg asked Aoife what she feared most. She hesitated before responding, "The North Wind's howling." The king used his powers to transform Aoife into the North Wind. Aoife's screams can still be heard during storms. To protect his grandchildren, Bodb Dearg issued a decree that no one in Ireland could kill swans.

Aoife's spell on her sister's children lasted for nine hundred years. Every three hundred years, they had to move to a different lake. The first three hundred years were peacefully spent on Lake Derravaragh, where their loving father visited them often. The children bade Lir a final farewell and traveled to the Straits of Moyle for the next three hundred years. This was a stormy and turbulent time, so the children were often split from each other while on the waterway between Ireland and Scotland.

For the final three hundred years of the curse, the children vowed to stay together on the Isle of Inishglora. This difficult landscape caused the four to live in tremendous pain. When the curse ended, they traveled back home, only to find that their father was dead.

As with many ancient stories, there are many iterations of this tale. What happened to the children after being cursed for nine hundred years is no exception. However, none of the endings find the children living happily ever after.

One end has the four flying to Erris after discovering their father is dead. Since their curse is over, they are in human form. In Erris, they meet St. Mochaomhóg, a kind Christian missionary. He baptizes the four, who are shriveled and very old. After their baptism, they die in peace and are buried in how they lived. Conn is on Fionnuala's right, Aodh in her arms, and Fiachra is on Fionnuala's left.

Another version depicts the children, who retained their swan form, meeting a stranger after the nine hundred years are up. This stranger is looking to find Tír na nÓg, or the Land of the Young. The children say there is nothing left there, but the stranger, Aibric, insists they travel with him. The swans lead Aibric to the land where they grew up. Once they have arrived, Aibric calls to the mountains to have pity on the children. The land is magically transformed back to the beauty of their childhood.

However, a queen from the south hears about the swans and demands her husband, a king from the north, find and capture them. When the king tried to seize the swans, their bodies turned to dust. The children's souls escaped and joined their parents in the afterlife.

Swans have been used throughout time and in various cultures to represent many traits that humans aspire to attain. Qualities attributed to swans often include love, loyalty, and trust. The children exhibit all of these attributes. These traits also prompted their stepmother to act on her jealous rage.

Loyalty and trust are important, as you well know. Initially, Lir is not supportive of the new king. He feels he has earned the right to lead the tribe. When he is not chosen, Lir is understandably angry. Some in Bodb Dearg's inner circle believe he should eliminate Lir. However, Bodb Dearg sought loyalty from all in his tribe.

To ensure that loyalty, Bodb Dearg offers his daughter to Lir in an arranged marriage. The union between Lir and Aoibh ensures Lir's loyalty to the new king of the Tuatha Dé Danann, who now trusts and supports the king.

True love is a product of this marriage alliance. The depth of love between Lir and Aoibh results in four beautiful children. After Aoibh's death, Lir's love for his children grows even deeper. Through time and seeing the wondrous success of the marriage of his first daughter, Bodb Dearg arranges a second union. The loyalty and trust between Lir and Bodb Dearg are two-sided.

A father's incredibly deep love for his children begins the path to their transformation, as a lack of love triggers raging jealousy. Their stepmother, Aoife, changes the children into swans, which represent all the traits that she does not possess.

Transforming from clumsy birds into graceful and elegant animals, swans demonstrate the need to exhibit inner love. The children's love for each other also allows them to survive nine hundred years away from home. Despite all the challenges the children faced, they continued to share their beautiful songs, never losing the voice of who they were. They remained loyal to themselves and their family, and their unwavering trust in their love for their father sustained them until their souls were eventually reunited with their father and mother.

Swans mate for life, and Lir and Aoibh were true mates for life. Lir could not nurture another marriage after the death of Aoibh. For three hundred years, Lir visited his children. And the children stayed with each other and were loyal to each other for nine hundred years. The love and devotion of a father to his wife, a father to his children, and siblings to each other are extraordinary.

The *Children of Lir* also illustrates elements of rebirth. Bodb Dearg is the king of the Tuatha Dé Danann. According to legend, in one of their last battles, the tribe was seeking to survive. Some stories tell of their disappearance, while others say they evaded the Milesians by going underground. These underground locations are referred to as *sidhe* mounds, which is the same song the children sang while traversing the waters. Even though the children's forms shifted into swans, they still retained the connection to their tribe.

From the underground mounds, the tribes were able to transport between Tír na nÓg and this world, which is also called the Land of the Young. This continued the lifeline of the Tuatha Dé Danann. Tales tell of the Tuatha Dé Danann living in the underground mounds to this day. But perhaps they were reborn as fairies, who populate many Irish myths.

The Irish believed in an afterlife or an Otherworld. In one version, the Children of Lir leave their bodies as dust in this world, their souls reuniting with their parents in the afterlife. Transforming from human form to that of a swan supports the Celtic view of the cycle of life, as shifting between shapes and worlds was done fluidly.

Sculpture in Ballycastle.
Michael Dibb / Children of Lir;
https://commons.wikimedia.org/wiki/File:Children_of_Lir_sculpture_Ballycastle,_County_Antrim_2017-07-29.jpg

Statues and jewelry depicting the children are available throughout Ireland. Surviving with grace and interconnectedness with one another are a few of the reasons this tale resonates with so many. The ability to reinvent yourself and adapt to your surroundings is the key to survival during any time period. Shifting between different worlds and trusting the form that you take will still represent who you are is a theme that resonates with many.

Chapter 6: Other Irish Myths of Note

Stories and myths from the earliest days in Ireland were shared from generation to generation. Tales of magnificent creatures who accomplished unbelievable feats were passed down in families and villages. Multiple layers of meaning can be gleaned from listening to and reading these stories today. Characters in Irish myths are complex, and their roles and lives can change from story to story. The intricacies in these stories that were once sacred to people thousands of years ago are more accessible when delving into them through the lens of the cycles of Irish myths.

We have mentioned these cycles briefly earlier in the previous chapter, but the four cycles or groupings of Irish myths are the Mythological Cycle, the Ulster Cycle, the Fenian Cycle, and the King Cycle. Each cycle has its own traits, characters, values, and belief system that were shared with listeners.

The oldest and, therefore, least preserved of the cycles is the Mythological Cycle. Stories in this grouping focus on five waves of invasions of Ireland. These are not to be confused with the conquests of Ireland by the Vikings, Romans, or Celtic tribes. Although they were not written down until 1100 CE, it is believed these events occurred over a thousand years before Christian monks recorded the exploits of supernatural beings and their exploits.

Several versions of the Lebor Gabála Érenn, also referred to as The Book of Invasions or The Book of the Taking of Ireland, talks about the battles of different groups who fought for control of Ireland. Irish origin myths differ from other cultures. In many cultures, origin myths explain how the world and what is in it came to be. Stories told in The Book of Invasions tell of people coming to settle the land from other places.

The invasions are sometimes conquests, while other times, they are colonization expeditions or the resettlement of people. Cessair, Noah's granddaughter, and her followers are the first settlers of Ireland in some origin myths. To escape the pending biblical flood, Cessair persuades her father, Bith, and their people to flee. They set sail for the western edge of the world. When they land in Ireland, their numbers include fifty women, including Cessair, and three men.

To balance the population and repopulate for survival, each of the three men is given sixteen wives. However, the members of the expedition soon perish from the flood, except for Fintan mac Bóchra. A shapeshifter, Fintan mac Bóchra survived the flood as a salmon in what is now referred to as Fintan's Grave, believed to be in the Arra Mountains near Lough Derg.

After the flood receded, Fintan transformed into a hawk. For over five thousand years, Fintan provided wisdom and guidance to the kings of Ireland. Fintan shared his advice through the era of Fionn mac Cumhaill in the 5th century CE.

For almost three hundred years after the demise of the first settlers of Ireland, the land remained uninhabited. Another descendant of Noah, Partholón, led the second invasion. Many accounts describe Partholón as a villainous leader who ruined his homeland and killed his parents before setting off for a new land.

Partholón, Dealgnaid (his queen), and his tribe settled near Dublin; they are credited with bringing farming and building to Ireland. After settling in the area, the Partholónians are attacked by a tribe of giants, the Fomorians. These magical people came from Tory Island. After achieving success in their battles against the Fomorians. s, The Book of Invasions recounts how the Partholónians were decimated by a plague.

Over nine thousand Partholónians died from the plague and were buried in an area that today is referred to as Tallaght. The name of the town is derived from támh leach, which means "plague grave."

Ireland again was unpopulated due to the plague. Partholón's brother's grandson, Nemed, decided to lead the next settlement of Ireland. The Lebor Gabála Érenn tells of the Nemedians and their battles with the Fomorians s. The Nemedians had more success against the Fomorians than the Partholónians did; however, the plague wreaked havoc on the Nemedians, killing thousands of them, including their leader. Eventually, the Fomorians forced the remaining Nemedians from Ireland.

The Fir Bolg was the fourth group to invade Ireland and attempt to establish their civilization. Stories in *The Book of Invasions* tell of these people bringing their judicial system and ruling hierarchy to Ireland. Their timing and story paralleled the Book of Exodus in the Bible. The Fir Bolg had been enslaved but managed to escape to Ireland. A tribe of peace, their time in Ireland was short-lived. The Fir Bolg were quickly outmatched by the Tuatha Dé Danann. The details are told in the First Battle of Mag Tuired.

The fifth influx of vanquishers and the most well-known are the Tuatha Dé Danann. *The Book of Invasions* details their arrival as being different from the first four groups, who came by sea. The Tuatha Dé Danann chose to demonstrate their magical and godlike powers and appeared in clouds of dark fog.

The Tuatha Dé Danann are said to come from the goddess Danu and established the first goddess culture in Ireland. Similar to the groups who arrived before them, the Tuatha Dé Danann faced the Fomorians in battle. However, the Tuatha Dé Danann were more powerful and kept the Fomorians at bay.

The Tuatha Dé Danann brought many gods, goddesses, magical treasures, and special places to the stories of Ireland's foundation. The Tuatha Dé Danann brought the Spear of Lugh, Dagda's Cauldron, the Stone of Fal, and the Sword of Nuada to Ireland. Gods and goddesses from the Tuatha Dé Danann include Lir, the god of the sea; Ogma, the god of learning and writing; Lugh, the god of the sun and light; Brigid, the goddess of fertility and health; and the Dagda, the god of death and life.

Ruling Ireland for many years, the Tuatha Dé Danann were the last immortals to control Ireland. When the Milesians, ancestors of the Celtic people, defeated the Tuatha Dé Danann at the Battle of Tailtiu, the Tuatha Dé Danann disappeared from Ireland.

Stories say the Tuatha Dé Danann were driven underground. Other tales state an agreement was reached between the Milesians and the

Tuatha Dé Danann in which the Milesians would rule the physical world and the Tuatha Dé Danann would control the spiritual realm. In the spiritual world, the Tuatha Dé Danann live in the fairy mounds that one can find throughout Ireland, or they have withdrawn to Tír na nÓg, the Otherworld. Since the Tuatha Dé Danann are immortal, they continue to live to this day.

The Riders of the Sidhe.
Sevenseaocean, CC BY-SA 4.0 <https://creativecommons.org/licenses/by-sa/4.0>, via Wikimedia Commons; https://commons.wikimedia.org/wiki/File:%22The_Riders_of_the_Sidhe%22_John_Duncan_1911_McManus_Galleries,_Dundee.jpg

The *aos sí* came from the Tuatha Dé Danann. Also referred to as *sidhe* or "people of the mounds," these descendants of the Tuatha Dé Danann include many famous characters in Irish mythology and folklore, such as leprechauns, banshees, and changelings.

Chronologically, the Ulster Cycle follows the Mythological Cycle, which transpired over two thousand years ago. More than eighty stories talk about the Ulaid. This group of people lived in the area of present-day Ulster, which is named after the Ulaid.

Previously, the grouping of stories was called the Red Branch Cycle or Rúraíocht. During this time period, there was no central king who ruled all of Ireland. Instead, many provincial kingdoms divided the land. The term "Red Branch" is a translation from Old Irish for the names of two of the ruling houses of King Conchobar. Throughout the stories in this cycle, a blend of semi-historical information is woven with mythological components.

Many tales in the Ulaid Cycle involve the actions and deeds of King Conor or Conchobar mac Nessa and his rivals. Conchobar ruled from Emain Macha, which is the location of Navan Fort in Northern Ireland, with the Red Branch Knights. His opponents were King Ailill and Queen Medb, whose court was located at Connaught.

Stories in the Ulaid Cycle take place around the time of Jesus Christ, around the 1st century CE. The timing of King Conchobar's life coincidentally parallels that of Jesus' time on Earth. However, it might not be all that coincidental. As you might have noticed, many of the myths have some aspects of Christianity in them. Since the tales were transcribed by monks years after they were shared through the oral tradition, it is likely the monks added their own slant to the stories.

In this grouping of tales, the events in the Celtic world meld together magical elements, similar to the Mythological Cycle, with powerful warriors and their legendary battles. Characters evolve from having traits of cleverness and enchantments to larger-than-life heroic fighters who battle for the adoration of their tribe.

Mosaic depicting the Cattle Raid of Cooley.
Leandro Neumann Ciuffo, CC BY 2.0 <https://creativecommons.org/licenses/by/2.0>, via Wikimedia Commons;
https://commons.wikimedia.org/wiki/File:Desmond_Kinney%E2%80%99s_mosaic_(6179099398).jpg

Typifying the elements and central figures of the Ulster Cycle is one of its key stories: *The Cattle Raid of Cooley* or *Táin Bó Cúailnge*. One of the fiercest and most well-known of the Red Branch Knights is Cú Chulainn, the nephew of King Conchobar. One day, King Conchobar's foe, Queen Medb, decides to steal Donn Cúailnge, which was renowned as the most fertile bull in Ireland, from her rival. At this time, wealth and status were determined by the quality and quantity of one's cattle.

Queen Medb sent her army to capture the bull, and they took Conchobar's forces by surprise. However, once Cú Chulainn returned, the tide of the battle quickly turned. Cú Chulainn was born to Lugh, the god of the sun and light who led the Tuatha Dé Danann to victory against the Fomorians. The seventeen-year-old Cú Chulainn dismantled Medb's army one by one.

Desperate to win the battle, Medb offered Cú Chulainn land and money to fight for her kingdom instead. Cú Chulainn refused; however, he offered to cease his attacks on her men if she sent one warrior to fight against him. Through trickery, Medb forced Ferdia, Cú Chulainn's foster brother, into battle. Medb goaded Ferdia by spreading the word that he was a coward. This enraged Ferdia, who came to see the queen and insisted that she stop. Prepared for his visit, Medb had a fabulous feast. After plying Ferdia with wines and food, he became enamored by Medb's beautiful daughter. Medb promised Ferdia her daughter's hand in marriage if he battled Cú Chulainn.

For days, a fierce battle raged. All of Ireland was captivated by the fighting. After Ferdia's sword was thrust into Cú Chulainn's chest, it was time for Gáe Bolga, the notched spear provided by Scáthach, the magical warrior queen, to end the battle. With all the force and power remaining in him, Cú Chulainn hurled the spear. This special spear required a technique that only Cú Chulainn knew how to perform. Ferdia was killed immediately.

In the end, Medb and her husband realize they cannot win the battle for Donn Cúailnge. A seven-year peace between the two kingdoms ensued. Cú Chulainn's reputation and legendary status were firmly entrenched among all of the kingdoms. He fought in many other battles until the witchcraft and trickery of Lugaid mac Con Roí defeated him at the age of twenty-seven.

Sharing some similar traits with the Ulaid Cycle, stories and characters of the Fenian Cycle include fierce warriors with supernatural powers. Cú

Chulainn, the hero of the Ulaid Cycle, fought for his tribe and people. The icon of the Fenian Cycle was Fionn mac Cumhaill (Finn McCool), the leader of the Fianna. This group of warriors consisted more of nomadic renegades than figures from early Irish myths.

Fionn mac Cumhaill comes to aid the Fianna.
https://commons.wikimedia.org/wiki/File:Finn_Mccool_Comes_to_Aid_the_Fianna.png

The High King of Ireland formed the Fianna. His intention was that the Fianna would work to protect him and his kingdom. Many clans were gathered together to form the Fianna, but joining the Fianna required a lifetime of allegiance. To be considered for membership to this band of warriors, one had to pass a number of different tests.

The Fianna were intelligent, as they needed to know the twelve books of poetry that contained the history of Ireland. As skillful bards and musicians, they could regal an audience with hours of entertainment. But they were also powerful and adroit warriors. The Fianna were required to be brave and could only marry for love. These traits and abilities made them welcome in many villages as they traveled the countryside.

High King Cormac mac Airt chose Fionn mac Cumhaill to lead the Fianna. Under Fionn's tutelage, the Fianna rose to their pinnacle of power. Fionn was an effective leader for most of his tenure. To be fair, he had an advantage. He was born to a Druid, who granted him wisdom. Fionn also gained otherworldly powers as a young boy.

Finnegas, a Druid, had spent more than seven years attempting to catch the Salmon of Knowledge. This special salmon contained all the knowledge of the world because it ate hazelnuts that dropped from nine holy trees surrounding the Well of Wisdom. One day, Finnegas and Fionn traveled along the Boyne River. Legend said that anyone who ate the salmon would gain the same knowledge that it had.

Fionn helped Finnegas finally catch the fish. Young Fionn was responsible for cooking the fish but was told not to eat it. While mac Cumhaill was cooking the fish, he burned his thumb. Instinctively, he put his thumb in his mouth to assuage the pain. The salmon's juices were on his thumb, causing its wisdom to enter Fionn. So, whenever Fionn sucked on his thumb, he could summon the insight of the Salmon of Knowledge, which offered him incredible protection.

Illustration of the Salmon of Knowledge.
https://commons.wikimedia.org/wiki/File:Salmon-of-Knoweldge-1904.jpg

Linking the stories to the next cycle is High King Cormac mac Airt, the king who selected Fionn mac Cumhaill as the leader of the Fianna. His exploits are a significant component of the last cycle of Irish mythology, which is called the King or Historical Cycle. Figures in this cycle of stories are a blend of historical people and mythological characters. The settings and exploits of the characters can also be a fusion of reality and magic. However, stories in this cycle are not always a mixture of mythical and historical; some can be purely historical, such as those about Brian Boru.

Stories in the King Cycle are, as its name implies, about the kings of Ireland. These tales were intended to provide examples of what it meant to be a good king, as well as depictions of ineffective kings. Details of kings' lives, including their adventures, their ability to lead in battle, their marriages, and much more, were shared with listeners. This collection of myths and histories includes tales from the 3rd century BCE until about the 11th century CE.

An important concept in this cycle is the imposition of *geasa*. These were restrictions often decreed in pairs. In the King Cycle, a *geis* (singular of *geasa*) is a vow that bonds the king to his people. Breaking the vow or committing an act that was forbidden meant the king had violated his sacred vow with the kingdom. Breaching the *geis* resulted in disgrace and could lead to death. However, following the expectations of the *geasa* caused a person to gain incredible power.

From the Book of the Dun Cow, one can find the story of High King Conaire Mór in Togail Bruidne Dá Derga or "The Destruction of Da Derga's Hostel." Conaire was the son of Eterscél Mór, and all signs at his birth foresaw a favorable future and kingship. With a kingdom in his future, Conaire had the *geasa* placed on him, as all kings did. The early days of Conaire's rule saw a kingdom that was peaceful and prosperous.

One of the *geasa* that framed Conaire's reign was that he could not hunt seabirds. The birds had visited Conaire and said they were part of his father's tribe of fighters, making them untouchable. While Conaire was king, he could never let a woman into his house after midnight. He also could not follow or listen to the three red warriors who rode red horses.

After years of leading Ireland, Conaire's rule came to a deadly end. He was forced to choose between following his *geasa* or aiding his foster brothers. Conaire violated his vows and chose to help his brothers instead.

The severed promise that hastens Conaire's demise was not following the warning he received about not going to Da Derga's Hostel. Along his way to the hostel, Conaire met the three men dressed in red whom he had been cautioned to avoid. These men were harbingers, warning Conaire of his impending death. After violating the *geis*, he continued to the hostel. Conaire's enemies met him there, and he was attacked and killed in the ambush.

Stories in the King Cycle tell the tales of many other kings. And as with other myths, these were intended to be a guide for people to live by.

Chapter 7: Samhain and Its Many Traditions

Celtic mythological traditions included the celebration of eight holy days throughout the calendar year, which was separated into quarters. The seasons divided the year, with four festivals noting the changing seasons. There were also observations of the two annual solstices and equinoxes.

Seasonal changes were marked by the four fire festivals of Imbolc, Beltane, Lughnasadh, and Samhain. Samhain started the new year, although it was celebrated at the end of the harvest season, not at the beginning of January like many of us celebrate today. February 1st signaled the beginning of spring with Imbolg. Summer or Beltane was recognized on May 1st. And wrapping up the four main sacred days of the year was Lughnasadh, which celebrated the beginning of the harvest season on August 1st. The most significant fire festivals were the commencement of darkness, noted with Samhain, and the beginning of light, which was celebrated at Beltane.

On the night before significant sacred days like Samhain, the ancient Celts believed the gods were closer to the earth than on any other day of the year. On the eve of Samhain, the curtain between this world and the Otherworld was thinner, which allowed for the easier transfer between the world of the gods and the *sidhe* to the earthly realm of the living. In other words, the fairy folk and the dead could intrude upon the world of earthly beings.

Windows and doors were left open and unlatched during the celebration of Samhain since the dead, who were viewed as revered guests, could readily travel between the worlds. Special foods and cakes were made in preparation for visitors. No earthly mortals were permitted to touch the food that was left for the dead visitors. If anyone violated this ritual, they were condemned to live their afterlife as a famished soul, as they could not partake in the Samhain feast.

To entertain the dead guests when they were not feasting, activities were planned. Games were played by the children in the village. Each year, the community leaders evaluated the engagement level of each of the activities. Only events that had positive feedback were offered again during the next Samhain, as the village elders wanted to ensure the dead would continue to be involved with the living.

When the summer crops were gathered, the ancient Celts left their hearth fires to extinguish on their own, which symbolized the passing of the previous year and preparations for the new one. A new communal fire was lit after the fields were harvested. Druid priests performed a ritual and lit a pure fire to celebrate Samhain. A wheel, which represented the sun, was used to light the sacred oak for the ceremonial fire. Community members cast symbolic objects into the flames as they prayed for the new year. Participants each took a pure flame from the community fire back to their abodes to relight their hearths. This flame lit a new start for the family.

Samhain was a brief transitional period between summer and winter. This transitory time is referred to as a liminal space. Since Samhain was the movement between summer and winter, it was not measured in time, as the hours and days of Samhain were not in either summer or winter. For the ancient Celts, this "floating time" meant that those on Earth were not tied to Earth. It was seen as a tranquil period; villagers and families did not argue with each other.

During the liminal space of Samhain, significant mythological events occurred. One key occurrence was the Second Battle of Moytura or Cath Magh Tuired. In this battle, two groups of supernatural powers battled for supremacy. In this epic showdown, the Tuatha Dé Danann triumphed. However, their king, Nuada, died as a result of the battle, giving rise to the leadership of Lugh.

The Tuatha Dé Danann's next foes were the Milesians, who are considered to be the ancestors of the Celts. After the Milesians defeated the Tuatha Dé Danann, the Tuatha Dé Danann were relegated to living underground. The Tuatha Dé Danann became known as the aos sí, the people of the fairy mounds. The sidhe, or mounds, were passageways to the Otherworld. The aos sí travel openly between the two worlds during Samhain.

Illustration of Aengus.
Internet Archive Book Images, No restrictions, via Wikimedia Commons;
https://commons.wikimedia.org/wiki/File:Heroes_of_the_dawn_(1914)_(14566173909).jpg

Another myth in which Samhain figures prominently is in one of the tales of Óengus or Aengus, a member of the Tuatha Dé Danann. He has ongoing dreams of a mysterious woman. When Aengus reaches for her, she continually disappears. Samhain's liminal time allows her, a shapeshifter named Caer, to go between the two worlds, transforming from a human to a swan.

Aengus searches for the woman of his dreams. Medb and Ailill assist him. Together, they find her father, Ethal Anbuail. However, he does not have control over Caer, the goddess of dreams and prophecy. Ethal tells them where they can find her, though. Caer will be with 150 other swans, and for Aengus to have Caer, he must be able to recognize her from all the other birds.

Aengus knows he can recognize the woman haunting his dreams, even if she has been transformed. He sees Caer and calls her to come with him.

Caer replies that she will only join Aengus if he comes into the water. His love for her is so deep that he transforms into a swan. Together, they sing lovely music for three days and nights. Legend says that people can still hear the hauntingly beautiful melodies of Aengus and Caer during Samhain.

Another well-known Celtic character, Fionn mac Cumhaill, influenced events by using the mystical powers available during Samhain. When Fionn was young, he learned poetry under Cethem. Every year, Cethem would travel to a fairy mound or a *sidhe*. Fionn noticed that Cethem would always stop at one specific location, the home of the fairy Éle.

Éle had an abundance of admirers due to her incredible beauty, and she found them all tiresome. During Samhain, many tried to gain her affection. Irritated by their attention, many admirers lost their lives in their vain struggle to court the legendary beauty.

Fionn is bothered by the death that Éle inflicted as he watches her procession of suitors. So, on Samhain, Fionn decides to retaliate. He conceals himself near Éle's *sidhe*. Fionn avenges the deaths of those who had met their deaths in their attempts to impress Éle, and in doing so, he garners the admiration of the other fairies.

Fionn mac Cumhaill battling Áillen.
Internet Archive Book Images, No restrictions, via Wikimedia Commons;
https://commons.wikimedia.org/wiki/File:Heroes_of_the_dawn_(1914)_(14750481494).jpg

Fionn is featured as a lead character in another myth connected to Samhain. His interactions with Áillen mac Midgna are shared in *The Boyhood Deeds of Fionn*. When the Tuatha Dé Danann were defeated by the Milesians, they were forced to live in the fairy mounds. One of the fairies, Áillen, was angered by their defeat and relocation.

An incredible musician, Áillen used his musical talents to wreak havoc on the incredible Great Hall of Tara as part of his revenge. Every Samhain, Áillen would use the liminal time to leave his *sidhe* and return to the mortal world. He would wear a magical cloak, which gave him the power to breathe fire, and go to the palace of the High King of Ireland. At this revered place in Tara, Áillen played his harp.

All in attendance at the great hall would fall under the spell of his music. Once everyone was asleep, Áillen used his fire-breathing powers, burning the magnificent palace to the ground. After he accomplished his mission, Áillen escaped to his *sidhe* in the Otherworld.

Every year, the renowned hall of Tara was rebuilt. But no one was able to stop Áillen because of how quickly he put people into a deep sleep. That all changed when Fionn mac Cumhaill came on the scene. Fionn made a deal with the High King. In exchange for leadership of the Fianna, a wandering band of combatants, Fionn would rid the world of Áillen. The king readily agreed.

However, no one was immune to the magical harp spell, even Fionn. So, he borrowed a spear from Fiacha, a warrior. When the next Samhain Eve arrived, Fionn breathed in fumes from Fiacha's magical spear. These magical vapors gave Fionn the protection he needed from the music. When Áillen arrived at Tara, he was met by Fionn, who refused to fall under his spell. Fionn took advantage of Áillen's confusion, piercing him with the bewitched spear. Fionn stabbed Áillen, ridding the High King of the annual destruction of his fabulous hall at the Hill of Tara.

Associated with the festival of Samhain and other feasts in Ireland is the fabled Dullahan, who was thought to be linked to Crom Dubh or Crom Cruach. Crom Dubh, the Celtic god of fertility, was known to be pacified by human sacrifices.

Tigernmas, the High King of Ireland who died around 1500 BCE, supported the worship of Crom Dubh in his kingdom. One Samhain night, Tigernmas and many from his kingdom worshiped Crom Dubh on Magh Slécht, a gathering place for followers of the god. The next morning, all who had assembled at Magh Slécht were dead.

It is believed that the Dullahan, with his connections to Crom Dubh, appears around midnight during the festival of Samhain and other feast days. Crom Dubh had expectations on the number of souls that should be given in worship to him. When Christianity arrived in Ireland, offering human sacrifices to the gods faded from acceptable practice. At that time, Crom Dubh transformed into the Dullahan so his death quotas could be fulfilled. According to tales from the ancients, Crom Dubh preferred his sacrifices to be decapitated, which is why the Dullahan appears headless.

While there are many descriptions of the Dullahan, some tell of him driving a spooky, dark coach that is pulled by four to six black stallions. His Cóiste Bodhar, or silent coach, connects him to the banshee. However, he is often depicted as a headless horseback rider. On the nights he rides, the Dullahan carries his glowing head in his hand. Raising his head high above him, the Dullahan's paranormal vision lets him search for his victim.

The Dullahan's whip, which is constructed from human spines, is used to force the stallion to move so rapidly that the horse's hooves spark fire. The Dullahan's massive mount emits flames from his nostrils and leaves a wake of burning bushes in his path.

When the Dullahan, or Gan Ceann (meaning "without a head" in Irish), stops riding, someone is about to die. He only speaks once on his journey, and that is to utter the name of his victim. By saying the person's name, the Dullahan has taken the person's soul.

Onlookers need to fear him as well, for there are two penalties for looking at the Dullahan. He either throws a pail of blood in your face or uses his horsewhip. If he strikes you with his whip made of human spine fragments, he will blind you in one eye.

The only protection against the harbinger of death is gold. In the past, people would carry some gold with them or wear gold jewelry to keep him at bay.

As with many other characters from Celtic mythology, variations on the tale of the "Headless Horseman" have been told in many countries and time periods. *The Legend of Sleepy Hollow* by Washington Irving is an American classic based on the Dullahan. These stories and others are perennial favorites that are shared on Halloween, which has its roots in Samhain.

Samhain has also been referred to as the Festival of the Dead or *Féile na Marbh* in Irish. Not all of the dead were peaceful visitors. There were many who desired revenge. For instance, revenants are corpses that rise from the dead to inflict terror on the living.

One such example of the walking dead or, in Irish, *neamh-mairbh* is Abhartach, Irish for "dwarf." Despised by the people he ruled, Abhartach was a vindictive and envious man. He believed his wife was having an affair, so he followed her, climbing out of a window in their castle to tail her in secret. In doing so, he fell to his death.

Relief spread over the kingdom. Wanting to rid themselves of Abhartach, the people buried him immediately. Decorum dictated that leaders of his rank should be buried standing up. The next day, Abhartach reappeared and demanded blood from his people. Panicked, his subjects complied and supplied him with their blood. But they knew they could not satiate the undead ruler forever, so they went to Cathán, a nearby chieftain. Cathán waited for Abhartach to reappear and killed him. Once again, Abhartach was properly buried. And once again, Abhartach, the vile *neamh-mairbh*, returned and insisted on more blood from the villagers.

Cathán sought assistance from Saint Eoghan. He said that since Abhartach was already dead, the only way to kill him was to spear his heart with a sword made from a yew tree. Yew trees held many layers of symbolism for the Celtic people. It represented intense strength and the contrast between life and death. Additionally, in ancient times, the tips of spears were dipped in the poisonous sap of the yew.

Cathán did as Eoghan instructed. After stabbing Abhartach, Cathán buried him upside down. A block of stone that could not be moved was placed on top of the grave. All of Abhartach's mystical powers were now eliminated. In pre-Christian versions, Eoghan is replaced by a Druid. In all stories, Abhartach's grave is called Slaghtaverty Dolmen. People still say strange things happen there. The Irish vampire is believed to have been the inspiration for Bram Stoker's Dracula.

The Dullahan and Abhartach were not the only unfriendly spirits who went between both worlds. During Samhain, the living used different means to try and keep antagonistic souls away from their homes. One way to do this was extinguishing the family's hearth fire on *Oíche Shamhna* or Samhain day (October 31").

Communities would then unite for Samhnagans or bonfires to emerge from the darkest night of the year. Relighting the fires commenced the new year. Druids would ignite the new fire, which contained bones from animal sacrifices (bone fires). It was believed the fires dissuaded the *aos sí* from returning to Earth.

Another means to ward off unwanted ancestors was wearing costumes. Many fairies were on Earth during Samhain to seek revenge on humans who had wronged them. People would disguise themselves as animals or monsters to fool them. Children and adults wore masks and costumes of frightening spirits. Animal skins, including the skull and ears, would be cleaned and worn as well. This protection kept the spirits from capturing humans and taking them to the Otherworld.

Turnip lantern.
Geni at English Wikipedia, CC BY-SA 3.0 <http://creativecommons.org/licenses/by-sa/3.0/>, via Wikimedia Commons; https://commons.wikimedia.org/wiki/File:TurnipJackolantern.jpg

Turnip or beet lanterns were used to ward off spirits holding grudges against the living. Frightening faces were carved into the root vegetables, and candles were placed inside the hollowed-out turnip or beet. People would carry them as they went from house to house or to the festival's activities. When at home, the lit lanterns were placed in windows. It was believed the lanterns with scary faces frightened the fairies and spirits from doing the household any harm.

The ancient peoples believed the rituals practiced during the festival of Samhain would help lead them through the upcoming season of darkness. A significant location for fires to light during Samhain was the Hill of

Tlachtga. Current research supports that this location, about thirteen miles from the Hill of Tara, where the High Kings lived, was used by the Druids to light the communal fires to celebrate the new year.

On the eve of Samhain, fires were lit at Tlachtga as a prelude to the events that followed at Tara. Samhain was an important festival for the Celts, as it provided assurance to the community that the days of light would return again.

Chapter 8: Botanical Folk Tales

From the fire of Samhain to the magical yew tree that could destroy Abhartach, tales that have their basis in nature form the grouping of botanical folk tales. The creatures that live in the woodlands provide fantastical stories and legends. Their view of life mirrors the unpredictability of what daily life can bring.

Haunted woodlands filled with spirits and ghosts explore the connections between humans and nature. These stories have been shared for generations, providing a shared common experience. Frightful and amazing escapades of fairies and other woodland creatures have been told and retold.

These tales are not usually categorized in the Mythological, Ulster, Fenian, or Historical Cycles of Irish mythology. Botanical folk tales are intended to delight and transport listeners and readers to another world. These stories are as unruly and unpredictable as nature itself. Some offer suggestions on ways to control the energy of nature. Others tell of ways to ensure that you stay in the good graces of the woodland folks. Fairies and other creatures remind listeners to respect and protect the lands of our ancestors.

One such tale is "The Green Mist." People believed that bogles, a mischievous group of supernatural goblins, lived amongst them. Bogles mainly lived indoors as house fairies, and the humans who resided with them followed rituals to appease the bogles and keep them happy. If any changes occurred in a bogle's household that it did not approve of, their friendliness vanished in an instant.

During the winter, bogles had more time for mischief. People would carry a lantern around the house before bed and chant words to keep the bogles pleased. Lullabies were sung so the bogles would remain in their nooks and crannies in the houses and fields. Bogles were always alert and listened to the families with whom they shared their homes.

Once upon a time, a family had a young girl who had become sickly over the winter. The young girl pined for the green mist, which was the new growth of spring. She and her family believed she would be healthy again once the sun and greenery returned. Day by day, she weakened until she needed to be carried. But she still performed the ritual to the bogles to welcome spring. Her mother carried her to the doorway, allowing her to crumble bread and salt, which was needed to harken spring's arrival.

All the townspeople, including the girl and her family, anxiously awaited the bursting of seeds and grasses to create the green mist. In the green mist, the bogles, if placated, worked their magic for the new growing season to commence. However, winter dragged on, and the girl's condition worsened. Hope was diminishing that she would live to experience spring's restorative powers.

She said to her mother that she wanted to live so that she could see the cowslips emerge from their winter slumber. Desperately, she said that she would be willing to live as long as the cowslips. When they wilted, she would as well. This panicked her mother, who knew the bogles were always listening.

The girl regained her health while the cowslips sprouted and grew. All were thankful, but her mother continued to worry. Her daughter became so attached to the cowslips that she prohibited anyone from touching them.

As frequently happens in spring, love flourished. The girl and her admirer spent hours daily with each other. One afternoon, the girl slipped off to sleep in the company of her suitor and awoke to find a flower crown of cowslips. Terrified, she cried and ran to her room, locking herself inside.

Her family and admirer tried to access her room. They smashed the door down and found her unconscious. The withered cowslips were held tightly in her hands. Later that night, she died. Apparently, the bogles had overheard her promise.

Betty Stogs fared better with the fairies, which appeared to assist her in the tale of "Betty Stogs and the Fairies." To recap what a fairy is, most accounts believe the *aos sí*, which encompasses fairies, are descendants of the Tuatha Dé Danann. This supernatural race was driven underground when the Celts arrived. Moving to the Otherworld, the *aos sí* live in fairy mounds. From this original group, many variances of little people or fairies, all with magical powers, have emerged.

Though they are not visible to the human eye, the work of fairies is apparent. They return to this realm to avenge any wrongs they believe that humans have committed. This is why Betty Stogs encountered fairies and pixies, another type of fairy.

Illustration of pixies.
https://commons.wikimedia.org/wiki/File:Page_83_illustration_in_More_English_Fairy_Tales.png

Betty was known for her laziness and lived a life that many would cherish. She was married to an admiring husband, lived in a cottage in the moors, and had a new baby. Betty was truly a fortunate young woman. However, she did not appreciate the gifts in her life. She did not nurture her baby or care for her home.

Betty's pet cat was more of a mother to the baby than she was. The cat shared its food with the baby and kept the baby warm. The baby was filthy from Betty's lack of care, as Betty viewed dirt as a way for the baby to remain warm.

While her husband toiled in the mines, Betty left the cat to care for the baby while she visited the local tavern. Returning one night after drinking, Betty found her home empty. The cat and baby were nowhere to be found. Desperately, Betty searched for her baby without success.

Later in the evening, her husband came home from work. He was incensed with Betty and her behavior. Seeking help from neighbors, they looked for the baby all night to no avail. At sunrise, Betty noticed her cat and followed it. The cat led Betty to her baby, who was lying happily in the grass. Betty was shocked at the baby's clean appearance and took her child home.

The village elders understood what had happened to the baby. They knew the fairies had seen how poorly Betty cared for it. So, the fairies took the baby. Throughout the night, they cleaned the baby with soaps, herbs, and flowers. They were not quite finished when the sun rose, but they had to return to their mounds under the earth. The fairies would return to finish their work. Once they finished cleaning the baby, they would take it to their home.

Betty learned her lesson. She knew if she did not properly care for her child, the fairies would return. This was a warning to all mothers. If one did not care for their child, the fairies or pixies would take the babies away. Infants who were removed from their homes would be raised as fairies.

Leprechauns are another magical force connected with the woodlands and natural forces. Pots of gold, "little people," and rainbows are often associated with leprechauns. It is believed that the leprechauns' tremendous wealth—the pots of gold—was an idea from ancient times. During wars and invasions by the Vikings, the Irish hid gold throughout the country. The leprechauns, one of the branches of fairies, resulted from the defeat of the Tuatha Dé Danann. When the leprechauns discovered the gold that was buried, they declared the gold to be theirs.

Luchorpán ("small body") is believed to be the origin of the term "leprechaun." Since leprechauns lived in the fairy mounds with others from the Tuatha Dé Danann, their size permitted them to reside underground. Tales involving leprechauns often show them meeting humans. During these encounters, leprechauns and humans frequently try to outsmart each other.

Drawing of a leprechaun.
Jean-noël Lafargue (Jean-no) Free Art License 1.3;
https://en.wikipedia.org/wiki/File:Leprechaun_ill_artlibre_jnl.png

"Tom Fitzpatrick and the Leprechaun" shows a leprechaun and a human attempting to outwit each other for a legendary pot of gold. During the harvest, Tom was out and about wandering through the fields of boliaun (ragweed). As he came closer to the hedgerow, he thought he saw a small pitcher of liquor. To his surprise, next to the pitcher was a leprechaun.

Of course, Tom had heard stories of leprechauns, but he had never met one before. Excited for his good fortune, Tom snatched the leprechaun and demanded to be taken to the gold. If the leprechaun refused, Tom threatened to kill him. Terrified, the leprechaun readily agreed.

The leprechaun promised Tom that the gold was only a few fields away. Traversing through hedgerows, down into ditches, and across streams, Tom steadfastly clutched the leprechaun in his hand. When they reached a massive field of boliaun, the leprechaun pointed to a plant. He told Tom to dig under the boliaun. Once he shoveled underneath the plant, he would find his pot of gold.

Tom was anxious to begin digging, but he realized he did not have a shovel. To mark the boliaun that held the promised gold, Tom tied his red garter to the plant. Before he rushed home, he made the leprechaun promise that he would not remove the garter. The leprechaun eagerly agreed.

To Tom's shock, when he returned to the field, every boliaun had a red garter affixed to it. Tom didn't even try to find which plant had the gold. Perhaps if Tom had not been so hasty to give up, he might have found gold under each plant. The leprechaun trickster bested the human and retained his control of the land and fields.

Slipping away from Tom was easy for the leprechaun. Fairy mounds were spread throughout Ireland (some believe they still are). These mounds were welcomed abodes for all types of fairies intruding on the boundaries marking the human world and the Otherworld.

Connecting their dwellings was a series of pathways. A network of trails crisscrossed all of Ireland. In addition to providing access to their homes, the fairy paths were also conduits for mysterious happenings. Fairies gave fair warning to the mortals about the borders between the two worlds. People were informed that unusual events would occur.

A farmer from County Kerry learned the hard way about the consequences of interfering with the fairy people or *sidhe*. The house in which he and his wife lived was in deplorable condition. The thatched roof would not protect them from another winter season of wind, rain, and snow. They knew they needed to build a new cottage.

The couple searched for a suitable piece of land. After finding a great location, the farmer sought assistance from his neighbors. Together, the community built the farmer and his wife a new home. As they wrapped up the project, an elderly man happened by. He stopped and looked over the new house. Strolling away, the man asserted that no one would be able to get a restful night's sleep in that house.

Unknowing, the farmer and his wife moved into their new home. Exhausted after all their hard work, the couple climbed into bed, ready for a good night's slumber. Just after midnight, loud clanging sounds emanated from the kitchen. Rushing to find the source of the noise, the farmer expected to see items from the cabinets strewn across the floor.

However, the kitchen was organized and tidy. Two more times that night, the couple was awakened from their sleep by a raucous commotion. The second night in their new home, the farmer went to bed in his clothes, ready to leap from his bed to catch the noisemakers. When the commotion occurred, he searched his house for the source of the sounds.

Not knowing what to do next, his wife visited the local pastor. The priest visited and blessed the house. Hopeful, the couple went to bed that night, but there was no change. They suffered another night of disrupted sleep due to banging and clanging. This pattern continued night after night.

One day, while the farmer was in town to sell cattle, he visited the local pub for a pint. While sipping his beer, the farmer noticed the old man who had made the strange remark about his house. The old man suddenly left, and the farmer rushed out of the pub after him. When the farmer caught up to him, the old man noted how tired the farmer seemed. The two returned and shared a pint while the farmer shared his tale.

The old man agreed to go with the farmer to his house to see if he could discern the problem. Upon seeing it, the old man immediately recalled his earlier concern. The house had been built on a fairy path. Nightly, the fairies tried to access their pathway. However, every night, the fairies collided with the house that acted as a wall on their trail.

Unbeknownst to the farmer, he had built his house between two hawthorn trees. Fortunately, there was a solution. The old man explained to the farmer that he needed to keep the front and back doors of the house open each night. This removed the obstacles in the fairy path. The farmer was more than willing to try the remedy and kept the doors open. He was never woken up again by the fairies.

The hawthorn tree, also known as the fairy tree, was a sacred meeting location for fairies. Cutting down a hawthorn tree is believed to cause incredibly bad luck. Conversely, having a fairy tree on your property is thought to produce prosperity.

To this day, you will see hawthorn trees dotting the landscape of Ireland. Legends tell of year-long road construction delays due to a hawthorn tree in the way. Respecting the sidhe is important in Ireland. Leaving a route for fairies to travel to the Otherworld maintains ancestral connections so ancestors can continue to provide guidance to their living family.

Fairies not only have protected and magical trees, but they also have fairy or hungry grass. Originating on Hungry Hill, hungry grass is also called *féar gortach* in Irish. The first known person to access Hungry Hill vanished. The person's disappearance created fear in others, and many refused to walk past the hill.

Hungry Hill overlooks the ocean, making it a beautiful location. One day, a young fisherman who was new to Ireland decided he wanted to fish in the ocean adjacent to Hungry Hill. Forgetting to eat breakfast before he left his home, the young angler was hungry while he was walking to the ocean. He decided that he would eat some of his lunch while he strode up the hill.

People nearby noticed the young fisherman. Knowing the perils of the hill, the locals shouted at the young man to get off. The fisherman ignored their screams. As the man kept climbing up the hill, the grass started to wrap itself around him. Not noticing the danger, the man continued to eat as he walked. With each bite of his food, the twisting grass unwound itself from the man.

When the man reached the shoreline, he met fishermen who came from the other direction. The young man told the story of ascending the hill. The others were amazed and shared with him the dangers and deaths caused by Hungry Hill. They all surmised that eating while on the grass must have protected the young man.

Angered that the mortal had ascended the hill, the fairies began planting more patches of hungry grass throughout Ireland. The fairies chose places where humans had slighted or offended them. To combat the effects of the grass, people always carried food with them. The food was eaten while one walked through the grass, although some people left offerings of food to the fairies.

Some people believe that beings from the Otherworld continue to travel between both worlds. To safely keep the passageways open, mortals must follow the expectations of the fairies or suffer the consequences.

SECTION THREE:
Scottish and Welsh Myths

Chapter 9: The Cailleach

Celtic mythology encompasses stories and beliefs from the ancient Celtic tribes. These peoples mainly lived in the areas of modern-day Ireland, Scotland, Wales, England, and parts of France and Spain. Narratives filled with fantastical creatures, gods, heroes, and villains framed the Celts' complex belief system. Enduring tales from the ancients influence and entertain us today.

Scottish folklore and stories connect today's readers and listeners to their ancestors. A country filled with varied and distinctive landscapes, stories from the past help explain how Scotland's spectacular terrains were formed. Scotland's craggy mountains and magical lochs continue to enchant visitors and residents, and its stories are as mystical as its scenery.

The Cailleach is a Celtic goddess who is credited with shaping much of Scotland's topography. One of the mother goddesses, the Cailleach represents many maternal symbols. In Scottish mythology, she is viewed as the creator of all gods and goddesses.

Considered the oldest of all gods and goddesses, the Cailleach, or the Old Woman of Béara, is older than the oldest human, Fintan the Wise. To escape the biblical flood, Fintan sought refuge in current-day Ireland with Noah's granddaughter, Cessair. Expecting a barren land, Fintan was surprised to find it occupied by the Cailleach.

Since the Cailleach has numerous responsibilities, she is referred to by an assortment of names. The Cailleach is known as the Queen of Winter or the Veiled One. She is also called the Hag of Béara (Cailleach means "hag"). It is difficult to discern the root meaning of her name, but most agree that it evolved from *caille*, meaning veil, and *caillech*, denoting veiled. The Cailleach is often depicted as an old, veiled hag.

There are also regional iterations of her name. The Scots call her Carline, Beira, Cailleach Bheur, and, mockingly, Gentle Annie. Other name variations include the Corn Maiden and the "one who controls the winter winds." Regardless of her name, there were four key areas that she commanded. The Cailleach's scope was vast, shifting from creation to destruction. She was the source of the seasonal change to winter each year. In all Celtic regions, the Cailleach was seen as a protector of animals, especially wolves. In Scotland, she was often seen as a deer herder.

Her intentions were as wide-ranging as the control she exerted. The Cailleach could be harmful to those in her path, yet she also worked to ensure that the harvest of grains would be sufficient for the long, cold winter.

The Cailleach is typically shown as an old woman wearing a veil. Often, she is portrayed with either one usable eye or just one eye in the middle of her forehead. Regardless of her depiction, her sight is considered extraordinary. Long flowing white hair can be seen under her veil. Her ghostly pale or dark-blue-hued skin tones are complemented by a rust-red mouthful of teeth.

As with many other Celtic deities, she is gigantic, which is in proportion to her abilities and powers. Portrayed as an old hag, the Cailleach never ages. Her clothing is dull gray, and she usually is wrapped in a shawl. Often, she is seen holding or using a walking stick or a shillelagh.

Traditionally, shillelaghs were shaped from sacred blackthorn trees. The sharp, long thorns easily wounded anyone who approached the trees. Allegedly, witches used dark barbs to stab those they sought to put under their spells. The thorns caused those who were pricked to fall into a deep slumber. These trees were believed to have been used in the crown of thorns that Jesus wore.

These ominous connotations link the blackthorn trees and their spikes to the darkness of winter. The Cailleach, the goddess of winter, will thump her blackthorn shillelagh to commence the beginning of winter. Very dark and cold winters are referred to as blackthorn winters.

Many Celtic myths contain tri-faced, two-faced, or dual gods and goddesses. The Cailleach is frequently thought to be a two-faced goddess, as it is believed that she and Brigid are two faces of the same goddess. One begins her rule at the festival of Samhain, and the other commences her control at the festival of Imbolc.

However, not all tales consider the two goddesses as two faces of the same deity. They talk of battles between the Cailleach and Brigid. Nevertheless, both ideas depict how the seasons change from darkness to lightness; some just saw it as a peaceful transition, while others saw it as more violent.

One story that describes the transformation of the seasons occurs in Scotland. During Samhain, the Cailleach takes her plaid, which is a woolen scarf worn in the Scottish Highlands, and washes it. Since she is of gigantic proportions, her plaid requires a significant amount of water and effort to clean it. So, the Cailleach uses the Corryvreckan whirlpool, which is located between the islands of Scarba and Jura off the west coast of Scotland, to wash her plaid.

The Corryvreckan whirlpool.
Walter Baxter / The Corryvreckan Whirlpool;

Using her incredible powers, the Cailleach scrubs her plaid for three full days. Due to the turbulent waters and the intensity of the Cailleach, the green and blue tartan pattern of the plaid is completely washed away. Once it is cleaned, she lays the plaid out to dry. Since it is now pure white, her plaid covers the land with the first snowfall.

A version often shared in Scotland detailing how winter occurs includes the Cailleach and Brigid, who is the personification of spring. In this tale,

Brigid is imprisoned in a cave by the Cailleach. Since Brigid is trapped underground, she cannot spread her warmth and light on Earth. The Cailleach maintains control of the world, spreading cold, darkness, and winter storms of snow and ice.

In these Scottish myths, power between the two goddesses is transferred annually. The Cailleach rules after Samhain. On the winter solstice, the shortest day of the year, the Cailleach's power begins to falter. Her subjects, having grown tired of the long dark days, begin to revolt. As she battles to maintain control, the Cailleach creates the storms that occur during January and February; these are referred to as A'Chailleach.

She realizes that she is losing her power and seeks strength from the Well of Youth. When the Cailleach drinks the special waters, she gradually becomes younger. These are the milder days of winter, as they are a sure sign that spring is approaching.

Another version of the transition of seasons involves the Cailleach, Brigid, and Angus, who is one of the Cailleach's many sons. The Cailleach abducts Brigid on the night of Samhain. To ensure Brigid will not interfere with the Cailleach's rule as the goddess of winter, she is confined beneath Ben Nevis, the tallest mountain in Scotland.

Ben Nevis.
Graham Lewis, CC BY 2.0 <https://creativecommons.org/licenses/by/2.0>, via Wikimedia Commons; https://commons.wikimedia.org/wiki/File:Ben_Cruachan_-_Flickr_-_Graham_Grinner_Lewis.jpg

In a dream, Angus has a vision of the beautiful Brigid, but he does not know where she is imprisoned. He seeks advice from the king on what he should do. The king advises him to go to Scotland and find his beloved Brigid. On the eve of Imbolc, Angus reaches Brigid and attempts to free her. The Cailleach and Angus battle for control, which mortals experience as the turbulent weather of February and March.

The early spring flowers grow when Angus and Brigid start to win the battle against the Cailleach. An old, tired hag, her power continues to diminish until she turns herself into stone. The Cailleach will rest as a stone until Samhain, when she will once again capture Brigid. The Cailleach will imprison her again and reclaim her place as the goddess of winter.

Other versions of the myth sought to reassure the Celts about how and why the seasons changed. In one story that clarifies the shift from winter to summer, the Cailleach shapeshifts into a crow. As a crow, she gathers firewood. If the Cailleach collects sufficient firewood to construct a large fire, she transforms the day into a sunny, beautiful one. When this happens, winter will last longer. However, if she is not successful in building a roaring fire or oversleeps, then the day remains dark and dreary. When this happens, winter will end sooner. A similar tradition continues today with Groundhog Day, which is celebrated in Canada and the United States.

Another variation on how long winter will be is dependent on a battle between the Cailleach and one of her sisters. Toward the end of every winter, the Cailleach's sister comes to the Cailleach's land to fight. Since winter always ends, the Cailleach's sister always wins. However, the length of the fight determines the duration of winter. The longer the battle, the more winter days there will be. Once the Cailleach loses, she roams the countryside to gather her strength. At the end of summer, the sisters battle again. This time, the Cailleach always wins.

Illustration of Cailleach.

In addition to her defense of winter, the Cailleach protects and guards animals. Her appearance frightens the animals each winter. They are so terrified that they hide from her hideous face. By scaring them into hibernation, the Cailleach saves their lives, as they would not survive the cold winter season.

Her goodwill toward animals is shown in her protection of deer. Since they do not hibernate in the winter, the Cailleach uses her walking stick to assist them. While she travels around Scotland, she pokes through the snow and ice with her shillelagh. This creates access to food for the deer, which enables them to survive the winter.

The Cailleach also impacted winter in her role as goddess of grain. For people to survive the cold, barren winter, a bountiful harvest of grain was imperative. The last sheath of grain that was reaped was offered to the Cailleach in hopes of a successful spring planting. That same sheath of grain contained the first seeds that were sown in the next planting season.

Every year during the harvest, the first farmer who completed their task made a doll from their last sheaf of corn. In Scotland at that time, corn is what we now call wheat. The corn doll was called Carline. By doing this, the farmers and villagers showed their admiration and worship of the Cailleach in the creation of Carline.

Carline's features varied depending upon the success or disappointment of the harvest. In years of good harvest, the corn dolly was configured to look like a maiden. Less successful harvests were shown through Carlene's creation as a hag.

Carline was tossed on the field of the last farmer to complete the harvest. It was the responsibility of the last farmer to care for the corn doll, which represented the Cailleach. Throughout the winter, that farmer and his family had to feed and shelter the hag of winter. Her erratic nature made this a responsibility that no one wanted. Her place in the home was next to the home hearth, where she remained until spring.

On the first day of the planting season, Carline was removed from the home. She was either planted with the first seeds or fed to the horses that plowed the fields. This was to bless the planting season and end the Cailleach's control over the house and winter season.

Legend states that the Cailleach used her shillelagh and/or hammer to create and destroy Scotland. Many attribute the formation of much of Scotland's natural beauty to the Cailleach, making her one of the Celtic earth-shaper gods. Along with eight hags that assisted her, the Cailleach used her shillelagh to create the lochs, mountains, valleys, and rivers. One of the well-known hags or maids is Nessa of Loch Ness fame. After Nessa did not fulfill her duties, the Cailleach turned Nessa into the body of water now called Loch Ness.

In some tales, the hags are actually the Cailleach's sisters. They all lived together in the center of Earth. When they started digging their way to the surface, they began to gather many rocks and stones, which they put in sacks they carried. Eventually, they broke through into the ocean waters. The eight sisters went their separate ways. When the Cailleach needed to rest, she placed her satchel down. The rocks were unloaded and shaped into today's Scotland.

The Cailleach played a prominent role in ancient people's explanation of why the lands of Scotland were shaped the way they were. There are many stories and landforms connected to the Cailleach. She is often depicted as striding across Scotland, dropping stones, either purposefully or accidentally, from her apron or creel (a wicker basket). Scotland's islands and hills appeared from these dropped stones. The Cailleach formed some mountains to assist her in her travels.

One chain of islands that is credited to the Cailleach is the Inner Hebrides. These were formed when the Cailleach released pieces of peat and rocks that she had brought from the center of the earth. She created this chain of seventy-nine islands in the Atlantic Ocean off the coast of Scotland. Another island that the Cailleach formed was Ailsa Craig. A fisherman sailed beneath the Cailleach, and his sail touched her. She was so startled that she dropped the large stone that she had in her hands. This boulder is the island of Ailsa Craig.

Another landmark still visible today that was supposedly created by the Cailleach is the Sgrìob na Calliach. Located on the Isle of Skye, Beinn na Caillich (Red Hills) is a mountain range in Scotland that the Cailleach frequented. From this location, she would inflict the area with her devastating winter storms. She also excavated stones and rocks from this site. While the Cailleach was gathering stones, she lost her grip and slipped. The pathway Sgrìob na Calliach means the furrow or wrinkled brow of the Cailleach.

Picture of Loch Awe.

Chris Heaton, CC BY-SA 2.0 <https://creativecommons.org/licenses/by-sa/2.0>, via Wikimedia Commons; https://commons.wikimedia.org/wiki/File:Loch_Awe.jpg

The Cailleach's many tasks and responsibilities often exhausted her. One day, she was working on the summit of Ben Krachan, one of the highest mountain peaks in Scotland. After using the well to draw water, she had to replace its cover, a heavy stone slab. If the slab was not replaced by sunset, the water from the well would flow over the top. Once it began to overflow, it could not be stopped, and the world would be flooded.

The Cailleach removed the top from the well to get her water. She sat next to the stone slab to rest for a few minutes. However, she was extremely tired and fell into a deep sleep. Once the sun set, the water flowed from the well. Heavy streams of water surged down the mountainside. The rumbles of cascading water awakened the Cailleach. Immediately, she replaced the cover on top of the well and prevented the flooding of the world. Though she was quick to stop the flow of water, it still flooded the Vale of Tempe. Today, that land is called Loch Awe.

With her multiple roles and vast abilities, the Cailleach appears in many tales. Her ability to transform from an old hag to a young maiden causes many to misjudge her and her power. The Cailleach is not a frail old lady; as two faces of the same goddess, she quickly changes into a beautiful young goddess each spring. She brings the renewal of life each year. Her story and legacy continue to be a part of Scotland and its history.

Chapter 10: A Monster in Loch Ness

Similar to many cultures, ancient people told tales about how their worlds were formed. Scotland's mythical beauty and history are shared through its folklore. Many of the stories were based on the topography of the land, explaining how the mountains, rivers, and lochs came to be. Additionally, the sea and coast function as prominent players in Scotland's culture and rituals.

As with other Celtic myths, tales that originated in Scotland, specifically the Hebrides, were based on stories about the oceans, seas, and other waterways. Characters in the tales were often water-based beings, such as sea monsters, water spirits, and mermaids. Frequently, the creatures' exploits warned people about the powers of the seas and explained the origins of storms.

Stories came from sailors, as some allegedly met their doom because of sea monsters who controlled and roamed the waters. Surviving sailors regaled listeners with tales of gigantic snake-like creatures that they encountered in the ocean. The serpents were described as having massive heads, over twelve-inch eyes, and incredibly long and sharp teeth protruding from their mouths. They could have humps on their backs and lengthy arms. Sea monsters were the nemesis of early sailors because of their power and enormous size.

Located off the western coast of Scotland, the Inner and Outer Hebrides played an important role in the creation and preservation of

Scotland's tales. The Hebrides are a collection of over forty islands, but there are countless uninhabited atolls woven throughout the island chain. Since the islands are secluded, the early peoples of the Hebrides were not as impacted by the waves of conquerors as other parts of the Celtic world. Thus, the Normans, Romans, and others did not influence the legends told by the Hebrideans.

For many years, sea creatures have been sighted off the shores of the Hebrides. In the late 1800s, multiple sightings of a sea monster off the coast of Lewis, one of the Hebridean islands, were reported. One group of German sailors said they saw a sea snake with numerous bulges down its back. Those on the ship suggested the serpent was over 130 feet long.

Other water monsters have been seen in the same area. Searrach Uisge is said to live in Loch Suainbhal. People have reported seeing this creature for centuries. Details about Searrach Uisge compare the creature to the size of a capsized boat. Others say that it is about forty feet in length and has similar features to an eel. Legends tell of lambs being offered in sacrifice annually to Searrach Uisge.

Loch Morar.

John Haynes / Sron Ghaothar on Loch Morar;
https://commons.wikimedia.org/wiki/File:Sron_Ghaothar_on_Loch_Morar_-_geograph.org.uk_-_190066.jpg

In the Highlands of Scotland, locals tell the tales of Morag. Living in Loch Morar, Morag has been spotted by many witnesses, often at the same time. In one instance, nine people at Loch Morar all saw the same sea serpent. In the 1960s, two men in a boat literally ran into Morag. She defended herself by attacking them. The men fought back, causing Morag to slink back into the depths of Loch Morar.

In the 1800s, her appearances tended to coincide with the impending death of a local resident. When a Morar resident died or when one of the Scottish clans suffered in battle, Morag would feel great pain. She would be heard weeping with sadness. She is viewed as half-female and half-marine-creature. More recent viewings of Morag describe her as having two or three humps on her back. She is thought to be about thirty feet long with bumpy brownish skin. Her head is over twelve inches in width.

Of all of Scotland's sea monsters, the most famous is the Loch Ness Monster or Nessie. The Cailleach, or the goddess of winter who shaped much of Scotland's natural landscape, is credited with forming Loch Ness. The Cailleach had eight maidens or hags who aided her in her duties. She reigned from on top of Ben Nevis, where she monitored the work of her maidens.

One of the Cailleach's eight maidens was Nessa. The Cailleach was responsible for the wells in Inverness, Scotland. Since she had so many duties, she needed assistance. So, she assigned the task of watching one of the smaller wells to Nessa. Nessa's task was to keep the well capped throughout the night. She had to ensure the cover of the well was placed on it every day at sunset.

Late one evening, when Nessa was returning to the well to recap it, she either fell asleep or became distracted. Nessa was known for having the most melodic voice of the maidens. Her singing was more beautiful than the birds and harps of the fairies. Often, she wandered while creating music that harmoniously blended with nature, which distracted her from tending to her daily tasks.

Either way, Nessa arrived at the well after sunset. She came upon a stream of water that gushed from the well. Uncertain of how to stop the flow of the water, she ran. Nessa knew that the Cailleach would be angry with her. And from her vantage point on the peak of Ben Nevis, the Cailleach watched, enraged. She screamed at Nessa, telling the maiden that since she did not fulfill her duty, she would forever be connected to the water. Cursed by the Cailleach, Nessa was transfigured into the River Nessa, which flowed into and formed Loch Ness.

Nessa's music can only be heard once a year. On the anniversary of Nessa's change from a singing maiden to a flowing river and loch, she sings a mournful tune. Gone are the days of rapturous songs, for Nessa only knows sadness now. Her carelessness led to her troubles, which Nessa shares with the people through song when she rises from the waters. As with so many other myths, people can learn from the mistakes and misfortunes of those depicted in the stories.

The first recorded sighting of the Loch Ness Monster was in 565 CE. There are varying versions of the encounter between St. Columba and the Loch Ness Monster. One account asserts that Columba encountered a monster terrorizing a man in the River Ness. According to the story, St. Columba was able to defuse the situation and free the man from the grips of the water creature.

Another version tells of St. Columba visiting Scotland from Ireland and staying near the River Ness. During his visit, a local resident told the story of a monster living in Loch Ness. To verify the tale's veracity, Columba sent one of his men to the loch. Once notified of a sighting of the monster, Columba went to the water's edge. Reports say that he made a sign of the cross when he saw the monster. It is believed this resulted in the monster's exile.

In a different recounting of St. Columba and Nessie, Columba was traveling across Scotland. During his journey, he had to traverse across Loch Ness. Upon reaching the shores of the loch, he encountered residents burying a neighbor. The man had died from a water creature's bite while swimming in Loch Ness.

Columba turned to his group of followers and requested that someone swim across the loch. Though the swim was fraught with danger and possibly death, one of Columba's devotees answered his call. The monk agreed to swim across the loch and return with a boat that had been anchored on the far side of the waters.

Once the man began his swim, the monster emerged from the dark depths. Seeking another victim, the monster rushed toward the monk. All on the bank helplessly watched in horror. The monster got closer to the monk, ready to attack and kill him.

While the incident was unfolding, St. Columba remained calm. He began making the sign of the cross. After doing so, Columba appealed to God. Then, in God's name, Columba ordered the monster to stop. Upon hearing Columba's command, the monster of Loch Ness immediately retreated. The monk and everyone on the banks of the loch were safe. Accounts from this time period say the monk's name was Lugne

Mocumin.

Many attribute Nessie's reluctance to appear to her chastisement by St. Columba. Others believe that it is the size of Loch Ness itself that makes it so difficult to find Nessie. All the water from the lakes and rivers in England and Wales combined does not equal the amount of water in Loch Ness. However, sightings have and continue to occur.

In the late 1930s, a road was built that provided easier access to Loch Ness for automobiles. Since the road allowed a clear view of the loch for motorists, reported sightings of Nessie increased. Soon after the road's completion, visitors to the area recounted observing a massive creature that was similar to a dinosaur or other prehistoric creature.

Watercolor rendering of Nessie.
Free for commercial use; https://pixabay.com/illustrations/nessi-sea-serpent-watercolor-hole-6030872/

Interest in locating Nessie continued to grow. In 1933, a newspaper paid a well-known hunter, Marmaduke Wetherell, to locate the Loch Ness Monster. Allegedly, the hunter discovered massive footprints near the edge of the loch. From the size of the prints, the creature was estimated to be at least twenty feet long. These prints were later determined to be fake. It is uncertain who was behind the scheme to mislead the public.

The next sighting of Nessie happened the following year. An investigative group of twenty men gathered. Each participant was paid for his role in the expedition. Nine hours a day for five weeks, the men positioned themselves around the loch. Each had a set of binoculars and a camera to photograph evidence of Nessie's existence. The search party took over twenty photographs. However, the pictures did not provide conclusive evidence of the existence of the loch's famous resident.

News of a photograph taken by Robert Wilson ignited worldwide excitement in the mid-1930s. The picture was published in a newspaper. From the image, the Loch Ness Monster had the physical attributes of an extinct reptile, appearing to be over fifteen feet long with an extended neck similar to a plesiosaur. However, decades later, it was revealed that the picture was falsified.

Still, in the early 1930s, another encounter with the Loch Ness Monster was reported. Arthur Grant was riding on his motorcycle when he saw Nessie. He described the creature as having features that were comparable to a plesiosaur. When the creature headed toward the water, Grant followed. Unfortunately, he did not observe the creature enter the water. However, he did notice the ripples that the creature's entrance into the water created. There is no concrete evidence to prove or disprove Grant's sighting in 1934.

A few years later, G. E. Taylor, a tourist from Natal, South Africa, was in the area. Taylor was one of the growing number of travelers who visited Scotland in hopes of getting a glimpse of the elusive Loch Ness Monster. He used 16 mm colored film to record his visit; this is thought to be the first attempt to obtain a colored still picture of Nessie. When Taylor believed he had Nessie in his sights, he recorded her for three minutes. Taylor sold the film and its images to Maurice Burton, a zoologist and science author. Only one image from the film has been used, as Burton included it in a book titled *The Elusive Monster.* Burton claims the picture is of a floating object.

It is believed that Burton sent the film back to Taylor, and none of his other pictures have been seen by anyone. As far as anyone knows, the film was only shared with Burton; no one else has ever viewed it. People who believe that Nessie exists are still searching for the film, even though no one knows if it still exists. The film is as mysterious as the secrets in Loch Ness.

During the late 1930s and 1940s, interest in and the ability to search for Nessie waned due to World War II. Lachlan Stewart's photograph in 1951 added credence to Nessie's existence. He and a friend noticed significant motion in the water of the loch. Stewart happened to have a camera with him and was able to obtain pictures of what was causing the movement in the water. The two claimed they saw a three-humped creature quickly gliding through the water. As suddenly as it appeared, the creature plunged into the depths.

There are contrasting opinions on the story. Stewart's daughter vouches for her father, saying that he would not participate in a hoax. His daughter also claims the pictures were valid.

A few years later, the crew of a fishing boat observed images that could have been Nessie. The *Rival III*'s sonar detected a large object. Sonar (sound navigation and ranging) employs sound waves to measure distances in water and detect movement and objects. The massive shape was following the boat at a depth of about 480 to 100 feet from the bottom of the loch. For almost half a mile, the object kept pace with the boat. Then, as in other sightings, the object, which was perhaps Nessie, disappeared from their screen.

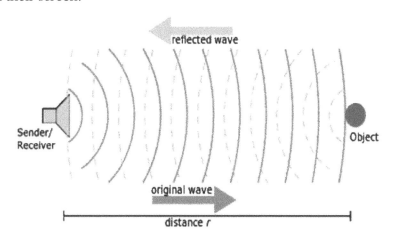

Sonar principle.
Georg Wiora (Dr. Schorsch), CC BY-SA 3.0 <http://creativecommons.org/licenses/by-sa/3.0/>, via Wikimedia Commons; https://commons.wikimedia.org/wiki/File:Sonar_Principle_EN.svg

Another sonar search for Nessie was conducted in 1967. D. Gordon Tucker, a sonar developer, positioned his team's equipment on Loch Ness, seeking answers on the existence of Nessie. Their trial was conducted over a two-week period. Sound waves from objects in the loch were detected by the sonar equipment. The sound waves identified large moving objects that quickly moved through the water. Because of the object's size and speed, Tucker did not believe it was fish or schools of fish. The length of the image viewed by Tucker supported previous views of Nessie's estimated size.

Twenty years later, Operation Deepscan was employed to search for answers about the Loch Ness Monster. In this search, echo sounder equipment, which is a type of sonar, was utilized. A significant mass was noted in the information received from the echo sounder. The images detected motion in the mass, which was located at the bottom of the loch. No unanimous decision had been reached on whether these images were of Nessie. There are believers who feel that this operation strongly supports the existence of Nessie.

Lastly, in 2014, an image appeared on Apple Maps. Located at the northern point of the loch, the impression was of something that reached almost one hundred feet in length. It does not appear that the image was altered in any way. Nonbelievers say the image resulted from the wake of a boat on the loch. Others feel that it continues to support the idea that the elusive Nessie lives in Loch Ness.

There are an average of twenty sightings of the Loch Ness Monster annually. Perhaps it will never be verified if Nessie is indeed in Loch Ness. Or maybe only believers are able to see her. Either way, she continues to entice visitors to optimistically search for her.

Chapter 11: Kelpies and Selkies

The Loch Ness Monster is not the only creature who lives in waterways in Scotland, nor is Nessie the only water monster whose tale is cryptic and uncorroborated. There are some who believe that Nessie was a story told to scare children. Some of the lochs in Scotland are incredibly deep, and the rivers flow very quickly. Tales of frightening monsters that capture little ones would stop children from going into the waters, as parents feared their children would be swept away in the rivers or fall into the deep lochs.

Another prominent character meant to warn of the dangers of water was the kelpies. Evidence from carved stones found near Loch Ness provides images of a strange aquatic beast. It is thought these carvings were the first depictions of kelpies. In most of the stone carvings found in this area of Scotland, the animals are clearly recognizable.

The Picts created these etchings, which are elaborately detailed. These ancient peoples lived in the northern and eastern parts of modern-day Scotland. The Picts did not leave any written records, but their stones have provided historians with information. Knowledge of the Picts has also been obtained through information left by Romans who attempted to conquer them.

There are two thoughts on the meaning of the word "Pict." One camp believes it is from the Latin word *picti*, which means "painted." The Picts often painted themselves with dyes and tattoos. The other theory is that the Picts referred to themselves as *pecht*, which means "ancestors."

Only one animal in the Picts' carvings is mysterious; it is often referred to as either the swimming elephant or the Pictish Beast. This same image can be found on over fifty of the stones left by the Picts, and it is believed the mystical and mythological kelpies are connected to these images.

Kelpies are aquatic beings with dolphin-like tails. When kelpies leave the water, they can shapeshift into a horse when on land. Nearly all bodies of water in Scotland have local stories involving kelpies. Interestingly, the greatest number of reported kelpie sightings in Scotland is near where the Picts' enigmatic carvings were found at Loch Ness.

The word "kelpie" itself probably originates from the word *cailpeach* or *colpach*, which means "colt" or "heifer" in Gaelic. These sea horses often appear to humans as friendly ponies or horses with dripping wet manes. However, kelpies are malicious beings. They lure people into taking a ride on them. Once the rider mounts the shapeshifting kelpie, they are literally stuck, as the hide of a kelpie is covered with a magical adhesive. Even when the unsuspecting rider realizes what is happening, they are unable to dismount. Unfortunately, these seemingly innocuous trips end in the watery death of the rider. Deaths by drowning were often attributed to the kelpies.

These mystical and malevolent sea horses prowl Scotland's rivers and waterways for victims. The only way to escape from being taken is by grabbing the kelpie's bridle. One needs to be lightning quick and control the kelpie before getting on its back. If one is fortunate enough to rein in the kelpie, then they can control it and prevent their death.

An apprehended kelpie has incredible power. Legend tells of one captured kelpie's strength being equal to one hundred horses. While in captivity, kelpies were used to assist locals in moving heavy supplies. Some kelpies assisted their captors in transporting stones to build walls and castles. Halters embossed with the sign of the cross were used to keep the kelpies under control.

Kelpies most often transform into horses. However, they can change their appearance into any creature it chooses. Sometimes, kelpies alter their form to look like a human. The human version of a kelpie wanders the banks of the water, posing as an alluring young man. Though beautiful, the transformed kelpie still has wet hair tangled with wild plants. Their goal is to entice a young woman to come near them. Once a woman is ensnared, she is led to her death.

Kelpies can also appear as women. As a woman, they follow the same scenario. Kelpies take on the persona of a gorgeous woman and stroll along the river's edge, seeking to attract the attention of a young man, who will be led to his death.

Painting of a female kelpie.
https://commons.wikimedia.org/wiki/File:Thekelpie_large.jpg

A kelpie could also morph into a shaggy-looking person. Following their usual modus operandi, the transformed kelpie would hang out by the water's edge. When a naïve tourist ambled by, the hairy human-like kelpie leaped out and attacked. An alternative method kelpies used to rid their area of tourists was to activate their magical powers. Kelpies beckoned the floodwaters, which snatched travelers and dragged them away.

The only warning that kelpies were in the area was the sound that emanated from their tails. When kelpies returned from their adventures to their watery homes, their tails echoed the rumbling noises of thunder. If you are ever in Scotland, listen for thunder or eerie shrieks. If you hear either, be careful; kelpies might be in the area.

There is no firm evidence that kelpies exist, but the tales involving them are fascinating. These stories involve people who did not heed the power and magic of the kelpies. One such story occurred in Braco. The local river was flooded, preventing a man who lived in the area from getting to his home. He needed assistance to cross the raging waters. Lucky for him, he spotted a horse calmly feasting on the grasses along the swollen river's edge.

Somehow, the man did not view the scene with any concern; he just felt relief at finding a horse. The man approached the horse, which willingly let the man scramble on its back. When the man was ready, the horse, which was actually a kelpie, sprinted into the water. The man was pulled into the depths of the roaring waters and was never seen again.

While most run-ins with kelpies do not end well for humans, some people manage to survive. In another story, the kelpie again used the ruse of a flooded riverway to enact its trickery. A husband was stranded on one side of the river while his deathly ill wife was sick at home, awaiting his return. Feeling helpless and overwhelmed, the husband collapsed in tears on the edge of the uncrossable river.

A kind Samaritan approached the desolate husband. Soaking wet, the Samaritan gave the appearance that he had been assisting others in their river crossings. The grieving husband gladly took his offer of aid. The Samaritan threw the husband over his shoulder and entered the water. Once in the middle of the swollen river, the stranger attempted to throw the husband into the river.

A battle ensued, and the two struggled. Still fighting, the two reached the far side of the riverbank. Able to touch the ground, the husband pushed himself away from the stranger. Sprinting away from the river and the "Samaritan," the husband hurried home. The stranger, furious that he had lost the battle and his conquest, reverted to his kelpie form. The kelpie snatched rocks from the side of the river and hurled them at the man who escaped.

After that incident, kelpie stones were stacked by people passing by the river's edge. These rocks were stacked until a cairn (a large stack of rocks) was created.

One kelpie continually roamed the woods and waterways near Loch Ness, frightening local residents. One local, James MacGrigor, sought to eliminate the threat. He snuck up on the kelpie and took its bridle, which is a kelpie's source of life. Without their bridles, kelpies can only survive for twenty-four hours.

This kelpie had the ability to speak. He pleaded with MacGrigor for his bridle but was met with a firm no. Unable to sway MacGrigor, the kelpie took another tactic and followed him home. Once the kelpie reached MacGrigor's home, it noted the cross nailed above the front door. The kelpie, thinking he had outsmarted the human, informed MacGrigor that he would not be able to enter his own home because he was carrying the bridle. MacGrigor threw the bridle into the house through an open window.

The kelpie's destiny was sealed. The bridle is now referred to as the "ball and bridle." Anyone who holds the bridle has access to incredible powers of healing. All a person has to do is place the bridle in water. Then, they turn the bridle three times in the water while blessing themselves "in the name of the Father, in the name of the Son, and in the name of the Holy Spirit."

The power of the kelpies is vividly captured in *The Kelpies*. *The Kelpies* are steel structures that stand almost one hundred feet tall. They were designed and constructed by Andy Scott, a Scottish sculptor. Each *Kelpie* required over 330 tons of steel in their construction. Over 1,300 tons of steel-reinforced concrete was necessary to hold the weight of each head. Eighteen thousand separate pieces are included in each sculpture; of those, nine hundred are the stainless scales.

The Kelpies can be visited in Helix Park, which is located between Falkirk and Grangemouth, Scotland. There is no danger of being lured into the waterways when viewing these massive structures. *The Kelpies*, with their size, strength, and tons of steel, only represent the power the mythical kelpies held and still hold (at least according to some) over the rivers and waterways of Scotland.

The selkies, another group of magical and mythical creatures, are said to inhabit the ocean waters off the western coast of Scotland. Thought to have originated in the waters around the Northern Isles, which are comprised of Orkney and the Shetland Islands, the selkies are shapeshifters, like the kelpies. The word "selkies" is a derivative of the Scottish words for seal: *selch* or *selk*. Selkies transform from a seal into a human and vice versa.

While most agree on where selkies first originated, there are many versions of how selkies came to be. Since stories from the Celts were not written down until later (being infused with Christian elements in the process), many conjectures have been formed over time. Selkies and their stories were likely the ancients' way of showing their respect and awe of the ocean's power, unpredictability, and beauty.

Some believers in the selkies view them as fairies. In Scotland folklore, fairies are closely linked with nature. For the selkies, their connection with nature was the ocean. Hundreds of years ago, people thought the selkies, like fairies, were disgraced angels. God had just not accepted them into heaven yet. While they waited for Judgment Day, the fairies lived as animals. The selkies lived as seals.

One tale says the selkies were once people. However, they committed a serious crime. For their horrible misdeed, they were cursed and changed into a seal. They were destined to live out their lives on Earth in the form of an animal as their punishment.

Another explanation for how selkies emerged comes from the Orkney Islands. Long ago, bards told stories about the selkies, who are actually people who have drowned. The souls of the deceased continue to live on as selkies. However, once a year, on Midsummer's Eve or the summer solstice, the souls can move between worlds. So, selkies can choose to cross over to the Otherworld, remain a selkie, or change back to their human form.

Myths of all cultures have helped people understand the mysteries of the world. Another explanation of how the selkies came about helped explain the unknown. For example, when children were born with webbed feet, selkies and their stories were used to help the parents understand their baby. Some babies are born with scaly skin or seal-like faces, and the legend of the selkies could have been used to explain why. Today, there are scientific names for genetic variations, but hundreds of years ago, the story of the selkies would have provided reassurance.

Statue of a selkie.
Siegfried Rabanser, CC BY 2.0 <https://creativecommons.org/licenses/by/2.0>, via Wikimedia Commons; https://commons.wikimedia.org/wiki/File:Selkie_statue_in_Mikladalur.jpeg

Regardless of the selkies' origins, these shapeshifters' tales include the allure of the ocean, romance, and heartbreak. A selkie's true home is the ocean. However, sometimes the glamor of life on land as a human causes a selkie to shed their skin. Selkies live in torment, wanting what they do not possess. Some selkies yearn for a life on land while they are in the sea; then, when they become human, they long for the sea. To complicate their situation, human-selkies are irresistible to human beings.

Selkies are seductive because of their beauty and personalities. They enjoy dancing under the moonlit skies and have gentle souls. When selkies leave the ocean and begin their lives on land, they take on a human form. If a selkie loses possession of its removed seal skin, it cannot return to the ocean. The human being who has the fur now controls them. If a selkie finds its skin, it always return to the waters. Thus, their stories always end with a broken heart.

Such was the tale of a Scottish fisherman. One day, he was wandering down the coast when he happened upon a group of women twirling under the moonlit sky. He tried to sneak up on them to get a better view. However, the fisherman snapped a twig, warning the women of a stranger's presence. The women rushed over to a pile of seal furs so they could run away.

But the fisherman reached the pile of furs just as the group of women did. He snatched the last fur in the pile. With tears in her eyes, the woman begged the stranger for her fur. However, the fisherman was aware of the legends of the selkies. He knew if he kept and hid the fur, then the selkie-woman had to remain on land and marry him.

The two married, and as the years passed, the couple had two children. The selkie was a loving mother and a dutiful wife. Yet she yearned for the sea. One day, her two children found a treasure. They eagerly showed their mother the surprise: a beautiful seal fur. Ecstatic to have her fur back, the woman knew she had no choice. Though the mother loved her children dearly, the ocean was beckoning her to return.

Sitting the children down to break the news, the mother started by explaining the heritage of the selkies. She told them that she had to go back right away. As soon as her husband fell asleep, the mother and her two children went to the water's edge. Holding back tears, she told the children how much she loved them and that when they heard her singing, they should come to the water to swim with her. Then, she swam away.

The next morning, the children told their father what had happened. Since the fisherman had loved his wife, he was filled with sorrow, yet he was happy for the time they had together.

Selkies are frequently females. However, there are male selkies who come ashore and transform into humans. Male selkies are known for their good looks and ability to mesmerize women. When they come on land, they pursue women who are unhappily married. When the disgruntled wife is ready for a new mate, she just has to cry seven tears into the ocean. A male selkie will shed his skin and come on land to rescue her.

When a woman has an affair or leaves her husband, it is believed that a male selkie has tantalized her. Male selkies also explain what happened to missing women, as a selkie must have taken a new lover to his home in the water.

All these love stories end with someone sad and forlorn. Selkies are passionate and kind lovers. However, for the selkies, there is no greater love than the sea.

Chapter 12: Nine Maidens and a Ghost Piper

Folk tales and myths that were orally shared from generation to generation in Scotland and other locales celebrated the natural wonders of an area and provided guidance on how to respect the environment. Parts of life that appeared incomprehensible were also explained through these stories. But not all of Scotland's magical creatures lived in lochs or oceans. Imaginary worlds filled with supernatural creatures flourished as well.

One area that was said to be filled with fairies was the Sidlaws, hills located north of the city of Dundee in Scotland. Fairies dwelled on Earth to intervene in the lives of their human neighbors. Sometimes the fairies sought to help the mortals; on other occasions, the supernatural beings were mischievous pranksters.

The Balluderon Stone, also known as Martin's Stone.
Val Vannet; https://commons.wikimedia.org/wiki/File:Martin%27s_Stone_-_geograph.org.uk_-_14993.jpg

At the base of the Sidlaws is Martin's Stone. The broken piece of stone is a remnant of a symbol stone craved by the Picts. The Picts were a group of tribes that lived in Scotland from 100 CE until around 900 CE. They carved details into stones that are still being deciphered today. Current research into the purpose of the Pictish symbol stones theorizes that the elaborately etched stones memorialized significant events, important people, and/or established property boundaries. The symbols on the stones may also have been used by the Picts to track information about people in their tribes.

Legend tells the story of the Nine Maidens of Dundee and Martin's Stone. The tale is set near the village of Dundee at the base of the Sidlaws. Years and years ago, a widowed father and his nine daughters tended their land at Pitempton farm. The family contentedly cultivated their plants and gardens. Whenever they harvested their crops, the family gladly shared with all in the village.

After a long, tiring day of weeding and working in the fields, water was needed from the village well. So, the farmer asked his eldest daughter to walk to the well to obtain a pail of water. Though the trip should have only taken a few minutes, the farmer was not concerned when his daughter did not return. He asked his second oldest daughter to go to the well and check on the oldest daughter.

Time continued to pass more slowly because neither the eldest daughter nor the second oldest daughter came back home. Next, the third oldest daughter was sent to the village well. She also failed to return. The father continued sending his daughters until he was left home alone.

Confused and distraught, the farmer knew he had to go to the well himself. He rushed into the village and ran to the well. One look overwhelmed him, and he collapsed in grief. All nine of his daughters were dead. Mangled and intertwined with each other, the bodies of his dead daughters were piled up next to the well. Leering over his daughters, the farmer saw a snake-like dragon.

Thoroughly devastated, the farmer knew he needed help. Gathering himself up, the farmer raced to the center of the village. On his way, he encountered Martin. He shouted about the wretched scene he had stumbled upon and informed Martin that his eldest daughter had died. Martin was betrothed to her, so he was as enraged as her father.

Martin was the village blacksmith, and he sprinted to his forge. There, he gathered his spear and horse to combat the dragon. He galloped to the well that the dragon had made into his den. Seeking to avenge the deaths of his beloved and her sisters, Martin fearlessly battled the vicious beast.

The dragon lunged at Martin, who quickly galloped away. Trying to confuse the dragon, Martin sprinted across the village's open fields. The dragon took the bait and stayed right on the heels of Martin and his horse. The two circled around each other as Martin tried using his spear to stab the dragon. However, the hissing dragon continued to evade him.

Martin knew he needed help to defeat the dragon, so he rode to the next village to gather assistance. Villagers ran out of their cottages, having heard the heartbreaking news of the farmer and his nine daughters. Many of the villagers also had family members who had been slain by the dragon, so they were eager to help.

With Martin leading the way, the throng of villagers baited the dragon, leading it to a nearby loch. With a frightening splash and wail, the dragon was submerged in the water. It wrestled its way out, spewing water on all of its pursuers.

The chase continued, but the dragon was slower now because of all the water it had ingested. Martin had the perfect opportunity to slay the dragon. The villagers, Martin, and the dragon all encountered each other at a nearby meadow. Fueled by anger and a broken heart, Martin clutched his spear tightly and readied to strike a blow. However, he hesitated for a second, which caused his throw to miss the dragon.

Thrashing about in a furious frenzy, the dragon started to lash out at the crowd. The villagers, sensing a change in who was controlling the battle, yelled encouragements at Martin. Eager to witness the death of the dragon, they shouted, "Strike, Martin!"

Martin knew he needed to act immediately. With all his strength, Martin heaved his spear, striking the dragon directly in its heart. Screeching in pain, the dragon collapsed. The crowd shouted in joyous approval; they were finally freed from the dragon's reign of terror.

On the spot where the final act occurred, a stone was placed in commemoration of the farmer's nine daughters and Martin's heroic actions. The etchings on Martin's Stone, which may have been made by the Picts, relate the details of the story. The stone can still be viewed today and is still situated in its original location. Only half of the original stone remains from when it was carved in the 8th or 9th century. Today, the stone is protected by an iron fence in the field where the battle between Martin and the dragon occurred. The worn images on the stone include a rider on a horse that appears to be trotting, a second rider beneath a Celtic cross, and the Pictish symbol for beast.

After the incident, the village was named Strathmartine in honor of Martin. The village's name is to remember the support Martin had from the crowd with the heralding of "Strike, Martin," which became Strathmartine. Today, the village is called Bridgefoot. Martin's Stone is one mile north of the village center.

In the center of Dundee on High Street, you can find the statue of a dragon that memorializes the legend. Throughout Dundee, you will find other dragons to complement the Pictish images from the battle.

Picture of the Dundee Dragon.
Kenneth Allen; https://commons.wikimedia.org/wiki/File:Dundee_dragon_-_geograph.org.uk_-_777300.jpg

Other tales and religious texts reference nine maidens. For instance, there is the story of St. Donald of Ogilvy. Ogilvy is a few miles north of the Sidlaws, so it is near where Martin's story transpired. Donald of Ogilvy also had nine daughters. After his wife died, Donald turned his home into one of prayer, sacrifice, and simple living.

This cloistered lifestyle was embraced until the nine maidens' father died. According to the story, after his death, the nine sisters entered the monastery in Abernethy. Some versions say the king of the Picts invited the sisters to join the monastery. Research has found that the Picts founded a cathedral in Abernethy as early as 700. Evidence of Pictish symbol stones was discovered at the site.

Legend also tells of Pictish King Garnard, who invited the sisters to live in his cloister, providing them their own prayer space within the monastery. While living there, the nine maidens continued the lifestyle they had with their father. Each of the sisters was buried at the monastery after they died. A sequence of engraved wooden panels was created to tell the sisters' story. They are displayed in the prayer room in the chapel. Unfortunately, the panels were destroyed during the Protestant Reformation.

The Nine Maidens have been revered for their monastic lifestyle and devotion to their father and each other. In another version of the Nine Maidens, Martin's love and act of vengeance for the eldest maiden is a poignant love story.

Just as their story haunts the area around Martin's Stone, so does the lingering melody from phantom bagpipers. Bagpipes and Scotland are synonymous to many. Many festivals and traditional celebrations include bagpipers. Records of bagpipes can be traced back to 1000 BCE. In the ancient and ghostly castles, caves, and tunnels from long ago, emanate legends and stories of mysterious bagpiper music.

One such story involves the Ghost Piper of Canard Bay. Stories from days long past tell of fairies inhabiting the caves and tunnels that can be found in the coves along the coast of Scotland. Some of these locations were later shared with pirates and smugglers. Buccaneers would hide their stolen stashes in the network of tunnels. To keep people away from the goods that had been taken from others, smugglers and pirates continued the tales of the haunted caves.

The stretch of alcoves and inlets from the Cove of Grennan down through Clanyard Bay was known to be inhabited by fairies. Residents of the area did not dare enter the realm of the fairies. However, one day, a young bagpiper willingly ventured into the caves. He fully believed that he would march through the caves and show up in Clanyard Bay.

The piper began to play a beautiful melody. While he filled the air with his music, he and his loyal dog headed toward the caves. For hours, the locals could hear the pipe's majestic notes. As if in concert, the piper's faithful companion howled along to the music. As time passed, the sounds began to fade as the piper wove his way farther into the caves.

Suddenly, the strains of the music resembled the sound of one keening. Just as quickly as that started, it stopped. Then, there was only silence.

The piper's dog sprinted from the caves. Barking and shrieking, the dog ran toward the people of the village. The terrified dog was hairless, and the piper was nowhere to be seen. No one ever laid eyes on the bagpiper again.

Now deserted, the caves are a forlorn place. Fairies have not been sighted or heard from in this area since the piper disappeared. Either the fairies have left this part of Scotland, or the supernatural beings have dug deeper caves.

On warm summer evenings, one can still hear bagpipe music in the distance emanating from Clanyard Bay. The piper lives eternally through his music.

A tale that ends in a similar manner occurred on the Isle of Skye. A school to train bagpipers was located there. A famous local family was seeking an assistant piper for their band. This was a highly sought-after, prestigious position. To make it more exciting, a student from the local piping college was to be selected.

With high hopes, all the students began practicing in earnest. Everyone wanted the position. One particular young lad coveted this job more than anything in the world. He took his bagpipes and practiced and practiced. Unfortunately, he was not a talented soul. But he kept trying. He took his pipes to practice near the local loch for inspiration. Even he could hear his music was lacking.

In exasperation, he threw his bagpipes on the ground. He laid down on the grassy knoll and cried. Suddenly, the lush green mound opened, and a stunning woman emerged from the world underneath. She asked the distraught young man why he was crying and so upset. He explained to the beautiful woman about the opening for piper and how much the position as assistant piper meant to him.

After pondering the young man's situation, the woman told the piper that she might have a solution. She asked him to think about two different ideas. While thinking, the piper had to determine which he thought was the better option for him. Did he want to be a well-known piper who did not really play well? Or did he want to be an incredible bagpiper who was not recognized or known?

The young piper thought about the choices and told the woman that he wanted to be a great bagpiper. However, he was concerned that he would never play well. She told him that she could help. Handing him a magical chanter (the part of the bagpipe that makes the melody), the fairy told him to start playing. The young piper put the chanter on his bagpipe and began to play.

Incredible music wafted through the air. Then, the fairy told him the deal. Whenever the piper was content with his life, his music would reflect his happiness. His melodies would make everyone sing and dance. Challenging days that made the young man sad would create melancholy sounds. The people listening would cry.

For the young man to keep the silver chanter and be able to control the music he created, he had to agree to one more thing. Whenever the fairy called the piper to her, he must immediately respond. She asked the young man if he was amenable to these conditions. He was so excited about his ability to play that he readily agreed.

As soon as he returned, he became the assistant piper at the local castle. Time went on, and his importance in the pipers' band at the castle increased. Eventually, he married and had children, who were also incredible pipers. He and his family became renowned, but he had forgotten all about the fairy who had given him the silver chanter.

Out of nowhere, the fairy beckoned him one day, summoning him to the cave near where they first met. Cheerfully, he headed to the grassy knoll while playing his bagpipes. His loyal dog trotted alongside him on his stroll. Even his family walked with him. They stopped at the bridge that led to the grassy slope.

He continued playing in view of his family until he reached the Golden Cave. Even when they could no longer see him and the family dog, they could still hear his melody. Suddenly, it was silent. The hairless dog sprinted back to the family, but the piper was never seen again.

Another tale of a piper is connected to the English Civil War. In Scotland, people were divided in this war; some were loyal to the Crown, while others supported the Parliament. Two well-known clans in Scotland differed on who they supported.

Duntrune Castle.

Their disagreement came to fruition at Duntrune Castle in Argyll, Scotland. One of the clans, the MacDonalds, was led by Coll or Colkitto. Coll had his own piper to lead his men in battle. At Duntrune Castle, Coll planned an attack on the Campbells. There are multiple versions of what happened next.

In one story, the piper was sent with an advance group to spy on the Campbells. The Campbells became aware of the intruders and captured them. Coll's piper was locked in the tower room. In another tale, Coll took control of the castle. Once the castle was secure, Coll left some of his men and the piper to retain control while he continued his battles throughout the countryside. After the battles, Coll planned to return to Duntrune Castle. However, the Campbells overthrew their attackers and regained the castle.

In either version, Coll approached the castle. The piper could see that Coll and his troops were advancing. Needing to send a warning to Coll, the piper began to play his bagpipes. He played with gusto, the melodies carrying into the distance. The music reached Coll. As he listened to the music, he observed there was something different with the sounds. His prized piper was sending a warning through his music.

Heeding the notes of caution, Coll and his troops retreated. When the Campbells saw their retreat, they realized what the piper had done. In retaliation, the clan took away the piper's livelihood. They cut off his fingers, and the piper eventually bled to death.

For years after the incident, the piper's melodies could be heard throughout the castle. Legend tells of a skeleton being found years and years later in the wall of the castle. The skeleton had no fingers.

SECTION FOUR:
Higher Powers and Superstitions

Chapter 13: Irish Gods and Goddesses

Gods and goddesses in Irish tales were often depicted as statuesque. Additionally, key figures were physically and intellectually compelling individuals. One extraordinary power that many of these supernatural beings had was the ability to alter their physical form. With their shapeshifting talents, gods and goddesses could elude captors and troubles.

Depiction of the Otherworld.
https://commons.wikimedia.org/wiki/File:Irishfairytales01step_0137.jpg

Even if the deities met their demise, they lived on in stories and were often reincarnated. Life after death was not just for the gods and goddesses; the ancient Celtic people believed in their transference to another world as well. Once one's soul transitioned to the Otherworld, life continued.

Multiple gods and goddesses were worshiped by the people of ancient Ireland. While the origin of many of the deities is unknown, others are connected to the Tuatha Dé Danann. The Tuatha Dé Danann were a race of supernatural god-like beings. The Tuatha Dé Danann inhabited Ireland thousands of years ago. In their battle for control of modern-day Ireland, the Tuatha Dé Danann lost to the Milesians, who are the ancestors of the people of Ireland.

The name, Tuatha Dé Danann, is believed to mean the tribe of the goddess Danu, one of the many goddesses of ancient Ireland. It is thought she provided the Tuatha Dé Danann with guidance and support. With Danu's nurturing, the Tuatha Dé Danann was able to develop their powers and magic. The mythical mist that swathed the Tuatha Dé Danann when they swooped in and settled in Ireland represented Danu's encouraging protection of her people.

A significant goddess, Danu is considered a mother goddess since all of the Tuatha Dé Danann are viewed as her descendants. Although she is seen as one of the first Irish goddesses, only fragments of information remain about her. Much of what is known and revered about Danu is through her lineage, which demonstrates her power and talents.

In the ancient Irish language, *dan*, the root of Danu's name, is connected to artistic talents and insightfulness. Therefore, it is believed the origin of the Tuatha Dé Danann's skills and abilities were favors Danu had bestowed upon her followers. All in the tribe relied on Danu for her prowess, and all in Ireland are connected to Danu, depending on her for wisdom and blessings.

One Irish creation myth tells the story of Danu and Donn, one of the first goddesses and gods of Ireland. Both of them emanated from the Great Void, the nothingness before the world was created. Created to be companions, the two became inseparable. One version tells of their great love for each other. Their love produced a blessed glow in their hearts.

Soon after, the couple had children. This created a problem since the couple was so attached to each other. One of the children, Brian, realized he and his siblings would not survive if they remained confined between their two parents. Time was running out; it was imperative that Brian convinced his mother to let them escape. Danu needed to decide between saving her children's lives or being with Donn.

Her love for her children triumphed over her love for Donn. Brian's only choice was to kill their father. Swinging his sword, Brian slashed his father into nine sections. Distraught by the sight and shock of Donn's death, Danu sobbed. Her cascading tears blended with Donn's blood. Known as the Waters of Heaven, Danu's tears created the oceans and seas of the world. Danu's children were swept away in the surging water and landed on Earth.

The nine sections of Donn's body formed other parts of the natural world. The skies were fashioned from his head. His brain shaped the clouds. The sun and moon came from Donn's face and mind, respectively. His bones created stones on Earth, and the wind used to be Donn's breath.

Some versions of the Celtic creation myth continue with Danu's formation of the Tuatha Dé Danann. When Danu cried over Donn's demise, she noticed seeds in her tears. Inside the seeds was Donn. Once Earth had been formed, Danu's tears began to inseminate Earth. Eochaidh, one of the seeds from Danu's tears, grew into an enormous oak tree. Two acorns tumbled from the great oak. Danu's tears nurtured the acorns, which became Nemed. It is from Nemed and his tribe that the Tuatha Dé Danann, or the tribe of Danu, originated.

Another important deity to the Tuatha Dé Danann was the Dagda. His name translates to good god, with good equating to how skilled and powerful he was. The Dagda was the leader of the Tuatha Dé Danann. As a warrior god, he had power over both the supernatural and mortal realms. The Dagda has a multitude of names due to his many talents. Each name provides insight into his talents and roles. His responsibilities and control span from life to death to the seasons, which makes him a "Father God."

In addition to his abilities, the Dagda possessed three revered riches. The first was one of the four treasures of the Tuatha Dé Danann: a magical cauldron of plenty. No one who traveled or fought with the Dagda would ever be hungry. Just the ladle of the massive cauldron could fit two of the Dagda's mighty warriors in it lying down. Food from the cauldron was always shared, representing the Dagda's goodness. In battle, the Dagda's troops were always satiated by a hearty feast. Its magic extended beyond food, though, as the cauldron could bring the dead back to life.

The Dagda's fierce club had the capacity to determine life and death. One end of the cudgel could kill any enemy. The other end could resuscitate the dead. The Dagda's club was so powerful it could kill nine men in one swing. His mammoth *lorg mór* (which might have been a staff, cudgel, or club) was transported from battle to battle on wheels. When it was pulled through the countryside, it left cavernous troughs that were used to denote borders between provinces.

A decorative oak harp was the third of his magical tools. When the Dagda played his harp, his music caused three different results. Listeners either ended up sleeping, laughing, or grieving. The harp also had the power to change the seasons.

Before battles, the Dagda would play music for his men to have them focus on their upcoming tasks. After the battle was over, the Dagda again played the harp. His music helped his warriors heal from their physical wounds and grieve over losing companions.

One of the enemies the Tuatha Dé Danann encountered was the Fomorians, who had heard of the Dagda's harp. The Fomorians knew that capturing the harp would ensure their victory. During a battle, some Fomorians were sent to the Dagda's home while the Tuatha Dé Danann were on the battlefield. Assuming their troops would be victorious, the Fomorians and their families absconded with the harp and waited for the good news.

The Tuatha Dé Danann overpowered the Fomorians and won the battle. As part of their after-battle routine, the Dagda went to play his harp. When it was discovered missing, the Dagda and his men searched for it. They located the Fomorians surrounding the harp in a deserted castle.

However, since it was a magical instrument, the Dagda just had to call it. At this point, the Fomorians grabbed their weapons, ready to battle again. Despite being vastly outnumbered, the Dagda calmly began to play.

His first song caused the Fomorians to sob. Then he changed the tune and played merry songs, causing great joy and laughter. This made the Fomorians relinquish their weapons. To wrap up his medley, the Dagda strummed songs for sleep. After all the Fomorians were asleep, the Dagda and his men returned to their homes. They had won the battle. No one ever tried to steal the harp again.

The Dagda's magical powers aided in the birth of his son, Aengus. Though married to the Morrígan, the Dagda's true love was Boann. However, Boann was married. Her husband, Elcmar, was a judge in the Tuatha Dé Danann. In his leadership role, the Dagda was able to influence where and when Elcmar had to perform his judicial duties.

To have time with Boann, the Dagda ordered Elcmar to meet with High King Bres. The Dagda and Boann consummated their affection for each other, resulting in Boann's pregnancy. Protecting himself, his lover, and his unborn child, the Dagda used his magical power to hold the sun in place for nine months. The Dagda made time stand still.

Therefore, Boann conceived and delivered a child in one day. Named Aengus for his vigor, he represents eternal youth due to his twenty-four-hour gestation period. In addition to his role as the god of youthful vitality, Aengus represents love and the poetic use of language. This talent was used by Aengus to conspire with his father to trick Elcmar.

Elcmar and Boann's home was at Brú na Bóinne. Aengus and the Dagda were traveling and stopped at Elcmar's home to visit. While there, Aengus asked Elcmar if he and the Dagda could stay a day and a night. Elcmar readily agreed. Later, Elcmar realized the error of his quick rush to be hospitable. In ancient Irish, the phrase "a day and a night" really meant all days and all nights. Elcmar had relinquished his home.

Aengus's first love caused him heartache. Étaín was a breathtaking beauty, but she was a mortal. When Aengus saw the lovely Étaín, he was enamored. Complicating the potential relationship was Midir. The Dagda was the father to both Aengus and Midir; Midir had actually raised Aengus. Further adding to the difficulties was the fact Midir was already married to Fúamnach.

The two brothers vied for Étaín's affection. In the end, Étaín chose Midir, who left his wife. In her anger, Fúamnach, an enchantress, transformed Étaín into a fly. She then created gusts of wind to sweep Étaín out of their lives. Aengus was furious with Fúamnach. He used his mystical abilities to locate Étaín. Aengus believed that he could care for Étaín and return her to her former beauty.

However, before Étaín could be transformed, she landed on a wine goblet. An Ulster warrior's wife drank heavily from the goblet, ingesting Étaín and becoming pregnant in the process. Étaín was reincarnated but did not recall Aengus or Midir.

Furious at losing the love of his life, Aengus searched for Fúamnach. In his anger, he decapitated her. The god who represents love killed to protect his love from any additional harm.

The Irish goddess of poetry is Aengus's half-sister, Brigid. The Dagda's daughter through his marriage with the Morrígan, Brigid was part of the Tuatha Dé Danann. She was connected to Imbolc and oversaw many areas of life. She was seen as the goddess of poetry, healing, fire, family life, and childbirth.

Depiction of Brigid.

In some myths, Brigid is married to Bres, who was also part of the Tuatha Dé Danann. Bres's father, Elatha, was a Fomorian, and his mother, Ériu, is Ireland's namesake. After the leader of the tribe, Nuada, was injured in the First Battle of Magh Tuired (also called Moytura), Bres was named High King.

Since Bres was part Fomorian, he was selected as king, as the Tuatha Dé Danann sought to improve their relationship with the Fomorians.

Brigid and Bres's marriage was also a way to end the feud between the two groups. Their relationship resulted in a son, Ruadan.

However, Bres was not an effective king. He favored the Fomorians and made the Tuatha Dé Danann work for them. He imposed high taxes, driving the Tuatha Dé Danann into poverty. Worst of all, his reign did not prevent the next battle.

Before the commencement of the Second Battle of Magh Tuired, Nuada resumed leadership of the Tuatha Dé Danann, and Bres allied with the Fomorians. The battle was going well for the Tuatha Dé Danann. So, the Fomorians sent for Ruadan, who was welcomed by both sides because of his lineage.

After each battle, the injured Tuatha Dé Danann returned with sharpened blades to fight the Fomorians. The Fomorians asked Ruadan how this could happen. He explained the warriors were treated by the Tuatha Dé Danann's physician, Dian Cécht. After the clashes, combatants were immersed in Dian Cécht's well of Slaine and restored to health.

Another resource the Tuatha Dé Danann had was their smith. Daily, spears and other weapons were honed by Goibniu, who operated the forge. The Fomorians convinced Ruadan that he needed to assist them by killing Goibniu.

Ruadan went to see Goibniu in the forge and asked for a new spear. Not suspecting any malicious actions, Goibniu readily complied. He and his fellow craftsmen created a beautiful and deadly spear. He handed the spear over to Ruadan, eager to hear his praise. Ruadan hoisted the spear over his head as if testing its weight before plunging the weapon into Goibniu.

The wounded smith yanked the spear from his body and thrust it into Ruadan. Since Ruadan had chosen to side with the Fomorians, he was not entitled to Dian Cécht's well of Slaine. And on the ground of the foundry, young Ruadan died.

There are multiple versions detailing his death. One tale says it occurred in the foundry, while in another version, the deed happened on the battlefield.

Brigid hurried to the scene of her son's death. Her inconsolable despair was heard by the Fomorians and the Tuatha Dé Danann. Her cries were the first time keening had been heard across the fields of Ireland. Her poetic wailing began the Irish tradition of keening (vocalized lamenting of the dead) at gravesites. The goddess of life and death, who guards cemeteries, demonstrated her connection to all with her display of grief.

The same battle that brought such sorrow to Brigid brought forth a new leader: the god Lugh. Similar to Ruadan, Lugh's lineage was a blend of Tuatha Dé Danann and Fomorians. In the Second Battle of Magh Tuired, Lugh had to fight against his grandfather, Balor. Balor, also known as Evil Eye, only had one eye. The massive eyelid weighed so much that four men were needed to open it. Enemies who dared look in the eye were incapacitated.

Lugh was empowered with one of the four treasures of the Tuatha Dé Danann: Gáe Assail or the Spear of Assal, which had magical powers. The spear never missed its target. After the spear had completed its task, it returned to the hand of its thrower. When the spear was not in use, it was immersed in a cauldron of water; otherwise, the spear would set fire to all that was near it.

During the heavy fighting, Balor beheaded Nuada, High King of the Tuatha Dé Danann. Lugh hurled his spear into his grandfather's eye, leading to the Tuatha Dé Danann's victory. The Fomorians were driven from Ireland, and Lugh was proclaimed king of the Tuatha Dé Danann. He ruled over a peaceful kingdom for more than forty years.

Chapter 14: British Gods and Goddesses

Today's countries that are part of Great Britain share many similar deities with each other.

Britain's most well-known physical manifestation of a mythical belief system is Stonehenge. Over five thousand years ago, during the Neolithic Age, Stonehenge was constructed. The Neolithic Age is the last part of the Stone Age. During this time, ancient peoples began to shift from their nomadic wandering to settling in villages.

As people began to create semi-permanent villages, burial locations for the dead became part of the landscape. Ancestry worship, afterlife beliefs, and connections between the living and the dead have been part of cultures for eons. However, it is not known if this type of belief structure began to develop during the Neolithic Age. Regardless, the formation of megaliths occurred. Megaliths are large stones assembled in some type of pattern. It is believed megaliths served as a monument or memorial.

While there is not a definitive answer to the question of why Stonehenge was built, it is part of the grouping of megaliths attributed to those who lived over five thousand years ago. Evidence supports that the final stage of Stonehenge's construction was completed no later than 1500 to 1200 BCE. The stones used for Stonehenge were moved 150 to 200 miles from their original location.

Many researchers use this as evidence that Stonehenge must have been created for a significant religious purpose. The arduous task of manually dragging rocks such a distance could only have been performed for the worship of ancestors or deities. Additionally, other cultures used only certain stones in their creation of monuments to their dead and gods. It was believed that some rock formations could transmit connections from this world to the supernatural world.

Picture of Stonehenge.
Free to use under Unsplash license. Jack B., https://unsplash.com/photos/aJj87xsnVQA

The orientation of the stones at Stonehenge correlates to midsummer sunrises and midwinter sunsets or the summer and winter solstices. Many other ancient cultures have gods and goddesses associated with the changing of the seasons. Any deities associated with Stonehenge could have been for ancestor worship, bountiful harvests, fertility, healing, or perhaps something else entirely.

Not unlike reading or hearing myths and stories of gods and goddesses, Stonehenge offers visitors a glimpse into a culture of the past. And just as some of these tales leave us in awe, Stonehenge does the same.

While there are no specific stories or deities tied to Stonehenge, there are many supernatural beings and tales from Britain. Many of these have evolved into folklore, but their origins helped ancient people develop their societies based on a value system. Often, people learned traits to emulate and avoid through these tales.

British gods and goddesses reigned over the humans of present-day Scotland, Wales, and England. Exploits of these deities exist mainly in the *Mabinogion*. A total of eleven stories appears in this collection. Originally, these tales were shared orally from generation to generation. As with other myths, the stories evolved as time passed, with variations infused by different storytellers.

Also referred to as the *Four Branches*, this collection of deities and their kingdoms and lands, languages, and deeds have inspired numerous other pieces of fiction. References to the legend of Arthur were first told in these works. Many gods and goddesses of England, Wales, and Scotland were captured in these stories, most of whom originated from two competing families: the Children of Dôn and the Children of Llŷr (Lir).

The Children of Dôn represent light. Their matriarch was Mathonwy's daughter, Dôn (Mathonwy was the king of Gwynedd). In some versions, Dôn's husband is unknown; in others, her husband is Beli, the god of death. The goddess mothered at least six children. They were family gods or leaders of the Children of Dôn. She is considered analogous to the goddess Danu, an Irish goddess. Both goddesses proliferated their leadership through their children.

Akin to Ireland's god Bile is Beli, son of Mynogian, who was the ruler of Britain. Frequently, he is called Beli Mawr. As with the stories involving Dôn, the number of children he fathered and with whom varies. Most sources refer to the children of both Dôn and Beli as the Children of Light.

Llŷr represents the Children of Dark in the tales of the *Mabinogion*. Llŷr was the patriarch of the family, and he and his family were often in conflict with Dôn and Beli's family. Llŷr was married to Penarddun, and they had three children. Their two sons were Bran and Manawydan, while Branwen was their daughter. It is thought that Penarddun was Beli Mawr's sister. Penarddun also had two sons with Euroswydd. They were named Nisien and Efnysien.

In the second branch or part of the *Mabinogion*, Llŷr's children play prominent roles. This section of the tale is titled "Branwen, Daughter of Llŷr." Bran, also known as Bran the Blessed and Bendigeidfran, was king of Britain. The king of Ireland, Matholwch (also spelled Mallolwch), sought a wife. In his travels, Matholwch lets Bran know of his desires. Bran nobly offers his sister's hand in marriage to Matholwch, who readily accepts the offer.

However, Bran's stepbrother, Efnysien, felt slighted. It was not because Branwen was given away in marriage; rather, Efnysien felt he should have been consulted in the decision. In retaliation, Efnysien assaulted and injured Matholwch's horses. The king of Ireland is offended, so he begins to leave without Branwen. To ensure that Matholwch would not leave without his sister, Bran offered him horses from his own stable. In addition, Bran presented Matholwch with a magic cauldron that could bring the dead back to life to make amends for Efnysien's actions.

Depiction of Branwen.
https://commons.wikimedia.org/wiki/File:Branwen.jpg

Matholwch accepted the gifts and request for forgiveness. Branwen was then married to the king of Ireland. The beginning of their marriage and life together in Ireland went well. Soon, they had a son, Gwern. Unfortunately, Matholwch's subjects felt he should have received more from Bran in compensation for the incident with the horses and Efnysien. Matholwch, wanting to appease his followers, agreed with them.

The mistreatment of Branwen began. She was treated as though she were a servant and not married to the king of Ireland. To ensure that Bran remained unaware of the abuse, Ireland no longer allowed ships from

Britain to dock at their shores. Desperate for respite, Branwen began training a bird. For three long years, she taught a starling how to fly a message to her brother, the king of Britain.

Once he heard the news of what happened to Branwen, an outraged Bran gathered his forces and set out for Ireland. As a giant, Bran could not sail on any of the ships because they would sink, so he walked in the water. Only Bran's head could be seen as he waded across the sea to free his sister. When Matholwch learned of the approaching ships and Bran, he withdrew from his castle and headed inland. On their way, Irish troops destroyed the bridge over the River Liffey.

Bran and his troops continued to pursue Matholwch. When Bran reached the River Liffey, he laid his body across the waterway, allowing the British troops to use him as a bridge. The king of Britain and his men made their way through the forests of Ireland as they continued after Matholwch. Bran was taller than any tree in Ireland, and his head rose above the tree line. The Irish knew he was on his way.

Realizing that Bran would not stop, Matholwch sent a messenger to Bran with a peace offering. Matholwch's proposal was that he would remove himself from power and that the title of king would be given to his son with Branwen, Gwern. Also, Matholwch would make amends to Branwen for how badly he had treated her.

To recognize the agreement, Matholwch built tents that would be large enough for Bran so he could be a part of the negotiations. Unbeknownst to the Britons, two hundred Irish troops were hidden in each tent. Bran and his men were told that each tent had large bags of flour. Efnysien knew the truth and went into each tent to squeeze the bags, killing the warriors.

The agreed transfer of leadership continued, except Efnysien contested Gwern's new role as king. So, when he could, Efnysien grabbed Gwern and tossed him into a fire. Shocked, Branwen lunged toward the fire to save her son, but Bran stopped her before she hurt herself. Fighting and chaos ensued.

Using the magic cauldron that Bran had given Matholwch, the Irish brought back the warriors Efnysien had killed. Any fighters killed during this battle were immediately reborn in the cauldron.

Realizing the death and ruin he had caused, Efnysien hid among the dead Irishmen. When the bodies were thrown into the cauldron, Efnysien elongated his body, shattering the cauldron of rebirth. His actions gave the

British their victory, but Efnysien was killed. The only Irish to survive were five pregnant women. Only seven of Bran's men lived, and Bran himself was fatally wounded.

Knowing that he was too large to be transported back to Britain, Bran asked his brother, Manawydan, to sever his head. Bran's head would join the seven on their trip back home. He assured the group he would provide entertainment in return for their help. Once home, Bran predicted that his head would remain in the Hall of Gwales for eighty years, where he would continue to amuse them. After eighty years, when the doors opened that faced Cornwall, people would need to bury his head.

The seven men, Bran's head, and Branwen returned to their county. Once they arrived, Branwen's traumatic marriage, the death of her son and brother, and weariness from battling caused her to die from a broken heart. The people were also told of the death of Caradog, Bran's son. Bran had left his son behind to lead Britain while he was in Ireland fighting.

However, Casswallawn, the son of Beli from the Children of Light's family, caused Caradog's death. Casswallawn wore his invisibility cloak while he killed Caradog's close companions and chieftains, which caused Caradog to die from grief. Manawydan, Bran's brother, was the only other heir to the throne. Since Manawydan was still away fighting in Ireland, Casswallawn seized control of Britain.

So, the group of seven survivors fulfilled Bran's prophecy. For eighty years, they savored delectable foods, enjoyed music and dance, and relished Bran's company. Most of their journey was spent in Gwales, which is analogous to the Otherworld. The royal hall had three doors; two remained open, and the one that overlooked Cornwall was always closed. Bran reminded the seven that if the third door was never opened, their stay in Gwales would continue. While in the royal hall, none of them felt sadness or unhappiness.

However, one day, Gwynn the Old decided to open the third door. As a result, memories of the battle between Britain and Ireland and all of their losses flooded the people. Now, they needed to satisfy the last part of Bran's prediction. The seven traveled to White Hill in London, where they buried Bran's head, which would protect Britain from invaders. The five pregnant women who had remained in Ireland after the battle to save Branwen gave birth. Gradually, Ireland was repopulated.

In *Lludd and Llefelys*, Britain's king continues to be crowned from the lineage of the god Beli Mawr. At the end of Caswallawn's reign, another of Beli Mawr's sons, Lludd, is appointed king of Britain. Lludd's brother, Llefelys, married into France's ruling family and was crowned king of France.

During Lludd's early reign, Britain prospered. He established his capital city, Caer Lludd, which is today's London. His subjects flourished; they were supplied with housing, food, and drink. All was going well for the new king. Then, he was besieged with three ordeals that threatened his peaceful rule. Lludd set sail for France to seek his brother's assistance.

First, Lludd needed to address the Coraniaid, a tribe of supernatural and malicious beings who had invaded Britain. One of the traits that made them seemingly invincible was their hearing. The Coraniaids' hearing was so acute that they could hear any noises moved by the wind's currents. With this magical ability, the Coraniaid were never at risk of injury.

Lludd's second misery to remedy was a frightening scream. Every May Day, a scream permeated Britain. The invisible horror caused havoc in the land. Experiencing the scream caused physical fragility in many. In others, the sound ravaged their minds, producing mental illnesses. As a result of the horrific scream, pregnant women miscarried.

The last condition Lludd was facing caused food to disappear. Regardless of the amount of food the king put in storage, it vanished by the next morning. The only way to remedy the problem was to eat all the food immediately.

Once Lludd arrived in France, he and Llefelys had to devise a means to communicate that the Coraniaid would not be able to hear. The two brothers used a long brass horn to smother the sounds of their talking. When they first began speaking, each could only hear the other use harsh, hateful words. They realized the brass horn needed to be cleaned, as a troll had infiltrated the horn, creating the miscommunications. After the horn was purified, the brothers began discussing their plans.

To address the issue of the Coraniaid, Llefelys informed Lludd that a special insect, when mashed and blended with water, would kill them. Though it was fatal to the Coraniaid, the concoction had no harmful effect on the people of Britain. Llefelys next explained the scream. Two dragons were ensnared in battle. If Lludd set a trap for the dragons and fed them mead, they would be put to sleep. Lastly, a magician was casting a spell on Lludd's guards. Once the spell had taken effect, the magician sneaked in and took the food. To fix this problem, Lludd needed to challenge the magician for ownership of his storage facilities.

Armed with solutions, Lludd returned to his kingdom. He smashed the insects that Llefelys provided and mixed them with water. Next, Lludd assembled everyone in his kingdom, including the Coraniaid. Once gathered, he sprinkled the potent blend over the crowd. All the Coraniaid died when touched by the concoction, but no Briton was harmed. Extra insects were kept in reserve just in case Britain was ever invaded again.

Next on the agenda was addressing the problem of the scream emanating from the warring red and white dragons. In Oxford, Lludd followed his brother's instructions and set a trap. He dug a large pit and filled it with mead from the best local brewer. Then, he covered the top of the hole. As usual, the dragons battled each other. While fighting, they fell into the pit. Thirsty from the fighting, they imbibed the tasty ale. Once they fell asleep, Lludd took them to Dinas Emrys, where they are held to this day.

Lastly, Llefelys had instructed Lludd to cook a wonderful banquet to lure the magician. Since the magician could make anyone sleepy, Lludd needed to have a vat of ice water. Anytime Lludd felt lethargic, he had to immerse himself in the water to reinvigorate himself. Finally, the magician arrived, ready to eat the feast and take all the food. A battle ensued, and Lludd emerged as the victor. The magician agreed to join Lludd's kingdom as a loyal subject.

Lludd confronting the magician.

Thus, Lludd, the god of healing, resumed his peaceful reign over Britain.

Chapter 15: Irish Celtic Deities

Irish mythology is replete with gods and goddesses and other mystical, magical creatures. Many of the other characters in Irish myths and folklore are grouped together as fairies. There are several spellings of fairy, and many people use the variants interchangeably. Historically, fairy is from Latin and referred to fate or the Fates. In Old French, the word fairy denoted magic and witchcraft.

The term fairies will be used here to refer to a broad category of creatures connected to gods and goddesses or mythology. These beings have supernatural powers; some are whimsical, while others can be malevolent. Often, their personalities are based on humans' treatment of them. The physical appearance of fairies differs and has changed throughout time.

In the world of Celtic fairies, one of the first groups of fairies resulted from the Tuatha Dé Danann. The people of Danu fought many battles for their land, which is in today's Ireland. Thousands of years ago, the Tuatha Dé Danann, a supernatural race, lived in Ireland after they were banished from heaven. The Milesians, viewed by many as ancestors of today's Irish people, invaded Ireland when it was occupied by the Tuatha Dé Danann.

Some stories say that the Milesian invasion was for revenge. In these tales, the people of Danu had killed the leader of the Milesians. When the Milesians landed, they conferred with the king of the Tuatha Dé Danann.

Amergin, the mediator for the Milesians, agreed with the Tuatha Dé Danann that the land was rightfully theirs. However, he suggested a resolution: he and the Milesians would withdraw from the land. They agreed to wait three days. After that, the Milesians would sail out into the seas over the nine green waves. Once the invaders were that far out, they could attempt another landing. If they successfully disembarked and conquered the island, then it would belong to the Milesians. Both sides consented to the idea.

Following the agreement, the Milesians boarded their vessels, but the Tuatha Dé Danann utilized their magical powers. Suddenly, the Milesians found themselves and their ships in the midst of a powerful storm. Their ships were hurled about on the rough seas, causing many casualties and nearly destroying the entire fleet. During the storm, Amergin's child and wife were killed. He began singing an invocation for his family. His incantation was stronger than the storm and parted the seas. Amergin and the Milesians landed in Ireland and conquered the Tuatha Dé Danann.

After losing their rights to the land, the Tuatha Dé Danann were relegated to living underneath the surface of the earth. In their underground world, the people of Danu recreated their kingdoms. *Sidhes* or earthen mounds mark the locations of their dwellings. *Aos sí,* or "people of the mounds," became the Tuatha Dé Danann's new name. In time, they became fairies and other magical creatures.

One group of magical fairies that lives in the fairy mounds throughout Ireland is the leprechauns. As with many other terms and characters from ancient literature, there are a number of spelling variations. Some versions are regional, but many believe that today's version of "leprechaun" originated with *lurchorpán* from the medieval Middle Irish spelling, which means "small body." Leprechaun is the spelling most often used today.

Others believe the word and group of fairies began with Lugh, the god of the sun and light. Lugh was a powerful warrior who fought valiantly for the Tuatha Dé Danann. He was a leader of the tribe for forty years. After his reign, he discovered that his wife had had an affair. He avenged his family name, having her suitor, Cermait, killed. In turn, Cermait's three sons retaliated and captured Lugh. After Lugh was drowned in a loch, now named Loch Lugborta, he became part of those dwelling in the Otherworld.

Lugh's status was diminished, as he was no longer the powerful trickster warrior. Some tales tell of Lugh, who was once the god of crafts, transforming from a fierce combatant into a shoemaker and tailor. In the underground realm of the *sidhe,* he became "Stooping Lugh" ("Lughchromain"), a fairy artisan or leprechaun.

Most stories agree with the depiction of leprechauns as slight in physical stature but quick and nimble. Historically, leprechauns were male and lived solitary existences. In their underground realm, they were skilled cobblers, fashioning footwear for the other fairies. Leprechauns were often the guardians of golden treasures for others who lived in the *sidhe*. Since leprechauns were known for their frugality, other fairies entrusted their riches to them.

Humans who sought leprechauns and their gold used two methods to find them. At the end of a rainbow, one could supposedly find a leprechaun guarding his legendary pot of gold. One could also listen for the sound of a cobbler's hammer.

Depiction of a leprechaun.
https://commons.wikimedia.org/wiki/File:Leprechaun_engraving_1900.jpg

These tricksters were challenging to capture; once in captivity, it was difficult for the abductor to keep the mischievous leprechaun in check. In case they were caught, leprechauns had an escape plan prepared. First, they appealed to the human desire for gold and riches, offering treasures for their release. To prove their trustworthiness, leprechauns showed where they stored their silver and gold.

The leprechaun's leather pouch contained a silver shilling. This magical coin stayed with the human until the leprechaun was freed. Once the leprechaun escaped, the silver shilling found its way back to the leprechaun's pouch. In another small sack, the leprechaun had gold coins. These were used to pay his way out of situations if he found himself trapped. When the leprechaun was safely away from danger, the gold coin disintegrated into ash.

Another ploy leprechauns used to escape from mortals was offering three wishes. These wishes tended to be fraught with misunderstandings. In the first acknowledged tale about a leprechaun, Fergus, King of Ulster, is tricked by the leprechauns. Termed sprites in this tale, a group of leprechauns finds Fergus asleep on the beach. After removing Fergus's sword, the magical creatures attempt to carry him over the water. Once Fergus's toes feel the coldness of the loch, he immediately wakes up. Quickly, he grabs three of the leprechauns.

The King of Ulster knows of the leprechauns' magic. So, he demands his three wishes in exchange for their release. Fergus's first wish is the ability to breathe underwater. The leprechauns tell Fergus that he will have this ability in all waterways except for Loch Rudraige.

Depiction of Fergus breathing underwater.
https://commons.wikimedia.org/wiki/File:7_Fergus_goes_down_into_the_lake.jpg

Believing himself above the restriction placed on his wish, Fergus decides to go swimming in Loch Rudraige. Proud of himself, Fergus thinks he has outwitted the leprechauns. Here he was, enjoying himself and breathing underwater in Loch Rudraige. Fergus's joy ends when he encounters Muirdris, a hideous beast. His fright is so profound that his face becomes permanently and horribly deformed from shock.

The disfigured king of Ulster drags himself back to his kingdom. His subjects are aghast when they view the king's face. No one in the kingdom is willing to tell Fergus what he looks like, so all the mirrors in the kingdom are covered, turned backward, or removed. As time wears on, Fergus becomes a cantankerous old man and treats those in his kingdom poorly. Finally, one servant cannot take the mistreatment any longer and tells him the truth.

Fergus realizes why he was not chosen to become High King, as he understands that his disfigurement has prevented him from achieving the highest rank in the land. Anger consumes him. In a rage, Fergus sets off for Loch Rudraige for vengeance. Muirdris and Fergus battle fiercely for more than forty-eight straight hours. But in the end, Fergus slays the monster.

The battle takes all of Fergus's strength. Valiantly, he swims to the shore. Once on the beach, where the leprechauns had found him years ago, Fergus collapses. He succumbs to death. In the end, the leprechauns prevailed by using their legendary trickery.

Some folklorists and mythologists believe the leprechaun has relatives, while others view them as a separate group in the fairy realm. One group of related fairies is the clurichauns. Another diminutive male figure, the mischievous clurichauns enjoyed imbibing on ales and wines and smoking. Often, clurichauns would slip into the cellars of homes to treat themselves to the beverages stored there. After indulging, clurichauns would light their clay pipes and relax. On other nights, inebriated clurichauns could be seen enjoying themselves by riding sheep or goats through the countryside.

Image of a clurichaun.
https://commons.wikimedia.org/wiki/File:Celtic_Fairy_Tales-1892-048-1.jpg

Clurichauns are depicted with ruddy faces, perhaps from their drinking and smoking, and are known to play pranks and create mayhem in one's home. His exploits can be problematic; however, if a clurichaun knows he is welcome in your cellar, he will protect your casks of wine and care for you and your family. If they feel slighted or offended by you, clurichauns will seek revenge. When clurichauns vacate a home, people report missing the sounds of Irish melodies the clurichauns sang after knocking back a few.

Considered similar to leprechauns and clurichauns are the fear dearg (far darrig), which means "red man." A fear dearg is a trickster who plays practical jokes on residents of larger dwellings, but their mischievous nature can be darker than the leprechauns or clurichauns. When one stops by your home, he enjoys sitting by the warm fire.

However, his visit foretells of changing fortunes for you since bad luck follows him. It is wise to appease the fear dearg. If he is unhappy with how he is treated, your luck will change more quickly and more severely. Because of the impending doom his sojourn foretells, nightmares are typically reported by those who encounter him.

Instead of the pouches of gold and silver carried by leprechauns, the fear dearg totes a burlap sack, which he uses to take newborns. The babies are replaced with changelings, a type of fairy. On other forays, fear deargs have been known to snatch people. Their dark version of mischief includes forcing the kidnapped person into a darkened, locked room. Once imprisoned, the person experiences the frightening sounds of the fear dearg. The fear dearg revels in the entertainment before releasing the tormented mortal.

Another ominous creature of the fairy world is the banshee. *Bean sidhe*, woman of the fairies, or a banshee is known as a harbinger of death. A banshee's cry signals death looms in the family who hears her screams. A banshee's wailing is also called keening, from the Old Irish word *caoine*. Though the banshee's cries are disturbing, they do not cause death. Sounds of banshee wailing vary throughout Ireland. It can range from mellow and soothing to so intense and penetrating that glass shatters.

Sightings of banshees are rare. It is believed she manifests herself as a beautiful young woman, an older motherly figure, or an exhausted elderly woman. These personas correspond to the Morrígan. A triple goddess who depicts all the stages of a woman's life, the Morrígan was a combination of three individual goddesses: Macha, Badb, and Nemain.

As a prophet and shapeshifter, the shriek of the Morrígan and her presence at the death of many men developed her connection to the banshees. The Morrígan was known to transform herself, and she was often seen as a crow or raven. When flying across battlefields, her blood-curdling screams instilled fear in the enemy. Other times, the Morrígan's physical appearance changed to that of a washerwoman. The warrior's clothes that ran red from blood was the one who would die in battle.

A banshee's cries mimicked those of the Morrígan. Years ago, many believed their families had their own banshee. A banshee would remain with them until everyone in the family had died and received a proper burial. Once a person was buried, the banshee would make certain the person's soul received the treatment the person earned. Self-centered, unkind souls would suffer, while good-hearted, kind spirits would transition to a tranquil realm.

Another Irish omen of death is Cóiste Bodhar, which means silent or death coach. The Cóiste Bodhar cannot return to the other realm without a passenger from the mortal world. The headless horseman drives the ghostly carriage. Those who have seen this spectacular sight tell of the ominous silence surrounding the vehicle.

Michael Noonan, a resident of Ballyduff in western Ireland, saw a black coach, six black horses, and a headless driver dressed in black gliding quietly through the villages in southern Ireland. Adding to the eeriness of the scene, Michael told villagers that all the horses lacked heads. Speeding away, Michael hoped the Cóiste Bodhar was just passing through his village. As quickly as the death coach appeared, it was gone from view.

Michael headed home with the dim hope that the scene had been his imagination. Early in the morning, he was in the fields, caring for his horse. He heard the thundering sound of a horse racing toward him. Madden, a neighbor in the village, was distraught. He needed medical assistance for his employer.

Michael ran to the local apothecary for provisions. Armed with supplies, Michael leaped on his horse and galloped to Madden's employer. He was too late; the death coach had already claimed another victim.

Another visitor who appears at night is the Pooka (Puca). A shapeshifter, Pookas can transfigure themselves into any being they choose, including as people. Often, Pookas show themselves as gorgeous dark silky horses with free-flowing manes and golden glowing eyes. To match the Pooka's incredible eyes, chains dangle from their horse neck.

Pookas relish in their ability to create bedlam. People never know what to expect from these goblin-like creatures. A trait that adds to their capability to cause confusion and chaos is their ability to speak like a person. They are naturally inclined to stretch the truth in their conversations with humans. Pookas are willing to mislead and swindle, making them crafty visitors from the fairy world.

Pookas willingly engage in perilous activities. As a horse, Pookas enjoy stopping by pubs in search of people who have drank one too many pints. Graciously, the Pooka offers a ride home to the unsuspecting person. Traveling home on a horse is much easier than walking, so many hop on for the ride. But the Pooka is ready for a rip-roaring adventure, not home!

Pookas are incredibly strong and talented, traits they love to show off. Once a human has mounted a Pooka that has shapeshifted into a horse, the escapade commences. The Pooka leaps over stonewalls, vaults over hedgerows, and sprints from meadow to meadow while the rider barely hangs on. The Pooka continues their lark until dawn, terrifying their passenger all the while. Then, the horse suddenly halts and tosses the person off. Stumbling to their feet, the human hurries away from the horse.

Legend tells of only one rider who was able to control the Pooka. The High King of Ireland, Brian Boru, accepted the Pooka's challenge to go for a ride. Before beginning the wild outing, the king quietly took three hairs from the Pooka's flowing tail. Then, Boru tossed them around the neck of the Pooka like reins. Once he started riding, he pulled the hairs taut, giving him some control. The reins and Boru's physical prowess were enough to allow the king to maintain his mount.

The Pooka conceded defeat. In turn, the king made the Pooka agree to two commands. The Pooka agreed they would not cause pain or suffering to Christians or their properties. Secondly, the Pooka would not inflict violence against the Irish. The Pooka was only permitted to do so if a person was going to commit an evil deed. Since Pookas are known for their deception and lies, it is unlikely the Pookas lived up to their agreement.

Though it may be a challenging ride, Pookas are great conversationalists. They have a terrific gift of gab and will gladly whittle away the hours chatting with you. Sometimes they offer wonderful advice, but remember, they do love an adventure.

Chapter 16: British Celtic Deities

Stories and escapades involving gods and goddesses from Wales, England, and Scotland are grouped together as Celtic Brythonic myths. From these tales, many well-known folklore legends have emerged. The origins of the heroic adventures of King Arthur and his knights began in Celtic myths.

Bards traversed from village to village, sharing these treasured tales. Listeners were entranced as the bards described incredible settings and larger-than-life characters. We get most British legends and stories from the *Mabinogion*, which consists of four main parts that are interconnected with one character, Pryderi, who appears in all four.

In addition to the *Four Branches of the Mabinogion*, there are seven other stories. Five of those stories introduce us to the earliest versions of King Arthur. Some tales are set in Arthur's court with his knights. Other stories connected to the *Mabinogion* show Arthur interacting with mythological beings and characters who appear in later tales of King Arthur and his Knights of the Roundtable.

The Welsh tale *Culhwch and Olwen* is thought to be one of the first stories in which Arthur is introduced. King Cilydd's son marries Goleuddydd, who becomes pregnant. Due to the problematic delivery of the baby, Goleuddydd dies. Motherless, Culhwch is raised by the kingdom's pig keeper.

King Cilydd wants a new wife and mother for his son. One of the men in the king's court suggests the wife of King Doged. Since she is already married, King Cilydd has to kill Doged. Cilydd does so, assuming control of Doged's kingdom, including his lands, widow, and daughter.

The new queen desires to ensure the succession of her and her husband's bloodline. When the new queen realizes that her husband already has a son, she thinks her problem is solved. To ensure their lineage continues, Culhwch's stepmother's resolution is for Culhwch to marry his stepsister. Culhwch refuses. Spurned, his stepmother places a hex on Culhwch.

Culhwch's curse is that he can only marry Olwen, the daughter of the king of the giants, Ysbaddaden Bencawr. However, the stunning Olwen has a complicated situation. It has been foretold that if Olwen marries, her father will die. Culhwch also cannot find Ysbaddaden Bencawr's kingdom without assistance. Only Culhwch's cousin, Arthur, can successfully aid him on his journey.

Culhwch leaves for his cousin's court in Celliwig in Cornwall. It is believed this is the earliest mention of the location of Arthur's court. Arthur agrees to assist Culhwch on his mission to find Olwen. Arthur chooses some of his most talented men to join him and Culhwch. Six of the most valiant warriors agree to aid them on their journey: Bedwyr (Sir Bedivere), Cai (Sir Cay), Cynddylig Gyfarwydd, Gwalchmei (Sir Gawain, who is also Arthur's nephew), Gwrhyr Gwalstawd Ieithoedd, and Menw, son of Tairgwaedd.

In their search, the troupe encounters Culhwch's aunt, his mother's sister. They ask for her assistance to locate Olwen. The shepherd's wife tries to tell Culhwch to stop his pursuit, as all of Olwen's suitors have never been seen again. Culhwch refuses to cease his expedition; he is besotted with Olwen and must find her. Realizing that her nephew will not be deterred, she provides information to the ensemble. Every Saturday, Olwen comes to Culhwch's aunt's house so she can have her hair washed.

On Saturday, Culhwch shows up at his aunt's house. He sees the pathways ablaze with white flowers. Wherever Olwen steps, white flowers arise, which illuminates the meaning of Olwen's name, "white track." Though Culhwch has never seen Olwen before, he is mesmerized. The two meet each other, and Olwen finds Culhwch to be an acceptable suitor. However, she knows of her father's destiny if she marries. For Culhwch to win her hand in marriage, he has to successfully complete the arduous tasks that Ysbaddaden selects.

Undaunted, Culhwch and his men continue their odyssey. With Olwen, they go to Ysbaddaden's castle. The king of the giants is ready for them. He has a list of requirements that must be met before Olwen marries Culhwch. For the wedding, Ysbaddaden wants to be able to shave his beard and prepare his hair. The only items that will accomplish this are a special tusk and a set of magical scissors, a razor, and a comb. However, the tusk needs to be from Ysgithyrwyn, and the hair grooming set is intertwined in the beard of Twrch Trwyth, a wild boar.

The first step to achieving this feat is to obtain the sword of the giant Wrnach. This weapon is needed because it is the only way to kill Twrch Trwyth. The men track down Wrnach, who is convinced the sword's blade requires sharpening. Sir Cai takes the weapon from Wrnach and swiftly decapitates the giant, proving him wrong.

Next, Culhwch and his men have to find the prison that is holding Mabon ap Modron, as they need his help to capture the boar. To find him, they seek assistance from a magical salmon from Llyn Llyw. The salmon is large enough to carry the whole group and transports the men downriver to Gloucester.

Outside the prison, they plan their attack. They know Mabon's location because they can hear him singing sad songs about his imprisonment. Cai and Bedwyr slip into the prison while the others attack the jail. Once Cai and Bedwyr have Mabon, the men flee the scene.

Now, they need to get Drudwyn, the fiercest hound in all the lands. He is so powerful that Mabon is the only human who can control him. The magical pup is the only creature that can locate and capture Twrch Trwyth.

On their way to find Twrch Trwyth, they pursue Ysgithyrwyn, an enormous boar with distinctive tusks. The tusks are the only way that Ysbaddaden can shave his massive beard for the wedding. They slay the wild beast and remove his razor-sharp tusk.

Sculpture of Twrch Trwyth.

Nigel Davies / Detail of Twrch Trwyth sculpture;
https://commons.wikimedia.org/wiki/File:Detail_of_Twrch_Trwyth_sculpture_-_geograph.org.uk_-_915217.jpg

The chase to capture Twrch Trwyth takes the band through many villages and across the entire county. Drudwyn leads them through many escapades and causes a lot of mayhem. After losing men and numerous injuries, they close in on Twrch Trwyth. Mabon grabs the razor from Twrch Trwyth's beard. In the River Hafren, one of Arthur's men seizes the shears. When they reach Cornwall, Arthur snatches the comb. Pursuing him with the giant's sword, Twrch Trwyth is driven out to sea, where he dies.

The group's last task is to get blood from the Black Witch. The blood is the only way to soften Ysbaddaden's beard before it can be shaved. Arthur is able to defeat her, taking her blood as a prize.

One of Ysbaddaden's subjects, Goreu, is chosen to prepare the king of the giants for Culhwch and Olwen's wedding. In an act of vengeance for the death of his brothers and the king's malevolent rule, Goreu decapitates him.

The wedding goes on as planned. Olwen, the gorgeous bride, and Culhwch, the happy groom, are finally married. After the celebration,

Arthur and his men return to their court to ready themselves for another adventure.

Connected to Arthur and some editions of the *Mabinogion* is a formidable goddess named Ceridwen. Ceridwen has the powers and capabilities of Awen. In ancient beliefs, Awen was a combination of prophecy, profound wisdom, and inspiration, which were some of the realms over which Ceridwen reigned. Other spheres of influence included death, fertility, and creation or rebirth.

Some of Ceridwen's forces came from her role as guardian of the enchanted cauldron. The bewitched kettle brewed ways to alter one's appearance, shapeshift, and grant the power of Awen. Since the ingredients and resulting concoctions were so potent, they had to be handled with great care; otherwise, there could be unintended consequences. In this magical vessel, Ceridwen created mixtures that were usually intended to benefit others.

In *The Tale of Taliesin*, which is often included as part of the *Mabinogion*, the cauldron plays an important role. Ceridwen and her husband, Tegid Foel, have two children: a son and a daughter. Creirwy, their daughter, is considered one of the three most beautiful young maidens in the land.

However, their son, Morfran, is not as fortunate. He was born with physical and mental deformities. The parents love both children for who they are, although they are concerned about Morfran's future due to his challenges. Thus, Ceridwen and Tegid seek a way to ensure that Morfran will have a good life despite his issues.

Painting of Ceridwen.
https://commons.wikimedia.org/wiki/File:Ceridwen.jpg

Using her powers as a goddess and the controller of the cauldron, Ceridwen develops a special potion to assist Morfran. Her potion will transform Morfran by infusing him with supernatural intelligence and wisdom. It is such a unique blend of ingredients that for the mixture to be effective, it needs to ferment for exactly one year and one day.

To stoke the fire under the cauldron, Ceridwen sets Morda, a blind man, to the task. Gwion Bach, a young servant, is ordered to stir the cauldron for one year and one day. To ensure that only her son will benefit from the elixir, Ceridwen adds a twist to the recipe. After all the herbs have been blended, only the first three drops of the mixture will provide the recipient with Awen. The remaining concoction is poisonous.

Finally, the last day of preparations arrives. When stirring the magical elixir for its final blending, Gwion Bach inadvertently splatters three drops on his finger. Without thinking, Gwion Bach puts his finger into his mouth to soothe the burning sensation. Instantly, Gwion is infused with the Awen that had been prepared for Morfran. Wise enough to know that Ceridwen will be furious, Gwion Bach flees.

When Ceridwen arrives, she goes to the cauldron for the first three drops. Since there was no sighting of Gwion Bach, Ceridwen realizes that something was afoot. She stops herself before feeding poison to her son. Enraged, Ceridwen begins to pursue Gwion.

Using his newly acquired powers, Gwion shifts into a hare. To catch up to him, Ceridwen changes herself into a greyhound. As she closes in on him, Gwion becomes a fish and leaps into the nearby river. Diving into the water after him is Ceridwen, who has shapeshifted into a starving otter. Gwion bursts out of the water as a bird, but the more powerful and experienced Ceridwen becomes a hawk.

Realizing how strong Ceridwen is, Gwion tries to hide. The best way to hide is to become very small, so he transforms himself into a single piece of grain. He intended to conceal himself amongst all the other kernels of grain scattered throughout the landscape. Since Ceridwen is a mighty goddess, she, as a hen, has no problem finding Gwion. To end the lengthy chase, she eats him.

However, the consumption of Gwion as a piece of grain did not end his story, only the hunt. Because of the incredibly formidable tincture, the seed inside Ceridwen impregnates her. Angry, Ceridwen vows to kill the regenerated version of Gwion when he is born. But when Gwion is reborn, he is so stunningly beautiful that she cannot bring herself to kill the baby. She also knows she cannot keep or love him.

Swaddling the baby and putting him into a leather pouch, Ceridwen hurls the baby out to sea. Eventually, the baby floats to shore. After he lands, Prince Elffin ap Gwyddno finds the baby on the beach.

Though Morfran never received the benefits of the mixture in his mother's cauldron, many tales tell of him becoming a member of King Arthur's court.

Ceridwen's baby appears in other tales connected to the *Mabinogion*. The baby's rescuer, Prince Elffin, was on the beach because he had been sent by his father to check the dam for fish. He was disheartened when all he saw was the leather pouch. That was Elffin's usual day because he was an unlucky person.

When Elffin saw the baby, he was shocked at how radiant the babe's brow was. The baby became known as Taliesin or "radiant brow." Elffin knew he needed to take the baby back to his father, Gwyddno Garanhir. However, he was uncertain what to tell him; after all, it had been another unsuccessful trip to the dam for salmon. While worrying about what to do, the baby began to sing poetry, a song of consolation.

In this song, Taliesin told Elffin that he had been sent to assist him. Taliesin also divulged that if Elffin utilized his abilities effectively, then Elffin would prosper and overcome his enemies. Lastly, Taliesin revealed that he would be a famous bard and prophet one day.

When the pair reached Gwyddno's house, Gwyddno asked Elffin how much fish he had caught. Elffin replied, "None, but what I found is much better than some salmon." Gwyddno was skeptical, thinking that his son's bad luck continued. However, Taliesin told Elffin's dad that Elffin was right; he was more valuable to them than fish. Shocked to hear a baby speak so well, Gwyddno believed him.

Taliesin was adopted by Elffin and his wife, and his prophesies proved correct; Elffin thrived with Taliesin's assistance.

King Maelgwn Gwynedd, Elffin's uncle, invited Elffin to Deganwy Castle for Christmas the year Taliesin turned thirteen. During the feast, the king insisted that Elffin acclaim the wonders of his court and wife. Instead, Elffin proclaimed that his wife was more beautiful and virtuous and that he had the more talented bard. Angered, the king tossed his nephew in jail.

Next, Rhun, the king's son, was ordered to go to Elffin's house. With a reputation as being irresistible to women, Rhun was to prove whether Elffin's statements about his wife's integrity were correct. Taliesin knew what had occurred at the king's court and understood Maelgwn's motives. So, he and Elffin's wife contrived a plot of their own.

They realized that Rhun would attempt to seduce Elffin's wife to show she was not honorable. When Rhun arrived, he plied Taliesin's adoptive mother with alcohol. Once she was drunk and passed out, he severed her ring finger, which was adorned with Elffin's signet ring. Thinking he was so clever, Rhun hurried back to Deganwy with the finger and ring.

Boasting, King Maelgwn revealed the ring and finger to Elffin. Unfazed, Elffin noted that the finger had rye dough on it and that the nail was not manicured. Therefore, it was not his wife's finger. Incensed, Maelgwn had Elffin imprisoned again.

Unbeknownst to Rhun and Maelgwn, Taliesin had his mother switch places with one of the maids.

Next, the king sought to prove that his bards were more talented than Taliesin. A group of twenty-four bards and Taliesin competed to create an epic poem and then perform it. When the royal bards attempted to demonstrate their poetry prowess, they blabbered uncoherent words and sounds. Thinking they were drunk, Maelgwn summoned the lead bard for punishment. Maelgwn's servant smacked bard until he came to his senses. The bard insisted none of them had anything to drink, saying it was a spell cast by Taliesin.

Maelgwn demanded answers. Singing a thoughtful ballad as a response, Taliesin explained that he wanted Elffin released from prison for all he had done for him. If the king refused, Taliesin would create an epic storm that would unsettle Maelgwn's kingdom. To prove his ability, Taliesin concluded his ballad with fierce gusts of wind. Fearing the worst, Maelgwn ordered Elffin's release from captivity. The winds immediately subsided.

Also in verse, Taliesin informed all present that he was the lead bard of the west. He also explained his lineage. His poem told of his many existences since the creation of man and woman. Taliesin became an advisor to many kings throughout the lands, including the legendary King Arthur. His prophecies about the future inspired the actions of many leaders.

Conclusion

Answering questions is what myths do best. Though the world has changed dramatically since the first telling of a story, our human heritage and connections continue through the common bond of characters and situations everyone can recognize.

People, regardless of who or where they come from, all have similar basic needs. Everyone wants to belong, be loved, and be safe. Reading and sharing these tales helps nurture these needs. We can develop a greater depth of compassion the more we understand each other. Knowing more about people can be garnered through experiencing the best and worst of humankind.

Solace can be found in the connection between all peoples. Every society has its own collection of myths. This compilation of characters and situations from Celtic myths and legends clarifies that people are both individuals and members of a culture. Reading myths today can inspire us, comfort us, teach us, and make us laugh.

While it is easy to pass mythology off as being too fanciful, reading about the stories long ago can help us understand history even more. So, don't be afraid to pick up more tomes on Celtic mythology to really understand what it means to be human.

Here's another book by Enthralling History that you might like

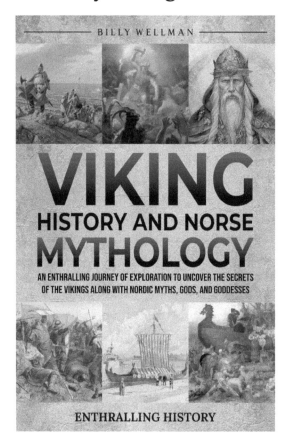

Free limited time bonus

Stop for a moment. We have a free bonus set up for you. The problem is this: we forget 90% of everything that we read after 7 days. Crazy fact, right? Here's the solution: we've created a printable, 1-page pdf summary for this book that you're reading now. All you have to do to get your free pdf summary is to go to the following website:

https://livetolearn.lpages.co/enthrallinghistory/

Once you do, it will be intuitive. Enjoy, and thank you!

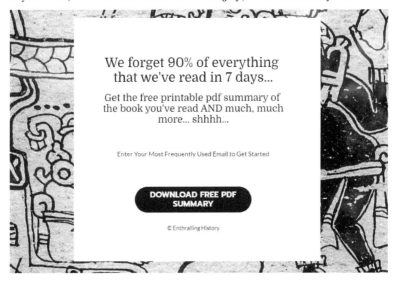

We forget 90% of everything that we've read in 7 days...

Get the free printable pdf summary of the book you've read AND much, much more... shhhh...

Enter Your Most Frequently Used Email to Get Started

DOWNLOAD FREE PDF SUMMARY

© Enthralling History

Works Cited

(IrishMyths.com), Posted byI. E. "Were There Female Druids?" *Irish Myths*, 14 Jan. 2023, https://irishmyths.com/2022/04/29/female-druids/

17, March, et al. "Who Was St. Patrick?" *Diocese of St. Augustine*, 17 Mar. 2022, https://www.dosafl.com/2022/03/17/who-was-st-patrick/?gclid=Cj0KCQjw8qmhBhClARIsANAtboccRKLcgJRz8Y3uxPcO0sbIp Qw9mInJbddIQf8WB75s2tV7PriTT1gaAuMZEALw_wcB

"8 Facts about the Celts." *History.com*, A&E Television Networks, https://www.history.com/news/celts-facts-ancient-europe

"Abhartach." *Wikipedia*, Wikimedia Foundation, 6 Feb. 2023, https://en.wikipedia.org/wiki/Abhartach

"Ancient Celtic Women." *Wikipedia*, Wikimedia Foundation, 14 Mar. 2023, https://en.wikipedia.org/wiki/Ancient_Celtic_women

"Ancient Celts Embalmed Enemy Heads as Trophies." *Nature News*, Nature Publishing Group, 9 Nov. 2018, https://www.nature.com/articles/d41586-018-07375-0

"AOS SÍ." *Wikipedia*, Wikimedia Foundation, 14 Mar. 2023, https://en.wikipedia.org/wiki/Aos_S%C3%AD#:~:text=Aos%20s%C3%AD%20(p ronounced%20%5Bi%CB%90s%CB%A0%20%CB%88%CA%83i%CB%90,com parable%20to%20fairies%20or%20elves

"Balor." *Encyclopedia Britannica*, Encyclopedia Britannica, Inc., https://www.britannica.com/topic/Balor

"Beliefs, Practices, and Institutions." *Encyclopedia Britannica*, Encyclopedia Britannica, Inc., https://www.britannica.com/topic/Celtic-religion/Beliefs-practices-and-institutions

Bhagat, September 20. "The Origins and Practices of Mabon." *Boston Public Library*, https://www.bpl.org/blogs/post/the-origins-and-practices-of-mabon/

Bisdent. "Epona." *World History Encyclopedia*, Https://Www.worldhistory.org#Organization, 2 Apr. 2023, https://www.worldhistory.org/article/153/epona/

"Brigid." *Wikipedia*, Wikimedia Foundation, 7 Feb. 2023, https://en.wikipedia.org/wiki/Brigid.

"Cailleach - Irish Goddess of the Winter & Her Trail in Ireland." *IrishCentral.com*, 4 Jan. 2023, https://www.irishcentral.com/travel/best-of-ireland/cailleach-irish-goddess-winter-trail-ireland#:~:text=The%20Cailleach%20is%20the%20goddess,we%20celebrate%20today%20as%20Halloween

"Cailleach." *Wikipedia*, Wikimedia Foundation, 5 Mar. 2023, https://en.wikipedia.org/wiki/Cailleach

"Canola (Mythology)." *Wikipedia*, Wikimedia Foundation, 14 Apr. 2022, https://en.wikipedia.org/wiki/Canola_(mythology)#:~:text=In%20Irish%20mythology%2C%20Cana%20Cludhmor,stroll%20to%20clear%20her%20head

Cartwright, Mark. "Ancient Celts." *World History Encyclopedia*, https://www.worldhistory.org/#Organization, 5 Apr. 2023, https://www.worldhistory.org/celt/

Cartwright, Mark. "Cernunnos." *World History Encyclopedia*, https://www.worldhistory.org/#Organization, 4 Apr. 2023, https://www.worldhistory.org/Cernunnos/#:~:text=Cernunnos%20was%20an%20ancient%20Celtic,a%20torc%20around%20his%20neck

Cartwright, Mark. "The Morrigan." *World History Encyclopedia*, https://www.worldhistory.org/#Organization, 3 Apr. 2023, https://www.worldhistory.org/The_Morrigan/#:~:text=Appropriately%2C%20the n%2C%20all%20three%20goddesses,of%20which%20contains%20a%20serpent

"Celt Timeline." *World History Encyclopedia RSS*, https://www.worldhistory.org/#Organization, https://www.worldhistory.org/timeline/celt/

"Celtic Calendar." *Wikipedia*, Wikimedia Foundation, 30 Mar. 2023, https://en.wikipedia.org/wiki/Celtic_calendar#:~:text=Among%20the%20Insular%20Celts%2C%20the,November%20in%20the%20modern%20calendar

"The Celtic Languages." *YouTube*, YouTube, 25 Dec. 2016, https://www.youtube.com/watch?v=ri1Vw3w1_10

"Celtic Metalwork Art (C.400 BCE - 100 CE)." *Celtic Metalwork Art: History, Characteristics of La Tene, Hallstatt Cultures*, http://www.visual-arts-cork.com/irish-crafts/celtic-metalwork-art.htm

"Celtic Religion - What Information Do We Really Have." *Celtic Religion - What Information Do We Really Have*, http://campus.murraystate.edu/academic/faculty/tsaintpaul/celtreli.html#BELIEFS%20IN%20CONNECTION%20TO%20CHILDREN

"Celtic Weapons: Art." *Celtic Weapons Art*, http://www.visual-arts-cork.com/cultural-history-of-ireland/celtic-weapons-art.htm

"Celts." *Wikipedia*, Wikimedia Foundation, 2 Apr. 2023, https://en.wikipedia.org/wiki/Celts

"CÚ Chulainn." *Wikipedia*, Wikimedia Foundation, 3 Apr. 2023, https://en.wikipedia.org/wiki/C%C3%BA_Chulainn#:~:text=C%C3%BA%20Chulainn%20(%2Fku%CB%90%CB%88,who%20is%20also%20his%20father

"CÚ Chulainn: The Legend of the Irish Hulk (Irish Mythology Explained)." *YouTube*, YouTube, 27 Apr. 2018, https://www.youtube.com/watch?v=GgHBGFL9v7s&feature=youtu.be

"The Dagda." *Wikipedia*, Wikimedia Foundation, 5 Mar. 2023, https://en.wikipedia.org/wiki/The_Dagda

Daly, Zoë "Who Is Ériu, the Patron Goddess of Ireland?" *Ériu*, Ériu, 21 Sept. 2022, https://eriu.eu/blogs/learn/eriu-patron-goddess-of-ireland

Dhruti Bhagat. April 30. "The Origins and Practices of Holidays: Beltane and the Last Day of Ridván." *Boston Public Library*, https://www.bpl.org/blogs/post/the-origins-and-practices-of-holidays-beltane-and-the-last-day-of-ridvan/#:~:text=Beltane%20is%20a%20Celtic%20word,well%20as%20increase%20their%20fertility

Dhruti Bhagat. June 18. "The Origins and Practices of Litha." *Boston Public Library*, https://www.bpl.org/blogs/post/the-origins-and-practices-of-litha/#:~:text=The%20Celts%20celebrated%20Litha%20with,the%20bonfires%20for%20good%20luck.&text=Other%20European%20traditions%20included%20setting,into%20a%20body%20of%20water

Did Iron Age Celts Really Hunt Wild Boar (Sus Scrofa)? - Jstor.org. https://www.jstor.org/stable/pdf/20557283.pdf

Dorn, Lori. "The Mythology behind the Royal Fairies of Celtic Lore." *Laughing Squid*, 13 June 2022, https://laughingsquid.com/supernatural-fairies-of-celtic-lore/#:~:text=The%20fairies%20of%20Celtic%20traditions,real%20ancient%20inhabitants%20of%20Ireland

"Druid." *Encyclopedia Britannica*, Encyclopedia Britannica, Inc., 15 Feb. 2023, https://www.britannica.com/topic/Druid

"Dullahan: The Headless Horseman of Irish Folklore - (Irish/Celtic Mythology Explained)." *YouTube*, YouTube, 14 Jan. 2019, https://www.youtube.com/watch?v=NEUCF-AA5WM

"Epona." *Encyclopedia Britannica*, Encyclopedia Britannica, Inc., https://www.britannica.com/topic/Epona

"Exploring Celtic Mythology: Children of Lir." *YouTube*, YouTube, 18 June 2018, https://www.youtube.com/watch?v=hROVjj0fX84

"Farming in Celtic Britain." *Roman Britain*, 26 Jan. 2023, https://www.roman-britain.co.uk/the-celts-and-celtic-life/farming-in-celtic-britain/

Fergus. "Tobernalt Holy Well, Sligo History." *The Irish Place*, 16 Feb. 2020, https://www.theirishplace.com/heritage/holy-wells/tobernalt-holy-well-sligo-history/

"Fomorians." *Wikipedia*, Wikimedia Foundation, 27 Dec. 2022, https://en.wikipedia.org/wiki/Fomorians

Gill, N.S. "Boudicca: A Mother's Revenge or Celtic Society's Laws?" *ThoughtCo*, ThoughtCo, 12 Aug. 2018, https://www.thoughtco.com/celtic-marriage-laws-4092652

"Glas Gaibhnenn." *Wikipedia*, Wikimedia Foundation, 4 Jan. 2023, https://en.wikipedia.org/wiki/Glas_Gaibhnenn#:~:text=Glas%20Gaibhnenn%20(Irish%3A%20Glas%20Gaibhnenn,yields%20profuse%20quantities%20of%20milk

"Goibniu." *Wikipedia*, Wikimedia Foundation, 10 Oct. 2022, https://en.wikipedia.org/wiki/Goibniu

hawk99. "History of Bees and Beekeeping - Bedtime History." *Bedtime History - Educational Stories, Podcasts, and Videos for Kids & Families*, 5 Oct. 2022, https://bedtimehistorystories.com/history-of-bees-and-beekeeping/

"Imbolc." *Wikipedia*, Wikimedia Foundation, 6 Mar. 2023, https://en.wikipedia.org/wiki/Imbolc

"Ireland in the Bronze Age." *Study.com | Take Online Courses. Earn College Credit. Research Schools, Degrees & Careers*, https://study.com/academy/lesson/ireland-in-the-bronze-age-life-houses-facts.html#:~:text=The%20average%20person%20in%20Bronze,break%20than%20any%20stone%20axes

"Irish Legends: Aine the Goddess Who Took Revenge on a King." *IrelandInformation.com*, https://www.ireland-information.com/irish-mythology/aine-irish-legend.html

Irish Monasticism, http://www.earlychristianireland.net/Specials/Irish%20Monasticism/

"Irish People." *Wikipedia*, Wikimedia Foundation, 3 Apr. 2023, https://en.wikipedia.org/wiki/Irish_people

"Iron Age People: Celts." *Ask about Ireland,* https://www.askaboutireland.ie/learning-zone/primary-students/subjects/history/history-the-full-story/irelands-early-inhabitant/iron-age-people-celts/

Jaideep.krishnan. "The Arrival of Christianity in Ireland: The Romans and Saint Patrick." *Wondrium Daily,* 7 Aug. 2020, https://www.wondriumdaily.com/the-arrival-of-christianity-in-ireland-the-romans-and-saint-patrick/#:~:text=Roman%20Britain%20and%20the%20Spread%20of%20Christianity&text=Since%20Britain%20was%20very%20tightly,spread%20out%20into%20the%20countryside

Liao, Jenny. "Introduction to the Gaelic Languages: Glossika Blog." *The Glossika Blog,* The Glossika Blog, 3 May 2018, https://ai.glossika.com/blog/introduction-to-the-gaelic-languages

"Linguistics." *Exploring Celtic Civilizations,* https://exploringcelticciv.web.unc.edu/linguistics/

"Lugh." *Wikipedia,* Wikimedia Foundation, 10 Mar. 2023, https://en.wikipedia.org/wiki/Lugh

"Lughnasadh." *Wikipedia,* Wikimedia Foundation, 30 Mar. 2023, https://en.wikipedia.org/wiki/Lughnasadh

"Milesians." *Encyclopedia Britannica,* Encyclopedia Britannica, Inc., https://www.britannica.com/topic/Milesians

"Monastic City." *Glendalough, Co. Wicklow, Ireland,* 20 Apr. 2020, https://glendalough.ie/heritage/monastic-city/

Moody, Sabrina. "Meanwhile, in Ireland: Ostara." *The Comenian,* https://comenian.org/7527/news/meanwhile-in-ireland-ostara/

"Morrigan: The Fearless Celtic Goddess of War." *ConnollyCove,* 7 Mar. 2023, https://www.connollycove.com/morrigan-goddess-of-war/#:~:text=Ancient%20mythology%20tells%20us%20that,dressed%20in%20a%20red%20cloak

"Muiredach's Cross." *Muiredach's Cross, the West Cross and the North Cross at Monasterboice,* http://www.megalithicireland.com/High%20Cross%20Monasterboice.htm

"Ogham." *Wikipedia,* Wikimedia Foundation, 23 Mar. 2023, https://en.wikipedia.org/wiki/Ogham

O'Hara, Author Keith. "Dearg Due (Female Vampire): Irishman's 2023 Tale." *The Irish Road Trip,* 4 Jan. 2023, https://www.theirishroadtrip.com/dearg-due/

O'Hara, Author Keith. "The Banshee: Origin + What It Sounds like (2023)." *The Irish Road Trip,* 4 Jan. 2023, https://www.theirishroadtrip.com/the-banshee/

"Oidheadh Chlainne Tuireann." *Oxford Reference,* https://www.oxfordreference.com/display/10.1093/oi/authority.20110803100247 501;jsessionid=E2B24DF9A20D347AA296ED414F8291EA

O'Neill, Brian. "Celts Arrive in Ireland - Iron Age Period - History of Ireland." *Your Irish Culture,* 1 Apr. 2023, https://www.yourirish.com/history/ancient/the-celts#:~:text=When%20the%20Celtic%20culture%20did,kingship%2C%20kingdoms%2C%20and%20power

"Pagan or Christian? Burial in Ireland during the 5th to 8th Centuries." *Home,* https://www.taylorfrancis.com/chapters/edit/10.4324/9781315087269-9/pagan-christian-burial-ireland-5th-8th-centuries-ad-brien-elizabeth

"Palladius (Medieval Ireland)." *Whatwhenhow RSS,* http://what-when-how.com/medieval-ireland/palladius-medieval-ireland/

"Pelagius." *Encyclopedia Britannica,* Encyclopedia Britannica, Inc., https://www.britannica.com/biography/Pelagius-Christian-theologian

"Pliny the Elder." *Encyclopedia Britannica,* Encyclopedia Britannica, Inc., https://www.britannica.com/biography/Pliny-the-Elder

Published by Tori On 9th August 2019. "All about Celtic Weddings- History, Handfasting and More! ★ Unconventional Wedding." *Unconventional Wedding,* 3 Apr. 2023, https://unconventionalwedding.co.uk/celtic-weddings-history-handfasting-and-more/

"PÚCA." *Wikipedia,* Wikimedia Foundation, 25 Mar. 2023, https://en.wikipedia.org/wiki/P%C3%BAca#:~:text=The%20p%C3%BAca%20(Irish%20for%20spirit,hinder%20rural%20and%20marine%20communities

Quinn, Eimear. "Irish Language Guide." *Wilderness Ireland,* 31 Mar. 2022, https://www.wildernessireland.com/blog/irish-language-guide/

"Sacred Grove." *Wikipedia,* Wikimedia Foundation, 25 Mar. 2023, https://en.wikipedia.org/wiki/Sacred_grove#:~:text=The%20Celts%20used%20sacred%20groves,Druids%20oversaw%20such%20rituals

"Saint Patrick." *Wikipedia,* Wikimedia Foundation, 28 Mar. 2023, https://en.wikipedia.org/wiki/Saint_Patrick

"Samhain." *Wikipedia,* Wikimedia Foundation, 16 Mar. 2023, https://en.wikipedia.org/wiki/Samhain

"Shield: British Museum." *The British Museum,* https://www.britishmuseum.org/collection/object/H_1857-0715-1

"Sluagh." *Emerald Isle Irish and Celtic Myths, Fairy Tales and Legends,* https://emeraldisle.ie/sluagh

"St Patrick's Purgatory." *Wikipedia,* Wikimedia Foundation, 12 Mar. 2023, https://en.wikipedia.org/wiki/St_Patrick%27s_Purgatory#:~:text=had%20substantial%20proof.-,St.,believe%20all%20that%20he%20said

"The Story of Tír Na Nóg." *YouTube*, YouTube, 12 Feb. 2018, https://www.youtube.com/watch?v=cSp-ihnpJ64

"Strabo." *Encyclopedia Britannica*, Encyclopedia Britannica, Inc., https://www.britannica.com/biography/Strabo

Thompson, Chris. "Pleasing the 'King-of-Bling!'' ˜ Notes on the Tasks of the Sons of Tuireann." *Pleasing the "King-of-Bling!'' ˜ Notes on the Tasks of the Sons of Tuireann – Story Archaeology*, 4 May 2014, https://storyarchaeology.com/pleasing-the-king-of-bling-notes-on-the-tasks-of-the-sons-of-tuireann/

"Traditional Irish Fishing Methods." *National Museum of Ireland*, https://www.museum.ie/en-IE/Collections-Research/Folklife-Collections/Folklife-Collections-List-(1)/Fishing-and-Hunting/Traditional-Irish-fishing-methods#:˜:text=Traps%20made%20of%20wicker%20or,salmon%20took%20place%20under%20licence

"Tír Na Nóg." *Wikipedia*, Wikimedia Foundation, 4 Feb. 2023, https://en.wikipedia.org/wiki/T%C3%ADr_na_n%C3%93g

"Wheel of the Year." *Wikipedia*, Wikimedia Foundation, 1 Apr. 2023, https://en.wikipedia.org/wiki/Wheel_of_the_Year

"Who Were the Celts?" *Museum Wales*, https://museum.wales/articles/1341/Who-were-the-Celts/#:˜:text=Where%20did%20the%20Celts%20come,and%20into%20the%20Czech%20Republic

World, Author Irish Around The. "Top 20 Irish Celtic Symbols and Their Meanings Explained." *Irish Around the World*, 19 Jan. 2022, https://irisharoundtheworld.com/celtic-symbols/

Sources for Part Two
Sources for Section 1
Sources were used between January 2022 and February 2022

The Complete Idiot's Guide to World Mythology

https://www.worldhistory.org/mythology/ 1/27/2022

https://global.oup.com/us/companion.websites/9780199997329/student/materials/chapter1/ 1/28/2022

https://www.worldhistory.org/Ancient_Celtic_Religion/ 1/9/2022

https://www.bbc.co.uk/religion/religions/paganism/history/spiritualhistory_1.shtml#h2 1/9/2022

https://www.christianity.com/wiki/cults-and-other-religions/pagans-history-and-beliefs-of-paganism.html 1/10/2022

https://www.paganfederation.org/what-is-paganism/ 1/15/2022

https://symbolsage.com/celtic-mythology-overview/ 1/20/2022

https://owlcation.com/humanities/Celtic-Mythology-Myths-of-the-Ancient-World 1/20/2022

https://www.learnreligions.com/gods-of-the-celts-2561711 1/18/2022

https://onthescreenreviews.com/2012/09/25/mythology-in-movies-the-celts/ 1/27/2022

https://www.historic-uk.com/HistoryUK/HistoryofEngland/Robin-Hood/ 2/14/2022

https://www.thegamer.com/best-games-inspired-celtic-mythology/

https://media.ireland.com/en-us/news-releases/local/united-states/assassin%E2%80%99s-creed-valhalla%C2%AE-takes-gamers-on-a-virtu 2/22/2022

https://irishmyths.com/2021/04/15/irish-graphic-novels/ 2/22/2022

Sources for Section 2

Sources were accessed between January 2022 and May 2022

https://www.irishcentral.com/roots/irish-myth-children-lir-swan-lake 1/20/2022

https://www.worldhistory.org/Samhain/

https://www.irishtimes.com/life-and-style/abroad/how-tales-of-the-headless-horseman-came-from-celtic-mythology-1.4060086 1/20/2022

https://www.irishcultureandcustoms.com/ACalend/Dullahan.html 1/20/2022

https://folklorethursday.com/folktales/farming-in-british-folk-tales-respect-or-revenge/

https://www.askaboutireland.ie/reading-room/history-heritage/folklore-of-ireland/carlow-folklore/the-story-of-mad-sweeney/the-children-of-lir/ 1/20/2022

https://www.wildernessireland.com/blog/irish-myths-legends-children-of-lir/ 3/10/2022

https://bardmythologies.com/ 4/23

https://www.celtic-weddingrings.com/celtic-mythology

https://seawitchbotanicals.com/

https://emeraldisle.ie/irish-fairy-tales 5/5/2022

Sources for Section 3

Sources were accessed between January 2022 and June 2022

https://mythopedia.com/topics/cailleach 1/20/2022

https://owlcation.com/humanities/TheCailleach

https://weewhitehoose.co.uk/study/the-cailleach/

https://folklorethursday.com/myths/the-cailleach-irish-myth/

https://www.livescience.com/26341-loch-ness-monster.html

https://mythology.net/mythical-creatures/loch-ness-monster/

https://www.historic-uk.com/CultureUK/The-Kelpie/

https://celticcanada.com/scotlands-ghost-trail/

https://www.connollycove.com/the-legend-of-the-selkies/

https://www.irishcentral.com/travel/best-of-ireland/cailleach-irish-goddess-winter-trail-ireland 1/20/2022

https://www.scotland.org/features/scottish-myths-folklore-and-legends 4/1/2022

https://www.scotclans.com/pages/the-loch-ness-monster

http://www.nessie.co.uk/htm/searching_for_nessie/search2.html

https://www.mysteriousbritain.co.uk/

https://theroseandthethistle.com/2019/09/29/the-ghost-piper-of-duntrune-castle2/

https://spookyscotland.net/nine-maidens/

Sources for Section 4

Accessed between January 2022 and August 2022

https://www.worldhistory.org/The_Morrigan/ 1/9/2022

https://www.worldhistory.org/Leprechaun/

https://mythopedia.com/topics/aengus

https://mythologysource.com/aengus-irish-god-youth/

https://brehonacademy.org/aengus-og-the-irish-god-of-love/

https://mythopedia.com/topics/brigid

https://bardmythologies.com/macha/

https://www.wildernessireland.com/blog/irish-folklore-fairies/ 1/20/2022

Wilkinson, Philip and Neil Philip. Mythology. DK Publishing: New York: 2007.

https://credoreference.libguides.com/c.php?g=139766&p=915787 1/30/2022

https://www.celtic-weddingrings.com/celtic-mythology/legend-of-the-banshee

https://www.worldhistory.org/britain/

https://www.english-heritage.org.uk/learn/story-of-england/prehistory/religion/

https://religionmediacentre.org.uk/news/stonehenge-a-neolithic-cathedral-a-healing-place-or-a-memorial-to-ancestors/

https://www.connollycove.com/banshee/

Ingram Content Group UK Ltd.
Milton Keynes UK
UKHW052133130723
425114UK00006B/74